INTERCULTURAL EDUCATION
IN THE COMMUNITY OF MAN

THE EAST-WEST CENTER—formally known as "The Center for Cultural and Technical Interchange Between East and West"—was established in Hawaii by the United States Congress in 1960. As a national educational institution in co-operation with the University of Hawaii, the Center has the mandated goal "to promote better relations and understanding between the United States and the Nations of Asia and the Pacific through cooperative study, training, and research."

Each year about 2,000 men and women from the United States and some 40 countries and territories of Asia and the Pacific area work and study together with a multinational East-West Center staff in wide-ranging programs dealing with problems of mutual East-West concern. Participants are supported by federal scholarships and grants supplemented in some fields by contributions from Asian/Pacific governments and private foundations.

Center programs are conducted by the East-West Communication Institute, the East-West Culture Learning Institute, and the East-West Food Institute, the East-West Population Institute, and the East-West Technology and Development Institute. Open Grants are awarded to provide scope for educational and research innovation, including a program in humanities and the arts.

East-West Center Books are published by The University Press of Hawaii to further the Center's aims and programs.

Intercultural Education
in the Community of Man

JOHN E. WALSH

Foreword by Edwin O. Reischauer

☰ AN EAST-WEST CENTER BOOK
THE UNIVERSITY PRESS OF HAWAII
Honolulu

To Utako

Contents

Foreword

Once men lived and survived in small family units, gathering food, catching fish, and hunting. In time the survival group expanded into a wandering tribe or an agricultural village. Then it became a small city state or little kingdom, and eventually it grew into the present large nation state. As the unit of survival grew, the individuals of which it was constituted became less directly known to one another and more diverse in their occupations, in their thoughts, and even in their cultural backgrounds. Thus each new stage required the development of new attitudes toward other people and new skills in cooperation.

In the past such changes always required centuries to achieve, but today headlong scientific advances force men to attempt to establish almost overnight an entirely new and much larger unit of cooperation. The community of survival is fast becoming the whole world, and the gravest question that man faces is whether he can develop the necessary attitudes and skills rapidly enough to achieve this community before disaster overtakes him. This time he does not have centuries in which to accomplish this giant step forward, but only decades.

The changing of attitudes and the development of new skills depend primarily on education. It is this educational need that Professor Walsh discusses in this volume. With the clarity and breadth of a philosopher, the understanding of an anthropologist, and the practicality of an educator, he grapples with the problem of developing the sort of "intercultural education" that our times demand. He argues that it is not enough that each person have the broadening experience of knowing about some other culture than his own. He believes that we must develop an overarching world culture made up of what is common to all mankind in values and perceptions, and that each person, while remaining true to his own particular cultural background, should also be educated through this world culture to perceive the common values all men hold, to feel a sense of shared traditions, and to command a common "world language."

The difficulties, Professor Walsh admits, are immense, but, as he puts it with both simplicity and accuracy, "there does not appear to be any acceptable alternative." To develop on a global scale new attitudes and, on the basis of these, new skills in cooperation is a prodigious undertaking—particularly if we are to achieve these in the short time that history seems to have allotted us. This volume does not provide all the answers to the problem, but it helps open up this crucially important subject to rational study and discourse. Let us hope that it will be answered by a flood of more specific efforts to achieve the goals it outlines.

Edwin O. Reischauer

Acknowledgments

This book was written while I was a Senior Fellow at the East-West Center. I acknowledge with deep gratitude the contributions of my colleagues at the Center from many cultures and many disciplines with whom I had the pleasure of discussing these ideas. Whatever its present shortcomings, the book has far fewer than it would have had were it not for the benefit of their criticisms and suggestions. My thanks, as well, to the East-West Center administration for its cooperation and encouragement and to the staff of the Center for its always pleasant helpfulness.

The manuscript went through several revisions, and typing it was a cooperative effort in the best tradition of the Center. I express my appreciation to all those who helped with the typing by mentioning Mrs. Miriam Gould, program assistant, Open Grants Program, and Mrs. Hazel Tatsuno, administrative assistant, Culture Learning Institute.

Quotations from literary works illustrating culture learning through literature are used with the kind permission of the publishers, identified in notes to the quotations.

1

The New Era of
Intercultural Education

A number of forces and influences have come together in the final third of the twentieth century to make the development of a new theory of intercultural education both mandatory and urgent. Intercultural education itself is not something new; it is the post-World-War-II emphasis on it which is new, spectacular, and profoundly revolutionary. In both formal and informal ways, people of different cultural backgrounds have been encountering and learning from each other since man's earliest beginnings. But even when intercultural education has been reflective and well designed, it has generally been regarded only as an interesting peripheral dimension of the basic educational process. Education per se has been *intracultural* and not *intercultural*. For centuries the central purpose of education was the distillation and the transmitting to the young of the ideas and values which were considered necessary to perpetuate the culture itself. Each culture appeared to assume that its way of interpreting the world and the life of man within it was the best or right way, if not the only correct way.

Contemporary man now realizes, however, that intercultural education must play a new role and be seen in a new way. Certain changes of thinking, required by the times, literally have opened up a new age of intercultural education.

One of the most striking changes centers on the fact that man now has it within his power to destroy himself and his planet. The hydrogen bomb's overkill has changed the world's thinking about war as a bargaining point in determining foreign policy, or as a means of settling international or intercultural disputes. Never before the nuclear age has man had such power, nor has such a monstrous possibility as total annihilation been in the forefront of man's mind as he searches for new ways of thinking and living.

Questions of war and peace are not reducible simply to understanding cultural differences, crucial as this understanding is. Cultural differences are facts of life in much the same way that air, water, and fire are. It is what men think about these differences, their attitudes and feelings toward them, and what they finally decide to do about them which determines whether there will be harmony or discord, peace or war. The essence of intercultural understanding and the whole burden of intercultural education in the new era is the realization that all men can and must come to live according to higher and more human laws and purposes than have heretofore been known or observed in practice. The destruction of one another is not rooted in man's nature. It is not a necessary decree of the historical or evolutionary process, nor is it an inescapable consequence of the competitive social and economic order that often pits one culture against another. Intercultural education would fall far short of the high objectives now demanded of it, if it did not bring about the understanding which leads to human, rather than purely cultural or national, values. Full understanding implies changes of attitudes, feelings, and emotions toward the peoples of other cultures and new, thoughtful, and generous ideas about ways of resolving conflicts without violence and in the interests of the general good.

A second fundamental fact of the new age and the change in thinking that it demands is best illustrated in man's landing on the moon. Man is now seen from a new vantage point, in one sense from outside and above his own natural sphere. There is great truth and great poetry in the thinking of a famous American poet, Archibald MacLeish, that since man has now seen himself from the outside he can at last see himself as he really is. Viewed from the moon, the earth and its inhabitants are adrift in a vast voyage through space. There are not many cultures and many different kinds or colors of men on the earth, but only one small planet, one struggling civilization, and potentially one brotherhood of all men.

The new task of intercultural education then, its responsibility and its context, is to help man achieve in fact what has already become an inescapable reality of the late twentieth century. The aims, purposes, and procedures of intercultural education must change in order to bring about in practice what is evident in theory. Intercultural education can no longer be regarded as a frill or a fancy in any contemporary educational system. It is essential to the survival and to the advancement of mankind. But it must be a different kind of intercultural education than what has been known in the past. Above all, it must have a sense of its new urgencies.

A new theory of intercultural education proposes the simple thesis that each human being ought to be introduced simultaneously to two cultures: the one of which he is a part because he was born into a certain cultural grouping—for instance, in China rather than in Latin America or Africa—the other of which he is part because he is a member of the human race.

The basic thesis presented here, namely that the modern world demands that each person should come to know two cultures—his own and the comprehensive human culture to which his own is directly related—is deceptively direct. This idea is, in fact, both revolutionary and far-reaching in its implications. There are immense theoretical and practical difficulties, and the work to be done would involve the effort and intelligence of all of the world's educators. There does not appear to be, however, any acceptable alternative.

Just as it has been a tragic mistake in the past to overemphasize intracultural ideas, values, and attitudes and to ignore those of other cultures, so would it also be a mistake to overlook or deny the beauty, strength, and depth which comes from cultural differentiation. Though a human being is first and foremost a man, he finds his home in a local setting which is of high importance to him.

To try to develop a single uniform worldwide culture is probably impossible and is clearly unnecessary. However to develop an educational system in which individual cultures are part of a wider, and broader, and transcendent human culture is not only possible but is a strict imperative if human beings are to continue to live together on this planet.

That finding a new approach to intercultural education is essential is pointed out by Henry Steele Commager, who says, "Clearly education is not getting the results that all of us deeply want and desperately need. Is this the fault of education or is the notion that these results are obtainable a delusion? Is prejudice so deep, interest so compulsive, zeal for power so ineradicable, that no education can counter or overcome their importunate demands? Or have we, perhaps, relied over-much on misguided educational philosophy and inadequate educational methods?"[1] And that a two-culture approach to intercultural education is at least possible is suggested by Rabindranath Tagore, who wrote, "In India what is needed more than anything else, is the broad mind which, only because it is conscious of its own vigorous individuality, is not afraid of accepting truth from all sources."[2]

Intercultural education requires a searching reexamination of the meaning of culture, the theory of knowledge, and the entire structure and process of education. It implies an end to the kind of education that teaches "this is the way *we* think and that is the way *they* think," as if it were inevitable that we will continue to think only in our way and they in theirs.

The purpose of this book is to examine intercultural education itself in greater detail, to explore some of the problems involved, and to set forth for further consideration some of the ways in which education might be reconstituted in order to achieve the intercultural understanding and appreciation so necessary in this day.

Before moving ahead, two introductory questions must be briefly discussed. These questions are crucial and propaedeutic to any analysis of intercultural education and what it should seek to achieve. First, is it inevitable that the rapid spread of industrial technology, communication, travel, transportation, and world trade will gradually tend to fuse into one universal culture, marked generally by a universal language, and a scientific, pragmatic, and broadly humanistic point of view?

The fusion of cultures and the dynamics of cultural change, interaction, and integration, have been widely studied, although the conclusions reached have not been satisfactory or consistent. Because there are so many variables, there are no known predictors of what will happen when two or more cultures come into close contact with one another.

Although there is no way of knowing with certitude what cultural changes and fusions the next few decades will bring, it is probable that a culture can accept the advantages of technological and scientific information without accepting the theological, philosophical, legal, moral, ethical, and social systems of the most technologically advanced cultures. In fact, even within those societies and cultures that have achieved high technological sophistication there is important and growing resistance to the impersonalization and the bureaucratization that advanced technology often entails.

The point is simply that each person is born into a particular cultural heritage and historical tradition. There is no such thing as cultural neutrality or indifference. Technology inescapably has a profound effect on cultural patterns. There is no turning back once technology has been introduced, but different cultures will accept or reject it in different ways and for different reasons. Whether his culture is closed, traditional, authoritarian, spiritual, artistic, logical, and scientific or whether it is open, free, experimental, innovative, permissive, materialistic, technological, and emotional, each person should know fully the principles on which his particular culture rests. Only then will he know how to evaluate it and how to improve it, what judgments to make relative to other cultures, and whether to stay within it or move apart from it.

Further, it would appear to be the advantage of a richer and fuller cultural life for all human beings if efforts are made to preserve certain cultural differences rather than to have them disappear in some vast fusion or standardization of cultures. Not only do differing cultural viewpoints and insights add beauty, interest, and diversity to human life, but also these differences form the background and starting point for a vital and meaningful general human culture. Uniformity of culture and conformity to the same set of cultural patterns would be intellectually and spiritually deadening and would, in fact, militate against the emergence of a broad and vigorous human community. The aim is not that everyone should think the same and become the same, but that starting with one's own traditions and convictions each one should share in the larger human community and contribute to it.

The second preliminary question is how is it possible to speak of a comprehensive or transcending culture when some of the most sacred and tenaciously held principles of one culture are in exact contradiction to the most essential principles of other cultures?

A comprehensive and inclusive world culture is in the process of emerging, and no one knows for sure what precise form it will take. The need for such a culture of cultures, as it might be called, is clear.

Even the most superficial analysis of the major cultures of the world reveals that they are sharply and deeply divided on certain fundamental cultural insights. Often enough these basic positions and premises do disagree with, or contradict, one another. For example, in religious or theological matters there is a clear contradiction between those cultures which hold that there is one personal God and those which hold that there are many gods or that there is no God. Some cultures place great emphasis on the dignity of the individual, while others give primary emphasis to the group and the role of the individual within it. Certain cultures tend to be very traditional, giving prestige and status to older persons, while other cultures emphasize youth and creativity, and value experience rather than age or custom.

Is it possible to conceive of a transcendent human culture which still preserves and encourages cultural differences? The evidence and experiences of the United Nations—particularly its Declaration of Human Rights—the World Court, the World Health Organization, the International Federation of Labor, and UNESCO, for example, while not conclusive, are illuminating and affirmative. Further, even some cultures which are both closed and self-contained, and which tend to be universalistic in concept have tried to find sound theoretical and practical ways for accommodating other peoples and cultures. In a similar manner, most philosophical and ethical systems, when dealing with the abstract ideas of the good life and the good man, tend to generalize for all men rather than to speak of man in individual cultural settings. To think of man as man, rather than of a particular man in a particular time and place, is as ancient as Plato and Aristotle on the one hand and Buddha and Confucius on the other. It is precisely because an author or a book can speak to people of any culture or all cultures that they survive and are regarded as classics.

It is clear that no transcending culture of the human community can be imposed by fiat or arrived at by a simple democratic voting process. It is probably clear as well that the process by which the peoples of the world arrive at a form of human culture and community is almost as important, if not equally important, as the substantive principles of that culture. Although after all these years still in its infancy, international law is one example of how common cultural principles emerge. The jus gentium, law of the nations, has an honorable history dating back to the Middle Ages and beyond, but the important point is that the present body of international law was not simply handed down or imposed by any one nation or lawgiver. Nor is it drawn exclusively from one cultural background or system of jurisprudence. It developed over many years through cooperative effort, dialog, and the exchange of ideas by legal experts from many different cultures. International law is constantly evolving; for example, the idea of a crime against humanity is relatively new, and it is arrived at by mutual agreement of those from many different cultural backgrounds who have something to contribute to its progress.

In his book *The Meeting of East and West,* F. S. C. Northrop suggests that all important culture differences can be subsumed under the question of how man views himself and the universe. He maintains there are only two fundamental views, one characteristic of the East and the other characteristic of the West. Northrop claims that each of these ways is incomplete in itself and that each is complementary to the other. He believes a general human culture is possible if the essential insights of the East and the West are combined. As he puts it:

> Thus, although the two great civilizations are different in a most fundamental and far-reaching way, there can nevertheless be one world—the world of a single civilization which takes as its criterion of the good a positivistic and theoretically scientific philosophy which conceives of all things, man and nature alike, as composed of the aesthetic component which the Orient has mastered and the theoretic component which it is the genius of the Occident to have pursued.[3]

Northrop's analysis is penetrating, and the scholarly evidence he brings to bear on his thesis is prodigious. Yet to many thinkers his conclusions will appear too forced, contrived, and oversimplified. A human culture, while based on ideas and a sound theoretical framework, will have to emerge more organically and creatively in daily human experience, communication, and intercultural contact. Nonetheless, Northrop's many pioneering contributions to the study of culture and civilization are valuable. Perhaps none is more important than his realization of the importance education plays in the ongoing process of shaping a world culture. He writes: "Education, and especially its application of the more objective, dispassionate method of science, even to the study of religions and the humanities, is an essential instrument by means of which the religious toleration and the democratic, theoretical, political assumptions necessary to make democracy function are propagated."[4]

AWARENESS OF CULTURE

Although the study of culture in any formal sense is a relatively recent development, its impact on worldwide thinking has been immense. The clarification of the concept of culture has led to a greater realization of the part that culture plays in shaping thinking and behavior and to the conclusion that diverse cultures derive from differing human perspectives on nature, on man, and on the self. In his autobiography John Stuart Mill wrote:

> I am now convinced, that no great improvements in the lot of mankind are possible, until a great change takes place in the fundamental constitution of their modes of thought. The old opinions in religion, morals, and politics are so much discredited in the more intellectual minds as to have lost the greatest part of their efficacy for good, while they have still enough in them to be a powerful obstacle to the growing up of any better opinions on these subjects.[5]

Mill wrote, of course, before the concept of culture had been as fully explored as it is now. The modern awareness of culture, however, might well be of such scope and profundity as to change, in Mill's words, "the fundamental constitution of man's modes of thought." If so, and if Mill is correct in his statement, there is now the possibility of a great improvement in the lot of mankind.

In more recent times Arthur W. Hummel expressed somewhat the same thought in these words:

> One who looks at our world today must realize that new movements of thought are taking place. The forces at work are not merely political and economic, but also cultural and spiritual. The awakening that we imagined would be confined to East has now come to the West. As communication expands and races mingle, we find that many of our old explanations are not large enough. We are forced to make new comparisons and to sort our old ideas in new ways. If in the first stages of this process, we seem to feel a sense of loss, of bewilderment and frustration, these are indications that we are on the threshold of something new. These are the first signs, it may be, of another Renaissance in the spirit of man.[6]

Among the new movements of thought now taking place is one that sees culture as an insight making for larger explanations. An older view which assumed that all men should see things in the same way has been largely abandoned. The awareness of culture as a concept that corresponds to one of the most basic realities of human life has made it possible to work toward an understanding of different cultures and different people and it has underscored the great contemporary need for intercultural education.

Cultural anthropologists have accumulated vast quantities of data about culture similarities and differences. It is probably accurate to say that there is no culture anywhere in the world, however remote, that has not been studied and analyzed. The findings of these investigations have not always been of equally high quality but each in its own way has contributed to the greater understanding of how the people of various cultures come to think and act in specific ways, and why they do so. Out of this vast body of culture information comes a totally new awareness of culture, its meaning, and its importance. It should be noted, nonetheless, that there is a sizeable group of theorists who maintain that socioeconomic status is a more important analytical tool than culture. They insist, for example, that the people in one culture tend to think much like people in any other culture of the same socioeconomic class. One study conducted by Rokeach and Parker concludes that "socioeconomic status is a more important indicator of values than is race."[7]

The systematic study of culture and the new realization of its power as an analytical tool has led to three important conclusions.

First of all, another culture, another way of seeing and doing things, does not necessarily imply a threat or a hostility. The people of one culture are not inevitably or naturally inimical to people of other cultures. Before cultural differences became well known and accepted, the general attitude of one people toward another was that of fear, if not of almost instinctive antagonism. There are important exceptions to this generalization, but until fairly recently fraternizing with members of another culture, and especially intermarrying, seemed to imply disloyalty to one's own culture. Prejudice against peoples of other cultures, even against those of subcultures within one's own country, was more the norm than the exception. The fear of the unknown or of the new can give rise to false stereotypes and strange myths regarding other peoples if there is little or no contact with them. Such distorted images can be intense and deeply rooted. But greater knowledge, communication, and closer and more frequent association of peoples have established that persons of other cultures are as likely to be initially friendly and cooperative as they are to be inhospitable, suspicious, or belligerent. In any event, they are simply reacting as their culture teaches them to react.

The heightened awareness of culture leads secondly to the conclusion that there is beauty, significance, richness, and expansion of the human spirit in the diversity of the world's cultures. It would be an altogether different and less interesting world if everyone thought and acted in the same way. It would be a loss to mankind if, for example, there were no Japanese gardens, Russian novels, Muslim architecture, Chinese food, Polynesian dances, and Buddhist philosophy and theology. Just as an individual culture benefits when it encourages the exercise of special and unique talents within it, so too the world is enriched by the distinctive talents and the intellectual and artistic contributions made by the various cultures. It is not suggested, of course, that any culture ought to remain technologically or scientifically backward just to preserve a diversity among the cultures of the world. Different modes and styles of life and thought ought to be respected even when the benefits of technology are available to all.

The third conclusion is that different cultures are a constant source of new thoughts and ideas. The thinking that one culture, no matter how self-sufficient and self-contained it might be, has nothing to learn from other cultures has long since been abandoned. Even the most dissimilar culture has something to teach, some intellectual and spiritual message, about how man encounters the world and adapts to it. Not all cultures are equally concerned with science and technology, but all have faced the same human problems of life, death, happiness, suffering, justice, values, meaning, and the transcendent. Any cultural interchange forces comparisons and judgments and opens up new ways of thinking, thus clarifying the cultural principles involved. There are many different insights into human nature, different views of the world and its history, different ways of arriving at intellectual positions, and each of them contributes something to the inexhaustible search for truth, knowledge, and love.

THE RELATIONSHIPS BETWEEN CULTURE AND EDUCATION

In order to arrive at an understanding of the new role of intercultural education in the forming of a human community, it is necessary first to understand the various interrelationships between culture and education. It is important to know what functions education fulfills within one culture before looking at its function among several cultures.

In general, education is the process by which a culture introduces its members to the skills, attitudes, information, knowledge, and values that will make it possible to preserve and enhance the culture. Those things that the older members of the culture feel are most necessary and most worthwhile are taught to the young. In this way, each member who lives within the culture comes to know what he can expect and what will be expected of him. Education is the principal means by which one learns a culture and becomes a member of it.

In simple and unsophisticated societies, the educational process is usually informal, indirect, unstructured, and random. A youngster learns which ideas and actions are acceptable and approved simply by observing and experiencing. The son, for example, sees his father fishing, or hunting, or tilling the fields and he imitates the way his father does it. Similarly the daughters learn their roles by observing and helping their mother. Instruction is largely by example and learning is through rudimentary experimentation. The learner quickly comes to know which actions lead to success and reward, and which to punishment.

In complex cultures, the educational process is more formalized and rigidly structured. The vast accumulation of knowledge and the intricate value system make the educational process the major activity and responsibility of the young. These cultures designate certain persons whose full-time responsibility is to plan instructional programs and to teach. Education, for the most part, moves outside the home and the world of chance experience and enters into the schools, colleges, and universities. There the young person learns what his culture requires of him now and what ideas, values, habits, and attitudes are going to be most helpful to him as an adult within that culture.

Even in advanced societies, of course, the student does not learn everything in school. The family, the church, the media, and his own peers teach him much of what he knows and values. The models or exemplars he seeks to emulate are those persons to whom the culture gives greatest respect. At all times and in all ways he is absorbing his culture. The atmosphere he learns in tells him much about which knowledge to pursue further and with which standards of action and behavior he ought to conform. It subtly lets him know the guidelines for his life, the people and things he is to treasure, the prejudices he is to share, and which actions are regarded as virtues and which as vices.

On the other hand, it is the educational process within a culture which shapes, forms, and molds the culture itself. The relationship is a reciprocal and constantly interacting one. A culture is only as strong as its educational systems and processes, whatever they may be, permit it to become. The culture that supports education, sees its value clearly, and gives it a high priority will be a vital and continuing one. Not only will its members be well informed, creative and contributing, but their culture will become more significant and a greater source of spiritual strength and satisfaction to them as individuals. Well-educated members of a culture will be able to build on its good points; they will be able to spot its weaknesses and move toward correcting them, thus enabling that culture to continue, to say something of value to the other cultures of the world, and to become a respected part of a world civilization.

Different cultures place different emphasis on education and give it different directions. For example, education is viewed variously as: the major instrument for socialization and increasing social mobility within the culture; the means for inculcating a particular ideology; the way of insuring a sufficient supply of trained and expert manpower in times of peace, and a source of military strength in time of war; or the privilege of a few, or the right of the many. Some see education as mainly directed towards the training of the mind and the deepening of the intellect, while others insist that the educational process involves the development of the whole person. The responsibility for education lies with the schools, the society as a whole, the church, or the public depending on the point of view.

How a particular culture views education depends, in part, on its stage of development; nevertheless, the two are intimately linked. As cultures develop they acquire certain needs that are unknown in less well-developed societies, and they also have greater educational opportunities. By its very nature a highly developed culture demands more of its educational system, but it could not have reached that stage without an already well-developed program. At the same time, because of technology, which greatly reduces the number of man-hours needed in providing for the basic necessities of life, it will be able to afford its younger people and its adults longer periods of time for preparatory study, in-service refresher courses, and updated educational programs. Those cultures that are less advanced do not have, at present, the same need for highly skilled manpower, although more and more they need educated leaders who will know how to coordinate the educational requirements and priorities with the development process.

There is another interrelationship between culture and education that merits attention. It is that relationship which deals with the highest and finest attainments of the human mind and spirit, those aspects of a culture which make it truly memorable and worthwhile. These have sometimes been referred to as the higher culture. Education here makes its greatest contribution to culture and receives in turn, when the culture is at its best, the greatest encouragement and support from it. A basic purpose of any educational system is to instill in its students a sense of the excellent, not as a way of proving superiority over others, but simply as a way of encouraging each person to achieve all that he is capable of achieving. Among the ancient Greeks it was called *arete,* that quality in anything which makes it the best of its kind. An educational system that succeeds in helping its students to appreciate excellence and to strive to achieve it serves its culture and the world well. On the other hand, to be content with anything less than the excellent, whether in the fine arts, the liberal arts, the lively arts, the practical arts, in science, or in ethics, is to miss one of the most noble, beautiful, honest, and luminous aspects of human existence.

In order to instill a sense of the excellent, however, education must be free. The culture cannot impose limits and constraints which are intended only to promote fixed political, social, economic, or religious ideologies. The culture should not prescribe limits beyond which the human mind cannot move or ideas from which it cannot deviate. The individual human spirit that is shackled and enslaved by a particular culture rather than liberated by it cannot achieve excellence; neither can an educational system as a whole.

WHAT IS INTERCULTURAL EDUCATION?

Intercultural education is the process by which one looks beyond his own culture and attempts to understand and appreciate how persons of other cultures interpret the life of man and the things of nature, and why they view them as they do. The words *transcultural* or *cross-cultural education* are also sometimes used. Although the emphasis may be slightly different, in general these terms and *intercultural education* are interchangeable.

As is true of all forms of education, intercultural education takes place at a number of different levels, in a number of different ways, and for a number of different reasons. In one sense, the person who casually reads about or visits another culture, even as a tourist, is learning something about that culture. In the modern world some forms of intercultural education are open to almost all people, because travel is becoming more common, because universal literacy is an accepted goal of most cultures, and because the radio and television make communication much easier and faster.

The major distinction in intercultural education, in the formal sense of that term, is the difference between specialized and generalized knowledge of another culture. It would be impossible for one person to specialize in the study of all the cultures of the world. Specialization here means learning the language or languages of the culture under consideration and studying the religious, legal, social, economic, political, psychological, and historical background of that culture. This kind of profound knowledge usually implies that the specialist, an outsider to the culture, has spent a considerable amount of time living within it. The specialist knows the culture fully, from its formal philosophers and thinkers to its characteristic popular wisdom. He seeks to know what the people of the culture value most highly and what its intellectual, spiritual, and political leaders advocate.

General intercultural education, on the other hand, is considered part of every person's liberal education. It makes no claim to profundity through an exact, detailed knowledge of a particular culture, but it seeks to create a degree of awareness, understanding, and appreciation of at least one culture other than the one into which the student was born. General intercultural education should start early in the educational process and should persist into adult or continuing-education programs. Not only is it an essential part of the educational process required by the exigencies of life in the modern world, but also it is one of the best means for insuring that a student will better understand and appreciate his own culture.

Area studies occupy a status between specialized and generalized intercultural knowledge, and encompass a geographical locale that, because of certain common characteristics, can be studied conveniently as a unit. It is possible in most universities to specialize in a given area or region. Though much more profound than general intercultural knowledge or education, these studies often lack the precision and depth that comes from intensive specialization in one culture. At the same time by noting comparisons and contrasts, area studies can lead to valuable information and understanding. Area studies incorporate and build on highly specialized and detailed studies, as for example, Clyde Kluckholm's study of the Navaho Indians or Jacques J. Maquet's study of the Ruanda in Africa. Like them, the search is always for insights and significant generalizations.

There is the long-standing and important question of whether intercultural education is a specific discipline or whether all disciplines are not fundamentally intercultural. The question stated this way is considerably oversimplified. Certain distinctions must be made among the recognized disciplines.

In mathematics, for example, there is a big difference between what might be called the substantive content of mathematics and the culture involvement of mathematics. To illustrate: the calculus as calculus is independent of its history and the culture which gave rise to it. How and why it came into existence, what its uses and implications are, whether the calculus or mathematics generally are highly valued in a culture, what the next developments in the calculus or mathematics generally will be—the answers to these questions are not part of the study of calculus itself. They involve the relationship between the calculus and particular cultures. There is no one-to-one relationship. A given culture might attain a relatively high level of mathematical knowledge and then turn its attention to other things so that there would be little, if any, further advance in mathematics. In the process of intercultural education, one culture borrows or learns from another those things it wants to learn or feels it needs to learn. Once the calculus is created, it is available to any or all cultures that might want to make use of it.

Mathematics, then, is both nonculture-involved and transcultural. It exists and will be learned or not learned as each person and each culture sees fit. This is true of all of the objective or experimentally verifiable sciences. However, there are many disciplines—namely, theology, philosophy, and the humanistic and artistic studies—in which the case is entirely different. The culture enters so intimately into these studies that they cannot be fully understood without an understanding of the culture which gives rise to them.

In a broad sense, even those disciplines or subject matters that are deeply culturally involved or oriented have an intercultural dimension. A student of literature or architecture, for example, should not be concerned with only American literature or Asian architecture. He must be concerned with literature or architecture wherever and in whatever forms it is found in the world. He cannot, in fact, know literature or architecture well if he knows only the American or Asian forms.

In a narrower and more realistic sense, however, intercultural study, especially in philosophy, theology, the humanities, and the arts, constitutes a special discipline. True, these are not like most other disciplines that move vertically from simple concepts to more profound generalizations. Rather, intercultural studies are necessarily interdisciplinary. The study of Asian culture, for example, is not part of any other discipline but it draws on many different disciplines. Most often, culture studies are either directly or indirectly comparative studies. In a world in which knowledge develops and accumulates rapidly, it is unrealistic to expect that individual professors will have the time or the knowledge to teach their special disciplines in an intercultural way. The American history professor, for example, may feel that he has all he can do to keep up with his field and teach it well. Further, intercultural studies and intercultural education must have their own purpose, their own methodology, their own integrity, and their own requirements.

Is intercultural education then a specific discipline? The best answer to that question would seem to be this: perhaps in an ideal intellectual and human world, there might not be any need for intercultural studies or education as such. Courses could be designed in most of the standard disciplines to highlight their intercultural meanings and implications. But such an ideal world does not exist, and intercultural education up to now has suffered greatly from lack of direction and emphasis. For the present, it appears theoretically possible and practically necessary to regard intercultural study as a distinct branch of knowledge drawing on many other disciplines, but having its own principles and processes. New types of courses will have to be introduced, and teachers and researchers will have to be specially educated to explore intercultural dimensions and relationships more deeply. New and distinctive ways of teaching will have to be devised.

Intercultural education is based largely on data supplied by those who attempt to interpret the principles of one culture to the people of another. It is greatly complicated by the fact that a satisfactory epistemology or logic of cultural interpretation has not yet been fully worked out. The implication is not that there is only one unchanging logical or epistemological system. The question is how does one learn about and understand another culture or cultures? What, in fact, does it mean to know another culture? Does one bring to this study the concepts, language structure, and the categories of his own culture, or does he devise entirely new concepts and strategies of investigation? Does one try to study another culture on its own terms and as it is from within? There is no one clear and necessary way of learning about another culture. Such a study in its deepest meanings and basic beliefs will depend on the ingenuity, intelligence, discrimination, and professional preparation of the investigator. Certain kinds of statistical information may be available to any who are able to make use of them; certain kinds of behavior will be readily observable. But to get at what the people of a culture really think, what they value, and how they feel is a subtle and difficult art. Part of the difficulty lies in the fact that all cultures are constantly changing, but more importantly, the investigator must make sure that he sees the formative principles and basic values in the other culture in the same way that the people of the culture see them, not as he thinks they do or should see them. Then, too, every culture has inconsistencies between its ideals and the way these ideals are practiced.

Some people ask whether it is ever possible to *learn* another culture rather than simply to learn *about* another culture? The researcher and his background always remain part of the problem. An observer with one cultural background, for example, might actually fail to see important aspects of another culture simply because he is not looking for them. They are entirely foreign to him and outside his range of interests or mental vision. On the other hand, he might attach undue importance to minor indicators which happen to coincide with his prejudices and preconceptions. It is always possible, as well, that any culture lets an outside observer see what it feels he wants to see or expects to see. Or, to complete the picture, it is possible in one sense, that an outside observer might come to know and understand a culture better than the people living within it. For example, though he was not a cultural anthropologist, Alexis de Tocqueville is said to have understood American democracy better than the Americans themselves. In fact, Americans still read his works for a better appreciation of the nature and functioning of their democracy.

Because of the difficulty of getting at valid and reliable data regarding another culture, including the difficulty involved in knowing how to go about gathering that data, the greatest possible openness, friendliness, trust, and mutuality is necessary in intercultural study. The observations of several investigators, taken together, are likely to be more reliable than those of a single investigator precisely because each

Economic, political, and social developments, as well as the need to keep the peace, have combined in recent years to make the world a global village and to underscore the urgent necessity and value of the emergence of the international mind. Even if all nations outlawed war as a means of settling conflicts and discontinued the production of all armaments, the shaping and strengthening of the international mind would still demand attention as a basis for solving other human and international problems. Among these problems are those of food production and distribution, of developing nations and the general problem of national sovereignty, of international law, of oceanography, of population density and dispersal, of human ecology and the pollution of the planet. But more pressing than anything else, and fundamental to all others, are the problems of education and of how to create the fullest and most satisfying life for every human being on earth.

GROWING REALIZATION OF THE POSSIBILITY OF A COMMUNITY OF MAN

Philosophers and theologians have consistently spoken in one form or another about the community of man. They have stressed the fact that all men everywhere belong to the same species, the same family. In fact, when the great philosophers and theologians of both East and West, whether, for example, Buddha or Plato, Tagore or Whitehead, speak about man, the way he learns and thinks and feels, the goals he ought to pursue, the universe of which he is a part, they speak about man as man, not about man as Caucasian, Chinese, African or Indian. Their philosophical and theological insights are directed not to men of a particular culture but to men in general. One reference will illustrate this point. With regard to Chinese philosophy, Thomé H. Fang writes:

> As to the nature and status of man, the Chinese, either as a unique person or as a social being, takes no pride in being a type of individual in estrangement from the world he lives in or from the other fellows he associates with. He is intent on embracing within the full range of his vital experience all aspects of plenitude in the nature of the whole cosmos and all aspects of richness in the worth of noble humanity. Anything different from this would be a sign of the impoverishment in the inner constitution of personality which is miserably truncated in development. This accounts for the concerted efforts of Chinese philosophers to advocate the exaltation of the individual into the inward

sageliness and the outward worthiness which together make up the intrinsic greatness of man as Man.[9]

Whatever the philosophers and theologians might have taught about the nature of man as man and the ideal of a community of all men, until very recently that ideal seemed so impossible of realization that it was almost meaningless. To most people, even those of great vision, it appeared to be a mystic concept that might possibly be valid in theory but had no practical implications or bearing on everyday life. Further, although many philosophers and theologians speak about man in general or what men have in common, the fact that they disagree so fundamentally among themselves about what man is and where he is going, casts doubt on the concept of the community of man among those who view human life through the eyes of common sense and everyday experience. It is clear to them that men are separated from each other by great geographical distances and that many men would in fact spend their entire lifetimes without ever coming into direct contact with a person from another culture or country. Men are separated from men of other cultures and races by differences in language and interest, and they find it difficult, if not impossible, to communicate even when they do come in contact with one another. Finally, lack of knowledge about men of other cultures led to the feeling that these men were truly *other* and that their existence was of no concern except insofar as it might in some way pose a threat to one's own existence.

The late twentieth century, however, brought a profound change in man's thinking about his fellow men on the planet. What the philosophers and theologians have spoken of in theory about the community of man or the world community, which before seemed almost pointless, now looms as a real possibility, indeed as a genuine necessity for both human survival and fulfillment. Technology has made possible what philosophy and theology could only dream of. Human interdependence is now recognized not just as a metaphysical concept but as a psychological and physical fact. Human solidarity may still take a long time to achieve, but almost no one now denies that a true community of man is at least possible.

Never before in history has the world been in such readiness for the development of a community of man. In the difficult, slow, and uneven evolution of man there have been many climactic moments in which the species might either make a major leap forward or unwittingly slide thousands of years backwards. The present moment is one such. The forces of the world have been moving toward it rapidly, although the achieving of a community of man is neither inevitable nor easy of attainment.

First of all, there is now sufficient anthropological and biological evidence to support the ancient philosophical and theological claim that all men are *essentially* the same and only *accidentally* different. The most important things that can be said of any one man can be said with equal validity of all men. The contrary statement, namely, that man does not have a nature but only a history, does not seem in accord with the conclusions of the best anthropological studies. For example, the desire and capacity to learn and to know, and the desire and capacity to love and be loved, are now known not to be limited to any one culture, race, or religious group. They are common to all men and, given the right environment and educational opportunity, to a surprisingly similar degree. Naturally, there are different aptitudes, motivations, and attitudes, different ways of looking at things and doing them, but these same differences are found within cultures as well as among them. Whatever man's origin, the hard empirical evidence supplies the basis for viewing all men as sharing a nature that functions in much the same way everywhere. There is nothing to support the contention that some races or cultures are *naturally* superior or inferior to others.

Second, the massive efforts that have been and are being made, by both international agencies and local governments, to eliminate illiteracy and to extend the levels of education are bearing rich fruit. Much remains to be done, since almost half of the world's population is still functionally illiterate, but what has already been accomplished shows what can be done, and the accelerated rate at which it can be done. Use of the new educational methods and technologies have helped show that certain peoples, formerly regarded as outside the mainstream of modern civilization, can bypass thousands of years of technical and cultural development and catch up in one or two generations. Any sound idea of a community of man implies, of course, providing the intellectual tools and the spiritual motives necessary for all men to participate, and only education can bring this about. The means to do so are already at hand; education is rapidly changing both man's knowledge of his fellow man and his attitudes toward them.

Third, the whole world is now tied together in a tight and rapid communications and transportation network. It is theoretically possible for any one place in the world to communicate with any other in a few seconds. People are transported from one part of the world to any other in a few hours. There is no longer any justification for the separatism and isolation that used to divide peoples and partition them off against one another. In fact, there is no longer even the possibility of such separateness. The readiness for the development of a community of man has been forced on us by technological knowledge and interchange, whether or not man wants it or is willing to accept it.

Finally, most of the intellectual leaders of the world have come to realize that the older forms of nationalism are no longer supportable in the twentieth century. While there would seem to be some psychological need for man to identify with a definite geographical area that he calls home and for which he has basic and almost instinctive loyalties, the exaggerated and chauvinistic nationalism of the past is no longer necessary or tenable. It could be very dangerous. For some time, many of the nations of the world, including those most recently created, have been confederating into regional groupings. These regional groupings, whether for economic, ideological, or military purposes, are proving helpful but even they are already recognized as insufficient and somewhat anachronistic. What is needed, and that for which the world seems poised and ready, waiting for inspired leadership and direction, is a new form of cosmopolitan man, who is a citizen of both the ever-shrinking world and of his own local community. The kind of nationalism that has been the cause of many misunderstandings, hatreds, and wars in the past is more and more recognized as an outmoded form of social and political organization.

THE MEANING OF A COMMUNITY OF MAN

To some people the idea of a community of man, though it might be theoretically possible, would seem to require such a change in human nature that the difficulty of achieving it makes it almost useless to try. They maintain that, historically, the only time in which people have come together to form a true community is when they are forced to do so by some outside intervention, some natural disaster, or to engage some common enemy. They hold, further, that people by nature are selfish and competitive and since the concept of a community is based on sharing, participating, communicating, cooperating, and sacrifice of self, a community in which all men would be looking out for and interested in the welfare of other men, simply because they are fellow humans, is asking something of human nature which history has not yet seen.

It has already been suggested that the new era is such that all men must live and work together to make sure that mankind itself does not perish. Even if it were granted that men form a community only when they are threatened, the fact is that a constant threat of atomic or hydrogen annihilation hangs heavily over the heads of the human race. Mankind together also faces the threat of environmental pollution, ecological imbalance, and the danger of large-scale mental disorientation, as well as large-scale poverty and underdevelopment. Thus, there is ample reason for working toward the growth of a community of man, even for these very practical, though somewhat negative, reasons.

More importantly, the ideal of a community of man grows not out of fear but out of the felt need and human desire for mutual assistance, protection, encouragement, enrichment and fulfillment. The historical record in this regard is not good. Throughout history man has been more self-centered and self-seeking, more acquisitive and exploitative, than cooperative. But if this is a turning point in history and if the next breakthrough in human development might be the community of man or the world community, it is important to know what that means.

Community does not in any sense mean that all men would come to think alike or behave in precisely the same way. That would be uniformity rather than community. Neither does a community of man mean that each man would somehow come to know each of some three billion people on a person-to-person basis as he does in the smaller community of the family, for example, or of the small business. In a community of man there might not be much more personal contact among individuals than there is right now. But the attitude of all men toward one another would be entirely different. One man seeing another human would literally see him not as a thing or an object but as a brother, whose concerns are necessarily his own concerns.

Each man would recognize the fundamental human dignity of each fellow man that he encountered. He would perceive him not as an alien, a stranger, or a present or potential enemy, but as one who deserves respect and assistance just because he is human and shares with all other human beings the same basic attributes and qualities. Community is indeed based on cooperation, sharing, working together for the benefit of all. Communication, too, is essential to community, and proper and common modes of language and communication would have to be—and could be—worked out. All men would understand thoroughly the *we* of inclusive mankind, and there would be no *we* pitted arbitrarily against the *they* of different races, colors, religions, or nations.

Community means basically a unity or oneness based on those things which people have and do in common. It is a matter of mutual reliance, of attitude, of confidence, and of shared purposes and expectations. It has no necessary implications of holding economic property in common, but it does imply that man is not simply economic man and that the economic order exists for the good of man and not for his enslavement. A community of man implies, positively, that all men are seeking the common good, the good of all, but not that the individual person exists totally and completely to serve the common good. A human community has as its core the reciprocal love or fellow-feeling which flows from recognizing what a man is and what he might become rather than considering what his race, religion, nationality, or culture might be.

The idea of the community of man is really the developing on the broadest possible scale of a unifying social philosophy or an active social consciousness and awareness. Some people reject the concept of the community of man because it seems to them to denigrate the role of the individual and to make him subservient to the needs and the dictates of the group. They fear that community would impede individual creativity and lead to a general uniformity and conformity. But this need not be the case. A true community at every level respects individual differences and encourages and supports diversity within an overarching unity, a unity of dependence and interdependence. For example, it is essential now to the welfare of the whole world that the developing nations, the have-not nations, be given whatever assistance the have nations may be able to provide, without any implication that somehow or other the people of these nations are inferior as human beings. A true community of man would take this one step further and extend all possible material, spiritual, and educational help as a way of recognizing a close and common bond among all human beings and the integrity and dignity of each.

The concept of a community of man is clearly an ideal. And like most other ideals, it probably can never be fully achieved. Mankind, on the other hand, has always needed ideals toward which to strive, and it can find a certain unity in the very pursuit of a clear ideal. Certainly a community of man cannot be achieved by fiat, and it cannot be achieved even in part unless its meaning is clearly understood and unless it is perceived by members of all cultures as a goal valuable in itself and deserving of all the effort and understanding that will be required to make it a reality. The great danger, of course, is that any one culture or ideology would be so convinced that its own interpretation of man in all his relationships is exclusively the right one that it would either attempt to impose its ideas on other cultures or choose to remain completely outside the community of man. The attaining of any community of man will depend on openness of mind, willingness to listen, to learn, to be persuaded, and to change one's thinking if such is indicated; it implies the use of reason rather than force, and it demands a kind of intellectual integrity which leads when necessary to making allowances and accommodations for ideas and behavior patterns different from one's own.

Most of those who have thought seriously about the developing of a community of man see the value and the beauty in it. That there is considerable disagreement both about how a community of man is to be envisaged and about how it is to be achieved is to be expected. The idea itself is still relatively new. The achieving of such a community will involve vast and fundamental changes in educational theory and practice throughout the world. But those who favor the developing of a community of man and are working toward it see in it benefits for all men that more than justify the efforts and the changes necessary to bring it about.

To exert every possible educational effort and to exercise the fullest possible intelligence in the developing of a community of man would be well worthwhile if it did nothing more than make the prospects for world peace more secure. It might in fact be the only practical way of preserving or insuring world peace. The deliberate and total, but often blind, destruction of the life of fellow human beings must be regarded as the exact antithesis of any idea of the community of man. War is the ultimate negation of human community. World peace cannot be maintained by any alignment of forces leading to a so-called balance of power. It can be gained and guaranteed only through mutual and rational understanding and trust, the elements which the striving for a community of man insists on and builds on.

World peace, however, is not simply the absence of war. It is not mere neutrality or negative indifference. To live in peace is to live in a state of positive regard for other human beings and of active, harmonious, and cooperative relationships among men.

If peace could be assured, the vast amounts of money which are now being poured into national and international defense could be redirected into the improving of man's physical and material well-being. Man's energies, talents and attention could be more fully channeled into constructive and productive purposes. A true community of man would work to make sure that all its members were free of the poor health, malnutrition, inadequate housing, and the grinding poverty that now haunts such a large percentage of mankind. Community implies that each person is doing his share and making conscientious efforts to contribute his unique capacities for the betterment of all; it is not a *welfare* concept based on centralized control over production and consumption for the good of the party, the race, the caste or class, or the nation. A community of man would function in such a way that all people would have the opportunity not just to provide for themselves the bare minimum necessary to subsist but also to share in a humane way in the comforts, conveniences, and goods of this world. A community of man does not depend on any one particular kind of social or economic organization, but it would aim to make sure that there was such a ready exchange of goods and services that they would be easily available where they were needed and wanted.

The development of a community of man would accompany and make possible a wholly new form of world civilization, not uniform but richly diverse and variegated and above all, open to all. Each man would share in the intellectual and spiritual richness of the various cultures of the world. No man lives just to make a living. It is rather in the delights of the intellect, the heart, and the spirit, and in sharing these with his fellow men and putting them in their service, that he finds his greatest human fulfillment and satisfaction. The community of man would be deeply interested in helping each man to find that which makes him most human and contributes most to his happiness and enjoyment of life. The arts and sciences, the humanities, philosophy and theology would flourish in a way never yet known to man because they would be respected and treasured as expressing the depths of the human mind and the creative powers of the human spirit for the greater benefit of all.

The Universal Person

There is no direct incompatibility between a theory of intercultural education which sees the purpose of that education as the producing of the intercultural person and a theory which sees its purpose as the producing of the universal person. Both are valid purposes. Traditionally, intercultural education has aimed almost exclusively at biculturality or interculturality; its new theory, demanded by the modern age, enlarges its vision and seeks to educate for universality. The bicultural person is certainly an educational advance over the monocultural person, but in itself biculturalism does not create the *world community of outlook* which is now so urgently needed. The purpose of this chapter is to clarify more sharply what a universal culture means by delineating the principal characteristics of the universal man. Simply put, the universal man is the product of an intercultural education that is universalistic in intention and by design.

In thinking of the universal man, it is necessary to avoid two mistaken beliefs which have deep roots in the past and are still widely held. The first is that the term *universal man* has often been interpreted in a univocal sense rather than in an analogical sense; that is, that some men were literally universal in their comprehension and in their viewpoints rather than that they participated in the idea of universality to a greater or lesser extent. The second is the belief that history proves that there are certain natural psychological barriers to the free exchange of ideas and of cooperative action among peoples of different cultures and that not much, if anything, can be done about it.

At one time perhaps, although even this is highly dubious, the range of human knowledge was so limited that a certain few people of exceptional intellectual capability could know everything that was known by the human race as a whole. Such men, whether they in fact possessed this rare ability or not, became the referents or the models when the term universal man was used. It was said of such people as Aristotle, St. Augustine, and Leonardo da Vinci, that they literally knew everything that anyone of their time could know—at least if it was worth knowing. As knowledge rapidly expanded, this or that individual intellectual giant was said to have been the last of the universal men. It should be pointed out that even in these cases the term universal man was not used strictly univocally. Little, if anything, was known by the universal man of the West about Eastern thinking and culture.

It is now clear, however, that to apply the term universal man to anyone in this simplistic and univocal sense is misleading and inaccurate. To be a universal man does not now mean, and probably never should have meant, that a man could be expected to know and be interested in everything. The term universal man is correctly used only analogously. This means that men share in, and contribute to, the entire universe of intellectual discourse and active knowing, each in his own way and to his own degree. The more fully, of course, a man shares in universal knowledge, the more of a universal man he is or becomes. The one-culture person who has not heard of, or thought about, anything other than what he has learned in his own particular culture, is a universal man only to a minimal degree, if at all. To be a universal man, to whatever extent, means not how much a man knows but what intellectual depth and breadth he has and what attitudes he has; how he holds the knowledge he has and how he relates it to other central and universally important problems; how he sees the wholeness and the unity of things. He is universal in that, knowing that each individual's intellectual ability and his capacity for feeling and doing are limited, he nonetheless shares most fully in the human universe of knowledge and emotion.

The mistaken idea that the term universal man can be understood univocally rather than analogously might at first seem a small matter. In fact it has been the source of great misunderstanding and has forestalled for generations the developing of men who might have been truly universal in their thinking and sympathies. Among other things it led to the conclusion that the concept of a universal man was too idealistic, and that an actual universal man was an impossibility. Even the most brilliant and large-souled men would have to give up any idea of trying to master all that is known. It became necessary to specialize in increasingly narrow fields in order to keep abreast of new theories and discoveries within these fields. Men became less and less universal, in the univocal sense, as subdisciplines grew out of subdisciplines. They also became less universal even in a proper analogous sense as they paid less and less attention to how knowledge fits together as a whole and is integrated even within one culture, to say nothing of among cultures or transculturally. In large measure men ceased to be concerned about universal knowledge or universal culture; thinking univocally about the concept of universal man, whenever they did so, they were overwhelmed by the prospect of knowing all there is to know themselves or of educating others to become universal men.

The second mistaken idea to be avoided in considering the universal man of the modern era is the very common one that there is something natural, right, inevitable, and almost sacred about culture differences. The classic statement of this idea goes something like this: if people were capable of thinking as human beings rather than as specific kinds of persons in their own culture patterns, they would long ago have shown more evidence of doing so. Cultural differences among human beings, it is held, are as natural as the differences among species of animals. The historical and psychological barriers to the emergence of universal man are thought to be so great that nothing could possibly eradicate them. The first thing that comes to one man's mind when meeting another for the first time is not whether he is human, but what culture or race he belongs to and what language he speaks—in short, whether he is the same or different. Consequently, the argument goes, each person will always preserve and promote the interests of his own group rather than those of mankind as a whole.

There is, admittedly, a certain cogency to this argument. The world has not yet had enough experience with either intercultural education or the concept of universal man to know quite how to accept these ideas or what to expect from them. It is hard for most people to see that they have much in common with other people who speak a different language and whose cultural background and way of life are so different from their own. Even at scholarly international conferences

of the highest level it is not uncommon for scholars to regard themselves as representatives of their particular culture first, as members of
regional groupings second, and as members of the whole human family
a far distant third.

This misconception arises from two closely related errors. The first
is to think that what has long been the case in international and intercultural activity is always going to be the case. While cultural differences may have seemed insurmountable only a short time ago, and
while even now culture conflicts still sometimes lead to armed conflict,
it is now becoming clear that men not only can but also must communicate across cultural barriers and work together. The thinking
that might have been true and tolerable in the old context of cultural
distances and differences is no longer true in the new world and human context. If anything, although it would be hard to prove from the
actual historical record, there is much more reason to think that the
unity of man ought to be held more sacred and inviolable than the
differences. And in fact, more and more people of all cultures are
coming to see that even their own best and most practical interests are
tied up with the best interests of all men rather than just with the
interests of a particular culture.

Further, the concept of the universal person does not at all eliminate
culture differences. Rather it seeks to preserve whatever is most valid,
significant, and valuable in each culture as a way of enriching and
helping to form the whole. The universal man is not separate and
distinct from his native or local culture. It is precisely because he is
deeply grounded in his own culture that the possibility of becoming a
universal man is open to him.

The universal man, then, and the universal culture, of which he is a
part and which he helps to fashion, are even now, though as yet dimly
recognizable only by the few, in the process of becoming. The vast
majority of people and even most of the scholars and prophets still
consider the universal man something of a phantom if not a figment of
the imagination. So how can the universal man be best described in
clear and convincing terms? To begin with, the universal man is a
man and like all men he functions at two different levels: the descriptive and the practical. These levels are equally parts of any ordinary
human problem-solving activity, but they can most easily be defined as
getting the facts or describing the situation (descriptive) and doing
something with those facts or about the situation (practical).

THE DESCRIPTIVE ORDER

In the descriptive order the universal man or the man of universal culture first attempts to adopt a viewpoint which permits him to see the general, common, or universal facts about all men. He seeks to *describe* the facts of the situation rather than *prescribe* what, if anything, ought to be done about them. He sees, for example, that there are roughly three billion people, almost equally divided between men and women, presently alive on this planet. In itself this is a simple fact, but the very realization that he can identify these creatures as human beings is no small matter because by this very identification he separates out, according to whatever his criterion for humanness is, these three billion people from all other forms of life on the earth. He recognizes that the same criterion he uses to describe all other people as human beings also applies to himself. He is a person, a human being, along with the other three billion people whom he recognizes as similar to himself.

He notices next that the people are distributed unequally over the face of the earth in ways that are strangely diverse. This distribution does not seem at all to have been rationally planned or organized. Some people live in very cold climates, some in very hot, and others live in all the inhabitable climates in between. He sees further that these three billion people have placed themselves together in groups of various sizes so that, for example, some are tribal, some are nomadic, some live on farms, some live in hamlets, villages, cities, and suburbs. Some groupings of people have come together to form small, medium, or large-size countries. He observes that these groupings have some things in common by which they are recognized as groups: language, land, customs, law, means of production and distribution of goods, arts and crafts, religion and philosophy.

At the same time that he becomes aware of the vast differences, he observes that not only do the people within the groups have much in common but also that so do the groups. Biologically the people are basically the same and have the same needs, although there are accidental differences of color, size, and physiognomy. Intellectually they function in much the same way, communicating with one another, and sharing ideas and feelings, although there are different degrees of intelligence and differing ways of using it among the groups. Psychologically they all appear to have the same basic fears, hopes, desires and loves, and insecurities. Socially they have much the same kind of basic relationships with their fellow human beings and each person both contributes to, and shares in, the work and life of the group. Economically, the groups are in vastly different stages of development and modernization, and some of the largest groups—in India, China, and Africa, for example—are among the least technologically developed on every economic index. Spiritually they all seem to ask the same fundamental questions about origins, ultimate reality, and purpose, although the answers to these questions vary considerably from group to group.

The universal man in attempting to see the facts as they are and to describe the situation as it is, notes that very often, although the people within the individual groups seem to get along among themselves reasonably well, which is not to say that there is no discord and conflict within the group, the peoples of one group tend to be uninformed about, and disinterested in, the other groups. As a result there is often distrust, misunderstanding, hostility, and from time to time, open war between groups. He is aware, however, that various attempts have been made to ease the tensions among national and cultural groupings by their coming together in some larger form of organization, the most recent being the United Nations.

This, in the broadest possible strokes, is the universe of man, as the universal man sees it. He realizes that even in observing the world in this way he is being selective in his perceptions of what is, and of what is important, and that he is using the modes of thinking which his cultural background and education dictate. He has no other choice than to do so. He knows it is entirely possible that other observers from other points of view might see this simple outline of man's universe in another way and with different emphases, but he feels that there is enough objectivity in what he has observed that most men of most cultures would see this much of the world situation in about the same way as he does.

The universal man will, of course, seek more and more knowledge, more and more data, both about individual cultures and about the universal culture which he sees emerging. He realizes the importance of hard data both in the developing of a theory of universal culture and in the confirming of it. A universal culture cannot be simply a grandiose or idealistic paper creation; it must be soundly grounded in the real world and unless it is psychologically acceptable and even inspiring to those who would share in it, it will mean little.

At the descriptive level, the universal man is not content to look just at the facts, however general or specific they may be. He wants, as well, to get at the reasons and causes behind the facts and to understand them. He asks not only what the facts are but also why the facts are as they are. For example, the universal man realizes it is not sufficient to know that the people of different cultures start from different premises as they begin to construct their systems of thinking and believing; it is only when he knows why they start from different premises that he will begin to understand both the premises themselves and the pattern of logic that connects the premises and the conclusions.

Among certain Western philosophers who identify the intellectual virtues of the speculative order as knowledge, understanding, and wisdom, the word *understanding* is used in a precise sense to mean the grasp, recognition, or intuition of the first principles on which all human cognition is based. Such principles are said to be either evident or self-evident as soon as the terms of the proposition are apprehended. For example, such statements or principles as "a thing is what it is" (the principle of identity), or, "every effect must have a cause" (the principle of causality), or, "a thing cannot be and not be at the same time" (the principle of contradiction), do not require proof and in fact cannot be proved by reference to principles more pristine or fundamental than themselves. One either recognizes and understands such principles or he does not; there is no way of demonstrating them.

In the present context, however, the word *understanding* is used much more broadly. The well-acknowledged fact that different cultures start from different premises does not imply that the universal man personally assumes the premises of all cultures to be evident or self-evident. He attempts to understand not the premises themselves, which might in fact be contrary to or in contradiction to his own basic premises, but the reasons which lead people of other cultures to accept as self-evident the premises from which they start.

Still in the descriptive order, the universal man seeks the highest intellectual attainment of all—wisdom. Wisdom is more than knowledge or understanding taken separately or together, though it includes them. The wise man both knows and understands, but he sees things with a deeper and broader vision. Traditionally, wisdom has been regarded at least in the West as that power or intellectual habit by means of which all things are viewed in the light of their ultimate, rather than their proximate, causes. Wisdom in this sense has been seen as resulting from either theological or philosophical study, since only these two disciplines, both in content and in way of knowing, are concerned with ultimate causes. To know things in their ultimate causes is to know them as *being* and how they participate in the principles which govern all being as being. Since wisdom is that power by means of which all things are viewed in the light of their ultimate causes and since the ultimate causes are thought to be the primary, governing, and most important causes, it is the role of wisdom to evaluate, order, and integrate all knowledge and all life.

The universal man himself aspires to be a man of wisdom. Additionally, he recognizes that the pursuit of wisdom and the continuing search for it is a common, if not universal, characteristic of men in every culture. This characteristic is, in fact, one of the principal reasons that leads him to think that the emergence of a universal culture is a genuine possibility. If anything, the East places more emphasis on the pursuit of wisdom in its fullest meaning, though it may define it somewhat differently, than does the West. For example, John C. H. Wu, after explaining that "the most deep-rooted desire of the Chinese people is for harmony. Whether they are speaking of self-cultivation or dealing with the affairs of the world *harmony* is the keynote of their thinking," then goes on to state:

> To put it the other way around, the investigation of the nature of things and relationships leads to true knowledge, which leads to sincerity in thought, which leads to purity of heart, which prepares for the perfection of the whole person, which conduces to an orderly family, which helps to make a well-governed State, which contributes toward the peace of the entire world. In fact, the whole process is a continuous harmonious movement from the innermost harmony to the outermost harmony. For the investigation of things and knowledge represent the harmony of subject and object; sincerity in thought and purity of heart represent the harmony of intellect and will; personal perfection represents the harmony of body and soul; while the orderly family, the well-governed State, and the peaceful world form a progressive series of concentric expansions of transpersonal harmony.[1]

Finally, the universal man, working with all the understanding, knowledge, and wisdom he can acquire, and using the imagination and creative power which they open up to him, seeks to determine what a universal culture would and should be like. Just as on the one hand he is not interested in vague and unrealizable utopian concepts, so on the other he does not at all concur with that thinking which holds that man's future is determined by an inscrutable and ineluctable historical process in which man is trapped. He thinks as a matter of fact that a universal culture would add immeasurable positive value to man's life. The signs of an emerging world culture are all around him, as for example in man's growing concern for a just social order and in such immediate and practical matters as ecological improvement, and he seeks to help create it, at first through imaginative construction and then through action devoted to that purpose.[2] He has no desire to shape the world according to his own image and likeness or that of the culture to which he happens to belong, but he has a passionate desire that the world be shaped to man's greater benefit, happiness, and fulfillment. Although he does not use the term universal culture, N. K. Devaraja puts the point well when he writes: "Culture, thus, may be described as the process or group of processes by which individuals participate in, and enhance, the conscious and creative life of the human race, or of one another."[3]

What the universal man, thus, envisages is a macroculture, or a culture of cultures, in which all men feel they have a part, with which they can positively identify, and to which they can look for encouragement and support. Such a culture of cultures would have its own inner dynamic principles. It would not in any way tyrannize over the minds of men by creating a central orthodoxy to determine which ideas, attitudes, beliefs, and actions are acceptable and which are not. Rather the universal culture would evolve openly and integrally so that all ideas would be examined on their merits and their power to capture and hold the mind and spirit of man. Among other things, it would entail a human literature which all men would read and understand and which would express the feelings and longings of man as man, rather than of Asian or Christian man, or wealthy or poor man; each culture would make a contribution to world literature at the same time that it preserved all that is valid and good in its own literature. Such a culture would see the coming into being of a world history centered again on man as man, not on man as African, Latin American, or Oriental, although history of individual cultures would also continue to be written. The macroculture would be, as all cultures and peoples are, greatly interested in theology and philosophy, but these areas would emphasize man's eternal search for God and for wisdom—which search would be greatly enriched by the particularized insights and systems of theology and philosophy that exist today. Even today persons of a theological and philosophical bent are coming more and more to realize the similarities of their goals and aims, but the emergence of a creative universal culture would give great new energy and depth to man's religious and philosophical impulses and fascinations.

THE PRACTICAL ORDER

The universal man, however, does not function at the speculative or descriptive level alone. He also functions at the level of practical affairs, of action, of getting things accomplished. In this case he is concerned not only with thinking about a universal culture or speculating about what it might be and what it might involve but also with helping to bring it about and with assisting it to flourish. He recognizes that knowledge is a good in itself, since knowing is a human perfection apart from whatever practical consequences might flow from it. But knowledge, knowing, is tested in, and by, action and practice to the extent that many question whether there is any genuine knowing which does not result in the solving of specific problems. Knowing, it is claimed, is not the passive viewing of the real or of that which preexists out there, but real knowing is a method of manipulating, changing, or interacting with the external environment. Whether knowledge precedes action or is born through interaction of some kind, the universal man seeks to combine the deepest and best knowledge with effective action. The question to which the universal man responds with his whole being, his thought and his action, is: what should a particular individual person do in the situation in which man now finds himself to bring about an improvement in the quality of life for all men? Each person is only one, but it is ultimately with each individual person that the responsibility and the strength exist.

The answer to this question takes many forms, some more general, others more specific.

In general the universal man is concerned with finding a modus vivendi, a way of life which would allow for, and make possible, the full realization of the potential of all persons on the planet. A culture is, indeed, a way of life but heretofore it has been taken for granted that each culture, each way of life, was largely complete unto itself. Each culture thought primarily about itself and assumed that each other culture should and would do likewise. Whether that assumption or hypothesis might have been tenable in the past is debatable. That it is now no longer so is clear if, in their reading of the world condition in the late twentieth century, people at large are not to fall into what the behavioral scientists call a Type II error, namely, the nonrejection of a false hypothesis. (A Type I error is, of course, the rejection of a true hypothesis.) The hypothesis that a world or universal culture is impossible must be rejected, at least until such time as it is proven that it is impossible to develop a culture of man as man that transcends individual cultures, but which at the same time respects their valid and appropriate differences and diversities.

The question is whether a way of life, a universal culture, can be found which will do for all human beings what the more successful cultures of the past and present have done for certain of their own members. This is not to say that any culture has yet been able to open up to all its members the quality of life that its own intellectual and spiritual leaders hoped. Even in the golden age of Greek culture, for example, although its achievements still astound the mind, there were many illiterate people, since education was regarded as a privilege and a responsibility of only the well-to-do; the franchise was extended neither to women nor to slaves. In ancient China as well the educational system was excellent but was limited to a small percentage of the population since it was offered principally to those who were to go into the civil service. Further, even those cultures that have been most successful have had constantly to worry about being overthrown or overridden by the hostile forces of other cultures which envied their success and sought to destroy them by force. In the modern age it has become more and more evident that no individual culture can be secure and can devote its energies to the improvement of its own civilization and the quality of life of those within it unless it is conscious at the same time of the needs and hopes of all other peoples of the world. A culture might be able to protect itself for a time against military invasion from without or revolution from within, but it can do so only at the expense of sacrificing other much more important goals toward which it should be striving. A sincere effort on its part at improving the standard of living and the quality of life for all mankind is the only sure safeguard against the overthrow of any culture that is now relatively successful; much more important and positive is the realization that significant improvement in the quality of life for all men everywhere is now a real possibility as well as a genuine responsibility.

In the practical order the universal man sees the possibility of a universal culture growing out of a functional or operational approach to the solving of human problems. People do not have to agree on the ultimate nature of the good, the true, and the beautiful in order to achieve practical results. Functionalism means simply that human beings ordinarily find it much easier to cooperate across culture lines on the basis of specific problems to be solved or of specific projects to be carried out or services to be performed than on the basis of prior agreement on metaphysical theory. Of course, the very decision to cooperate functionally is in itself a part of a pragmatic and realistic theory. The concept of functionalism, however, is not maintained for its theoretical validity but because it is often impossible to reach consensus on philosophical or theoretical or historical grounds, and because working together on important projects tends to make people forget, or at least relegate to secondary importance, culture differences.

One classic example of international and intercultural cooperation that has worked exceptionally well along purely functional lines is the Universal Postal Union which began in 1875. This union has worked so well, despite the fact that the delivery of mail internationally is an extremely complex matter, that one now tends to take for granted that a letter mailed from almost any point in the world will arrive at its destination safely and reasonably quickly. This example of international functional cooperation is used because it has been successful over a long period. People seem to agree that the delivery of mail speedily and without its having been intercepted or censored is more important than the matter of who is correct or incorrect in an ideological dispute; nonetheless, the right to free access to information, including even the mail, is in itself an ideological question of great consequence.

The number of examples of beneficial cooperation along functional lines among nations and cultures could be extended indefinitely. The list would cover practically every phase of human existence, including both research studies and projects and the direct execution of specific programs, for example, in health, food, engineering, and water control. Functionalism at the practical level in no way precludes continuing dialog and communication on humanistic, artistic, and spiritual matters; in fact, it encourages them and lays the groundwork for them. Perhaps the best general example of functional intercultural cooperation has been the work of specialized agencies of the United Nations.

In these agencies people of various cultures work side by side on large numbers of specific projects in the hope of achieving results that will be beneficial to all.

The principle of functionalism is not, however, without its grave dangers and difficulties. There will never be any shortage of important and worthwhile projects to be undertaken, but there is not likely soon to be enough money and talent to undertake all such programs. The principle of functionalism itself supplies no way of identifying priorities and as a result projects or programs undertaken are often those in which the persons with power have some special interest. Functionalism sometimes leads to randomness, to duplication in some cases and complete neglect in others; to a kind of crisis mentality in which projects are undertaken to meet an emergency rather than to prevent its arising in the first place; and to outright conflict when a given project, however good in itself, interferes with what other interested parties consider their rights. Much more important, however, is the fact that functionalism, the carrying out of specific projects and programs as a felt need arises, sometimes sets in motion a chain of events or creates structures which make later long-range and more comprehensive planning much more difficult. Once a project has been undertaken or completed, certain processes, often irreversible, are set in motion.

Nonetheless, the universal man sees functionalism as setting the stage and developing the habits of cooperation that will make it possible for men of different cultures later to come together in the much more difficult matters of theoretical, intellectual, spiritual, and emotional cooperation from which the essentials of a universal culture might emerge. The person of universal outlook and awareness points to the fact that functionalism is already so far advanced and so widespread that a major breakthrough in the direction of a world culture could well be imminent and might be one of the greatest achievements of the twentieth century.

At the practical level the building of a universal culture or a program of truly intercultural cooperation requires creating institutions and organizations that can effect the necessary changes. The individual can do some things on a person-to-person and friend-to-friend basis, but it is only when an idea becomes institutionalized and an organization becomes effective that major change can be accomplished. In practically all areas of possible intercultural interest, of course, efforts have already been made. But here again, many of these efforts have been abortive because they were born out of due season or they were entered into with considerable reluctance, perhaps even out of sheer necessity, and seemingly almost always with an eye toward protecting or promoting the culture's own interests rather than those of the human race as a whole. The assumption generally seems to have been that cooperation should be hesitant and minimal out of a fear that it would lead to a loss of sovereignty or independence of action.

It would be impossible here, of course, to attempt to discuss in any detail all the institutions and organizations which a universal culture would necessitate. Though some new institutions would have to come into being, it might be more a matter of creating a new mentality and of giving a new orientation to those international institutions and organizations which already exist, at least in some stage of development. Probably the United Nations would have to be replaced by an entirely new type of institution or organization[4] since it now appears to have been founded on an untenable principle, namely, that the nation is the basis of international organization and order. It is in fact national interests and loyalties that make international cooperation and world loyalty so difficult to achieve. But many other international institutions and organizations would simply become more truly, deeply, and reciprocally international or intercultural than they now are.

A UNIVERSAL OR COSMOPOLITAN VIEWPOINT

Every human being has certain implicit or explicit viewpoints on all matters that affect his existence and that of his fellow men. Sometimes he is not even aware of what his viewpoints are, but as a result of education, experience, and a general growth of intelligence, he comes to articulate his viewpoints and to defend them. A viewpoint is a more or less consistent way of looking at things, although one purpose of all education is to open the mind of the student to deeper, more comprehensive, and hopefully more liberating viewpoints. One's viewpoint determines what falls within his range of vision; it determines what he sees and how broadly or narrowly he will envisage it; it determines the context within which he will select some ideas for further consideration and reject others. The universal person will have had the kind of learning and experiences which permit intercultural and universal, rather than rigidly one-culture viewpoints or perspectives. The universal viewpoint is epitomized in the term *cosmopolitan,* which comes from two

Greek words: *cosmos*, "world" and *polis*, "city." Both in the ancient Greek and the modern English usage of the word the cosmopolitan person is one whose city is the world. For the Greeks the city was the basic political unit rather than, as is now the case, the nation or the state. To be cosmopolitan does not mean that one does not have an origin in a particular city or a particular culture; nor does it mean that one completely separates himself or his loyalties and affections from the place of his origin. It means instead that he views things not only from the perspective of his local city but also from the perspective of the world at large. The cosmopolitan, a citizen of the world as well as of his city, realizes that he shares in, and contributes to, a greater unity which is that of the wider world, the whole of mankind. Intercultural education, of course, aims to inculcate a cosmopolitan viewpoint.

Respect is the first element in the cosmopolitan viewpoint. The monocultural person tends to view other cultures with fear, mistrust, and suspicion, if not outright hostility. The cosmopolitan views every culture with respect in that he realizes it has its own tradition, integrity, validity, and dignity. He sees each culture as yet another effort of the human mind to come to grips with the problems that confront all men. It is probably more correct to say that he regards the people of other cultures as capable, intelligent, and responsible persons, who may or may not share his feelings and insights, but who are to be respected as persons in any event. Other ways of seeing and doing things are not viewed as threatening his way of life but as complementary to it, as part of the whole of human experience. At the very minimum he respects other people enough not to try to impose his culture on them in any imperialistic or authoritarian way, but he also respects them enough to discuss with them openly and freely ideas that might be mutually beneficial.

Respect for other peoples and other cultures does not imply that all cultures or systems of thought are taken as of equal value. One can see in a culture much with which one does not agree and yet respect the people who subscribe to it and their reasons for doing so. To respect another culture does not mean that one accepts uncritically whatever the culture holds and advances. Genuine respect is mutual and it implies a willingness to inquire, to listen, and to learn. One of the first fruits of mutual respect is the agreement to disagree agreeably.

The cosmopolitan viewpoint entails not only respect but a serious effort at understanding other cultures. Respect, in and of itself, can be distant and aloof, bordering on indifference. Understanding, on the other hand, implies a desire to go beyond respect and enter into a deeper awareness of what the people of another culture think and feel and why they do so. Understanding is based on knowledge, of course, and the more one knows about a culture the more likely he is to understand the ideas and the attitudes of the people of that culture. But there is more than one way of acquiring and holding knowledge, and knowledge and understanding are not synonymous. To know a culture from within, or as the philosophers say, connaturally or through love, is to know it in the way that best leads to understanding. One can never fully know another culture, in the same way as its members do, but insofar as this is possible, it most closely approximates the knowledge which leads to genuine understanding. To know another culture in such a way as to identify with it and to seek truly whatever is best for it, rather than simply to observe it as an outsider, is the goal of intercultural education and derives from the cosmopolitan viewpoint.

Appreciation is the third and final element in the cosmopolitan viewpoint. Appreciation, of course, follows from both respect and understanding. But it is quite distinct. It means that another culture is regarded as a positive and highly valued good. The cosmopolitan person not only is at home in the other culture but also comes to take delight in the ideas, the people, the art, music, literature, drama, the theology and philosophy of that culture, and to view them as making a special contribution to the advancement of human civilization. To appreciate anything is to hold it in high esteem. The best evidence of the appreciation of another culture is to want to make its ways and its works better known among all the peoples of the world, not as a way of replacing one culture with another but as a way of enhancing the spiritual worth and value of all cultures.

MODES OF THINKING

The universal person is distinguished from the one-culture person not only in his habitual viewpoint, which is cosmopolitan, but also in his habitual modes of thinking.

Each culture has its own logic, that is, its own premises or postulates and its own way of achieving internal consistency. Granted the original premises, and granted the validity of the thinking or reasoning process, the conclusions are appropriate and admissible. In one sense each of these is a mode or method of thinking, a total way of bringing intelligence to bear on knowing and living. The claim has been made, but by no means proven, that the culture so determines the modes of thinking that changes in ways of thinking are virtually impossible. The fact, indeed, seems to be to the contrary. Ways or habits of thinking are learned and they can be, at least to a significant extent, reversed and relearned or greatly modified by education and experience.

The scientific mode of thinking, or scientific method itself, is said to be culture free, although different cultures will give different degrees of prominence to science and will bring scientific method to bear on different problems. The essence of scientific method is that both the process and the conclusions are publicly verifiable; they are thus transcultural, objective, or universal. Any person of any cultural background who repeats the process or the experiment in exactly the same way as reported by the scientist will get the same results. If he should get different results, the problem will be traced not to his culture but to his competence as a scientist. Science is based on the assumption that nature is regular, orderly, and predictable however much the cultures of the world may differ one from the other.

The modes or habits of thinking under consideration here in connection with the development of the universal person, however, are those which have to do mainly with arriving at policies for the organizing of human activities, interactions, and interrelations. Because they concern human interactions, they do not follow any set scientific or natural laws, although there is a certain predictability even in human interactions, as the social scientists and the psychologists are coming more and more to demonstrate. Further, these modes of thinking are not exclusively intercultural; they are present as part of the intellectual equipment of each person in every culture, to a limited degree, but they are essential to any person who is to function effectively in an intercultural context and dimension. Though separable for the sake of analysis, in actual operation the modes of thinking are not to be thought of as separate faculties or powers which one calls on as required and which one develops individually through some specific technique. Rather they are phases of a general intelligence factor which is improved and strengthened by the kinds of experiences proper to intercultural education.

These modes of thinking are three: goal-directed, developmental, and projective or inventive.

Even the naming of these three modes of thinking reveals a distinctly

Western approach to the problem; nevertheless, various interpretations of the same general concepts can be found in most if not all cultures. A member of another culture, studying the same subject, might well use different categories; there are, in short, different modes of thinking about even the modes of thinking. Betty Heimann, the renowned Sanskrit scholar, makes this point clear in writing of the differences between Western and Indian logic.

> Yet another difference between Western and Indian logic can be indicated by the comparison between two Greek and Sanskrit terms. The Greek term *heteros* means literally the "other." As such it gains with Aristotle the meaning of "the worse," "the lesser." Western logic clings to the established order and is reluctant to accept the vague otherness. The Sanskrit equivalent is *para*. It, too, means the "other" but as such the "higher and better." It is here where the fundamental difference between Western and Indian logic and its ethical implications lies. The thing in hand, while being clearly observable and distinct, is of definite value for the Westerner. The "other" for him, is thus something disquietingly vague, while the "other" is of positive value for the Indian because of its very vagueness. It opens the view on further unlimited potentialities.[5]

It is readily seen in just this one example that certain modes of thinking in India are quite different from those in the West. Intercultural education is concerned with understanding the modes of thinking of the different cultures and seeks even further to clarify why different modes of thinking exist.

While it is true that much thinking tends to be goal oriented or goal directed, it is also true that this mode of thinking takes on special meaning and importance in intercultural education. The universal person is very much aware of the part that goals play in human life, and his thinking is greatly influenced by the goals he sets for himself and for his society.

A goal is something good to be done, achieved, or attained. It has, of course, long been known that setting goals and keeping them clearly in mind helps attain them. It has only recently become more apparent that thinking is directed not only *toward* a goal but also *by* a goal. Goal-directed thinking is the opposite of random, ad hoc, or simple survival-type thinking. Thought selects and sets goals, but once that happens, the goal to be achieved penetrates, informs, and guides the very process of thinking about how best to achieve it. In one sense most thinking is goal directed in that it has some point or purpose beyond itself that leads to one or another form of action. In the broader and more subtle sense goal-directed thinking implies not only a conscious concern for the proper or best possible goals but also an intense effort at clarifying the goal fully, sharply, and realistically in operational terms so that one will know at all times whether in fact he is moving toward the goal.

Goals are short range or long range—proximate, intermediate, or ultimate. They may be, as John Dewey suggests, simply ends-in-view, that is, things that one wants to do or feels he should do. Man is a purposive animal, and when he acts he has some goal, however vague, in mind. There is much less agreement on whether nature itself, and man as part of nature and of history, has an ultimate goal toward which it is or should be directed.

The monocultural person tends to accept without question the goals and objectives that his culture sets before him. Whether these goals are the kinds of proximate goals which relate to his specific role as an individual in a culture—for example, how to make a living or how to raise a family, or to his broader ultimate role in the universe as a whole—the majority of men tend to concur easily with the dominate thinking in the culture of which they are a part. Some cultures include a world view which assigns the same ultimate goal to all men; other cultures see different final goals, or ultimate destinies, for different men depending on who they are and what they do. In those cultures which present more alternatives and options, the individual person will have wider choices among both proximate and ultimate goals within the culture, but even in those cultures which are most open, the number of acceptable goals is still limited. The one-culture person is confined by the goals which his single culture creates for him and more or less requires him to pursue.

On the other hand, the universal person finds himself facing a much wider range of possible goals, again both proximate and ultimate. He discovers that another culture, other cultures, or a universalistic culture open up vast new perspectives to him and add wholly new dimensions to his thinking about his goals and those of other men. Most often he does not at all want to relinquish the values and goals of the culture into which he was born, but at the same time he finds himself drawn toward, and directed by new goals which transcend any one particularized culture. The intercultural person, who makes the transition from a monocultural to a multicultural type thinking or to universalistic thinking successfully, without becoming a marginal man in the process, feels the impact of new goals in which his basic culture loyalties now become part of a much greater whole—that of humanity, human civilization, or universal culture itself.

The universal person is especially goal directed and goal conscious because he more or less freely accepts or rejects the goals which alternative cultures present to him. He determines for himself what the goals of his life should be. Having freely and with full knowledge chosen the goals, his actions in working toward their achievement are very deeply influenced by them. They are not goals which he accepts, unconsciously, simply because they are there; rather, they are goals which he makes fully his own.

The second mode of thinking characteristic of the universal person is called *developmental*. This mode of thinking is not exclusively intercultural; some developmental thinking goes on within each individual culture, especially in the modernization process. Businessmen, for example, tend to think in the developmental mode as they plan the progress and expansion of their business. But intercultural education highlights and stresses developmental thinking, and the intercultural person comes to think developmentally with a consistency and force which the one-culture person finds hard to comprehend.

The word *development* is used in so many different ways that it is loaded with ambiguities. Most frequently in the context of modernization it refers principally to economic development, and it is the process by which various cultures and countries strengthen and improve their economic positions. So much is this the case that the countries of the world are classified by economists as either developed or developing, although the development process moves ahead, at different rates of speed to be sure, in all cultures. Economic development is universally regarded as one of the most pressing problems of the modern age; at the same time there is general recognition that not all human problems are solvable by economic development alone.

A good example of developmental thinking is that which went into the "Report to the President from the Task Force on International Development" under the title, *U.S. Foreign Assistance in the 1970's: A New Approach*. The task force, composed of sixteen distinguished citizens, had been commissioned by the President "to recommend policies that will serve the best interests of our Nation through the decade ahead" (p. 3 of the report). The task force concluded, among other things, that foreign assistance programs should not be expected to influence others to adopt U.S. cultural values or institutions. The task force studied the entire field of American foreign assistance and attempted to set priorities and programs on a rational basis, not only for the 1970s but for the indefinite future. The report goes on to state:

> The United States shares with other nations concerns that call for common action. Problems related to population increase, poverty, public health, child development, literacy, natural resource exhaustion, rural backwardness, environmental pollution, and urban congestion exist in the United States as well as in the developing countries. Participation in both international development and domestic development can result in an exchange of useful experience. This has been demonstrated by government programs and by the work abroad of private organizations, such as universities, foundations and voluntary agencies.
>
> Participation in international development can promote progress toward the kind of world in which each country can enjoy the rewards of its own culture and the fruits of its own production in its own way, without infringing on the right of any other country to the same freedom for human fulfillment.[6]

In a much more general way, and as it is used here, development is synonymous with growth. While developmental thinking is and should be concerned with the future, the person who is thinking developmentally is more immediately and directly involved in trying to understand how things came to be as they presently are. He sees the present state or condition of things as resulting from certain developments or changes during the course of the history of the culture which brought it to its present status. He knows that the culture, barring violent revolution or sudden annihilation, will develop in the future along somewhat the same lines as it has in the past. But even apart from future developments, a culture can be really understood in the present only if one has come to know its developmental patterns over the years. Strong cultures change much more slowly than weak cultures for the very reason that they have the strength either to resist change or to adopt new ideas and make them part of the culture.

Developmental thinking is in the broadest sense historical, evolutionary, or dynamic thinking. There is a tendency among one-culture people to think only in the present and of the present, although they are often profoundly influenced by the past and attached to it. Education and wider experience do much to counteract this thinking in any culture, but the tendency to think that things are now as they always were and always ought to be dies hard. This is particularly true where the culture has a long and perhaps glorious past. That it has existed for so long tends to confirm its validity and confer value on it. To think developmentally, on the other hand, is to come to detect the trends and the stages of development, and to analyze and evaluate them. Each culture seems to have its cycles, its flourishing and its ebbing. This rising and falling of cultures is sometimes thought of as a natural phenomenon, but some cultures, by taking cognizance of, and exercising diligence in promoting the welfare of their people, have sustained themselves for long periods of time.

To think developmentally means to discover what forces and factors brought the culture into existence and were present at its birth. What have been its strengths and weaknesses; what are the unifying bonds and the disintegrating elements; what are the culture's genetic or physiological characteristics, what are the collective experiences that have either inspired the people or led to their dispiritment; what kinds of leaders have they selected or accepted and why; what emphasis have they placed on education and the higher culture? In short, the answers to these and similar questions give the developmental picture of the culture.

Realizing that in knowing the causes one can somewhat anticipate effects and help to control them, developmental thinking concerns itself more with causes and reasons than with effects. While in no way neglecting empirical and statistical data and while helping to find ever better ways of compiling and using them, the intercultural person who thinks developmentally is more interested in why people think and act as they do than he is in simply knowing what they do think and how they act in certain circumstances. The intercultural person in looking at a culture almost immediately asks what causes it to be as it is, and if the original causes are still functioning to give the culture its coherence and vitality. A culture will sometimes profess nominally or ritualistically an idea or presumed value which has long since ceased to effect any significant difference in what the people really do and believe. To think developmentally rather than in a static way leads the universal person to seek out the causes for the differences of thinking within a culture as well as among cultures and to understand what forces and influences have brought about changes of thinking in the past, and are most likely to do so in the future. Developmental thinking

is not idle utopia building or simple prediction, speculation, or futurism. It is intimately bound up with the creating of realistic programs or projects which can be expected to achieve the projected results.

The more complex life becomes and the more unitary the world becomes, the more necessary it is to think projectively, not only as a way of maintaining mental health and stability but also as a way of making sure that to whatever extent possible man controls his own future. It is not a sterile complaint, for example, that bigness, whether of business, education, religion, government, or international organization, creates a whole new kind of world, a world different in kind and not just in degree from the small world. Bigness makes its own demands and left to itself it determines how it will be served. Though bigness has many advantages, it becomes a human problem, that is, the disadvantages begin to outweigh the advantages when people begin to feel impotent and insignificant in the big, and often bureaucratic, structure. The person who thinks projectively does not simply take for granted that bigness is a fact of life about which he can do nothing. He looks forward to see whether, in fact, bigness in all human organizations is necessary, and, if so, how much bigness. If he forsees that bigness is an essential aspect of modern life he attempts to create ways of living with bigness without being swallowed up in it. He designs new forms to compensate the individual person for what he has lost in becoming part of the bigger system.

In very early times and, in fact, until fairly recently, projective thinking, though always a part of the intellectual process, was not nearly as important as it is today. A young person, born in a certain place and into a certain family background, could be fairly sure of what he would be doing and of what the world he knew would be like until he died. Change was slow and gradual, but in the modern world the forces of change challenge almost everyone, and both defining the directions of change and shaping them for man's benefit call for the widest possible projective thinking. The setting of priorities, of both time and importance, demands projective thinking of the highest type.

As the world moved into the 1970s, and the thought occurred to many people that the year 2000 was less than thirty years away, the year 2000 became an interesting target date for much projective thinking. What would the world be like in 2000, if indeed it existed at all? What would the university, the church, the school, the family, the media, the economy look like in that year? What major changes would take place between now and then, and what trends already set in motion had reached the point at which they are irreversible? Probably more major projective thinking took place at the beginning of this decade than in the entire seventy years of this century which preceded it. All of this thinking and writing was of importance, of course, but much of it stressed only one side of the projective thinking process. Often the question was, "What will the situation be in A.D. 2000?" Speculating about the answer to this question, almost as if certain events or developments were predetermined, could be of some value in forward planning. The much more important question, however, is "What *ought* the situation be at that time?" or, "What do the best interests of all people require that the situation be at that time?" Projective thinking at its best is concerned with what changes ought to be made and how they can best be made to insure the building of a better future world.

The intercultural person thinks projectively because he is necessarily concerned about the future. The monocultural person, if he thinks projectively at all, tends to see most change coming within his own culture; he is unaware of the broader influences of one culture on another as a source of new ideas about change. The objective of the universal person is not merely to understand other cultures, important as this is, but to assist in bringing about a much better relationship among the peoples of the various cultures. He knows this will not happen automatically; it calls for forward thinking of the most innovative form.

There is another way in which intercultural education helps to develop projective thinking in the universal person. Though it involves looking to the future, it is at first more lateral and contemporary than projective. It is a subtle and difficult form of education and there are no sure ways of achieving it; many who are intercultural persons in every other way never succeed in achieving it. It consists of the student's "projecting" himself into another culture in such a way that he comes to think and respond as the members of that culture think and respond. The great majority of students, many who have lived for years in another culture, still end by being regarded by the host culture as outsiders. But in a number of cases, the student, without becoming a member of the other culture and without losing his own cultural identity, comes to function in a way that both he and the members of the other culture consider or accept as quite natural. People of the other culture will speak with him as they would with any member of their own culture without being aware of any difference. Because he knows the culture and its people well, through a form of projection or empathy, he can anticipate or predict how they will react under practically all circumstances. He can judge correctly their feelings and emotions, and what they will regard as most important in any transaction.

This phenomenon has no relationship with what psychiatrists refer to as projection; rather it is a distinctive form of knowing. It is also a form or mode of thinking in which a person almost literally projects himself into the minds and hearts of the people of the other culture. He reaches a degree of understanding of himself and of them in which mutual respect and trust are easy and natural. The intercultural person becomes identified with the needs and aspirations of the other culture and he is particularly sensitive to its feelings, its ways of thinking, and its beauty.

THE UNIVERSAL PERSON AND WORLD LAW

The universal person sees law both as a foundation on which the structure of universal culture will have to be based and as a present instrument for promoting further harmonious relationships and cooperation among all men. In general, law, though it is developing and dynamic in itself as world conditions change, is that organizing influence, the rule of reason and the concern for equity, in society or culture by means of which the members of the society learn to live together and come to know what the society permits and expects. Law embodies in a practical way the ideals of what the society regards as the common good or the general welfare, while at the same time preserving the widest possible freedom for the individual person. Law, at its best, is not a burden but an opportunity, affording as it does the protection of the human rights of each person in the interests of the fullest good of the group as a whole.

The concern of law, of course, is for the establishing and perfecting of justice within a community or culture, and in the case of a universal culture it would be concerned with insuring justice for all. Though a good society goes far beyond the bare requirements of justice in promoting the common good, there can be no viable society which is not founded on justice. The question of the nature and meaning of justice has tormented the mind of man through the centuries since Plato first directly explored the subject. Since that time there have been a number of important theories of jurisprudence which attempt to account for the way in which justice is achieved through law, whether in its making, or in its interpretation and application. At the minimum, all valid systems of law insist on due process and on the equal treatment of all before the law. The right to justice is a right which inheres in the person as a human being and is not bestowed on him by the individual culture of which he happens to be a member. The constant struggle of the human race in its efforts toward civilization has been to achieve a rule of law and reason rather than of man or power.

A universal culture, of which universal law and the achievement of justice for all would be essential components, would have to be based on the concept that the world exists for the good of all, not just for the good of individual powerful, intelligent, or wealthy men, or for privileged or superior races or cultures, or for chosen peoples. Such a concept, of course, calls for a much different form of thinking than has prevailed throughout most of human history. The practical guiding principle in the development of man to this point seems to have been that the world and its resources are here to serve the interests of those who, through whatever stroke of fortune, are in the best position to take advantage of them and use them for their own purposes. Never, however, have the peoples and cultures of this world been so close together, geographically and psychologically, as they now are. Never before have they been forced to think beyond family, tribe, clan, nation, and culture, and to view man and the world as a whole. Previously, men have usually acted out of a spirit of taking care of themselves, their families, and close friends first, almost as if the world existed for them exclusively rather than for the good of all. This thinking, naturally enough, has resulted in the greatest inequities and injustices and has led to the fact that those with the most power, ingenuity, and luck have been able to benefit disproportionately from that which should benefit all. The heightened awareness of this disproportion and the demand for greater justice in modern times is not a claim that the world owes anyone a living. It does require that all have a chance to a fair share in the goods of this world and that all have the opportunity to work for the improvement of themselves and of all their fellows.

Good beginnings have been made in the development of the theory and practice of international law. A consciousness of the need for a system of international law that would be effective in both making and applying laws is becoming universal. Certain written and unwritten dictates of international law are already observed by most nations and persons who want to be known by the comity of man as civilized. The difficulty with the growth of international law has principally been that it still rests on the theory that each state is sovereign and that international law exists to protect the rights of nations and to govern the interrelationships among sovereign nations. Obviously there does not exist at this time an international legislature that could make laws binding on all nations and persons. International law has confined itself by and large to those questions that the individual nations have not claimed as their exclusive domains, for example, the law of the seas and the skies, and it has been assumed that the nations themselves had the right and the duty to make their own laws and to control their relationships with other nations through agreements, contracts, and alliances. A breakthrough in international legal thinking of the most profound significance came with the Nuremberg trials, however, at the end of World War II, when it was decided that the individual, rather than the state of which he was a citizen, was responsible before the law and before all men for his crimes against humanity, even though these were committed under orders from the governing authority of a sovereign state. This decision established the principle that there is a direct line between one man and all others that does not go through the intermediation of the state. It is doubtful that people at large throughout the world are as yet fully aware of all the implications of this doctrine; nevertheless, it opens the thinking on which a true law for man can be built.

A major practical difficulty in building a political system within which international or universal laws aimed at the achieving of justice for all could be written and applied is the suspicion that no man is capable of rising above the dictates of his own cultural background and the interests of his group in order to represent the thinking and the goals of man as a whole. The thought that any legislator or judge would naturally make laws or apply them in such a way as to enhance the particular good of his race, religion, class, nation, or culture is deep-rooted and tenacious in man's mind. Yet it is an assumption based on a reading of history that fails to take at all into account how much the world has changed because of recent developments in technology and because of man's newer philosophical, religious, and humanitarian thinking about the unitary nature of mankind itself. More and more men are coming to see the world as one in space and in time, and to realize that a system of universal law having the confidence and support of all is crucial if the world is to survive.

Each of the great civilizations has produced some few men who could be considered authentically intercultural or universal, in spite of the general thinking and the educational systems of the times. Further, the world view of most cultures, and especially of the intellectual and spiritual leaders within them, has included some explanation of man's relationship to all other men whatever their culture. Though these views have been the creation of the world as seen through the thought patterns and systems of a particular culture, the concept *all men* has not been alien to them; in fact, the basic appeal of most of the great religions of the world has been the universal applicability of the doctrines and the ethical standards they enunicated. The possibility of the development of increasing numbers of men who are genuinely universal in their world view, as a result of direct educational efforts and in the light of the needs and opportunities of the times, is not as remote as it might at first seem.

Law itself is one of the most powerful educative influences in any culture. Through the culture's laws and the degree of its observance of them, the young person quickly comes to know what the culture holds as sacred, what as important, and what as indifferent. The law makes some of the values of the culture explicit, for example, laws which make education compulsory to a certain age show the importance those cultures attach to education. The very fact that there is at present only a meager, though expanding, body of international law indicates to the young people of the world that it has not been considered of any great importance; it tells them vividly the kind of world in which they are living. On the other hand, it is the development of a system of international law which over a period of time will play a large part in the formation of a true world community and give recognizable form to it. Just as individuals with a universal outlook lead the way in the building of a universal community of man, so, in its turn, international law becomes a powerful educative force in giving shape and substance to man's universalistic aspirations and identities. Whether one takes the viewpoint that law arises out of the wisdom and foresight of legislators, or out of the desires of the people for it, or straightforwardly out of the deep need for new law and the pressures of events, the evidence seems to be clear that the greater interdependence, which the nations of the world feel as the world grows smaller, will bring into existence both new theories of international law and more practical means for creating, codifying, and implementing it. Barbara Ward makes this same point with her usual cogency. She writes,

> What we lack is any kind of moral community to match the community of potential death. Yet if we prefer the prospect of living together to that of dying together, then the common interest we have in creating genuine institutions of international order far transcends the differences of culture, even of ideology, that divide us now. . . . The concept which we have to achieve is that of international law with the support of an international police system. This, I believe, is the greatest task of this generation, in both East and West. . . . The task of institutionalizing man's higher energies for truth, for beauty, for goodwill, above all for love, are far more important for human survival and it is by compassion and justice, not by pride and conquest, that the good society shall be known.[7]

THE UNIVERSAL PERSON AND MODERNIZATION

The universal man is also greatly concerned about the substance and the process of modernization. Indeed, modernization in the present world requires the coming forth of the universal man in a way that earlier historical periods could not have known; a new era, with new world opportunities and problems, calls for a new type of educated intelligence, a new view of the world and a new world view. Today's modernization process, properly conceived, both demands and produces the universal man. The problem of poverty, for example, which modernization in its economic aspects seeks to alleviate or eliminate is a world problem, not simply a national or regional one, as Gunnar Mydral so well explains in *The Challenge of World Poverty*.[8]

Modernization, however, is much more than an economic problem. Difficult as it is to solve the problem of poverty in the midst of a plentiful world, there is good reason to think that economic answers can be found through the right kind of planning, assistance, and cooperation. Resources are not unlimited, but productivity can be greatly increased—as is witnessed by the Green Revolution, by the assembly line, and by improved machinery and equipment in both agriculture and industry. Distribution of economic and consumer goods of all kinds can be greatly facilitated through trade agreements and common markets, through loans that increase purchasing power, through private and public savings which make possible the accumulation of investment capital, and through education that supplies the necessary technical and managerial skills. The problem is not beyond human inventiveness. But its solution will necessitate universal men, men who see the economic problem and beyond it; men who realize that, even apart from all idealism and humanism, in the modern world the economic good of all depends ultimately on the economic well-being of each person.

One of the great problems of economic modernization has been that cooperative economic assistance programs have been tied too closely to national and ideological and military interests. Perhaps this was inevitable in the past; it is tragic in the modern world because it means that the economies of many countries cannot develop fully and freely as they should. Unilateral economic assistance programs, rather than multilateral, intergovernmental, or universalistic ones—as through the United Nations and other worldwide agencies—have not only impeded economic development in a great number of instances but have also served to make the developing countries dependent on those countries which, to win their ideological support, are willing to assist them.

Modernization includes economic development and industrialization of whatever kind is appropriate, but extends far beyond them. Modernization means being up-to-date in every way and looking to the future. Modernization in the present age involves a universalism in thinking and living, in which many of the older one-culture ideas no longer fit or serve, simply because of the nature of the new age. New thoughts cannot be unthought; new discoveries cannot be undiscovered; new visions of world unity cannot be suppressed. Each age, each decade in fact, has to modernize, but as Quincy Wright stated in the beginning of the 1960s, long before the moon landing with all its implications for mankind, ". . . the structure of peace requires a certain loyalty to mankind as a whole. We must realize that while we may be citizens of California and the United States, we are also members of the human race and citizens of the world. This implies that we have in our minds a picture of that world which is moderately acceptable to all the nations and ideologies and can therefore command a measure of loyalty from all."[9] And about the same time Georges Fradier was pointing out that "no one is so vain of his national culture as he who knows no other; conversely, it is difficult not to respect a people whose masterpieces one loves, whose joys and sorrows one senses."[10]

Modernization means awareness of the fact that science and technology have opened up new possibilities for human betterment and have posed a fundamental challenge to many older theological, philosophical, and cultural principles. It means not that everything new is good but that many of the older concepts and ways are no longer adequate. It would be as unfortunate for some of the developing countries to imitate certain of the principles of those cultures which consider themselves modern as it would be for them to fail to incorporate certain of the modern features of those cultures. Modernization is inescapable but it is not an unmixed blessing; it can, indeed, if not properly directed and controlled, destroy the spirit of man at the same time that it eases many of the burdens of living. The universal man realizes that modernization is not automatic improvement, that it brings in its wake its own set of problems so that he attempts to do whatever is possible to direct the process toward goals that will unite men rather than divide them, at the same that it gives full range to cultural differences. A world community of outlook, which he seeks and represents, is not the same as uniformity or monotonous standardization, but is rather the widest diversity within an all-encompassing unity.

Toward a New Theory of Intercultural Education

There has never been a consistent and carefully thought-out theory of intercultural education. Formal and widespread interest in such education is of recent origin, and more attention has been paid to the essential step of gathering data about the world's cultures than to theorizing about the purposes and methods of intercultural education and about how best to disseminate or communicate this data to others. An immense amount of data has been accumulated by the cultural anthropologists and by those engaged in comparative education. But the constructing of an overall theory of intercultural education remains to be done, and the new era gives urgency to the need for a theory according to which intercultural education can become integral, inspired, and more effective.

The term *theory* is used, as is customary, in contradistinction to the term *practice*. It implies a concern for what ought to be taking place rather than emphasizing what is actually taking place. Theory implies a set of principles or concepts according to which a discipline is delimited and distinguished from all other fields or disciplines. The theory of an academic discipline establishes the goals and objectives of the discipline, outlines the best practical means and methodologies for achieving these goals, and determines the criteria by which progress toward these goals is evaluated. The theory of anything is that intellectual framework or system of ideas that keeps any project, program, or investigation moving in the intended way. Both the theory of theory and the relation of theory to practice are general philosophical questions of considerable subtlety, but here it is necessary to point out only that theory both directs practice and is informed and checked by it.

Intercultural education is that process by which the people of one culture arrive at new and deeper knowledge of, and at a better understanding and appreciation of, the nature and functioning of different cultures. Intercultural education includes the study of past as well as of contemporary cultures: study of the culture of ancient Greece or Egypt, for example, is as much a part of intercultural education as is the study of the culture of contemporary New Guinea. Like all education, too, intercultural education can be either by another, whether through a book or other medium or a living teacher, or by means of one's own discovery without the direct assistance of a teacher. Like many other forms of education, as well, intercultural education can be formal and systematic or it can be incidental and peripheral to some other form of study or activity. Intercultural education can be education *in* a culture or *about* a culture.

Intercultural education is particularly difficult to analyze and specify because it takes place in many different ways and at many different levels. For example, the cultural anthropologist who spends years in the field, learning the language and other aspects of a culture directly, is engaged in intercultural education; so are the people with whom the anthropologist speaks and works; so are the graduate students who assist him. The student who reads the anthropologist's book about that culture as part of his education is also taking part in intercultural education. The same is the case with the teacher who uses the anthropologist's book as background for a lesson, a lecture, or as recommended reading. In short, anything that contributes in any way to one's better and fuller understanding of another culture is a form of, and a part of, intercultural education.

PROXIMATE GOALS

Constructing a theory of intercultural education has to start, of course, with consideration of what it is that intercultural education seeks to achieve. Intercultural education must be understood as one specific form of the educational process; it has its own objectives and its own means to them. In this sense it is roughly comparable to consumer or health or religious education, although each of these can also be intercultural in outlook. The term *intercultural* specifies horizontally a form or type of education, indicating its proper object, but it does not directly specify the level of education on a vertical or learning-age scale, indicating when intercultural education should or could best take place. Unless the goals of intercultural education are clearly delineated and constantly kept in mind, the means to the goals will be uncertain and inconsistent.

Simply to know, to be aware, that peoples of other cultures have different ways of thinking and behaving is to share more fully in the wider world of education. It is a use of intelligence which extends one's view beyond the practical work-a-day boundaries of one's local and immediate environment. To come to know *why* peoples of other cultures think differently and by what historical and psychological processes they have arrived at their modes of thought and their behavior systems is an exciting and vital part of the deeper wisdom and understanding which is a proper aim of all education.

The question immediately arises: what does it mean to know another culture and can one ever be said to know it fully? Like knowledge in any other field, intercultural knowledge is virtually limitless. Each individual comes to know a culture according to his own capacities and interests, and always in part. One could literally spend one's entire lifetime studying a particular culture and still not know it fully. But there are certain knowledges about a culture that are more revealing than others and that are central to all intercultural education. Most authorities agree that to know another culture fully one ought to know its language. The student of a culture furthermore must come to know its history, its literature and drama, its myths and tales, its theological and religious system, its stage of technological development, its customs and folkways, its psychological and educational conditionings, its energies and motivations, its hopes, loyalties, and values. These and many other aspects enter into the knowing of a culture. Knowledge of a culture is superficial or profound depending on how well one grasps these kinds of knowledge and the relationships among them.

Intercultural education also aims to change the negative attitudes of the people of one culture toward those of another, and to reinforce positive attitudes. Attitudes themselves are not directly observable, but the behavior which results from them is. Attitudes are based in part on knowledge and in part on feelings. They indicate a willingness to approach something or a desire to avoid something. Very often, too, attitudes stand in the way of arriving at accurate and genuine knowledge. Attitudes or feelings, such as superiority-inferiority, fear, hatred, distrust, jealousy, resentment, and aggressiveness prevent genuine understanding; in fact they may even preclude the possibility of any understanding. In many cases such negative attitudes are irrational, the result of long-standing myths, preconceptions, prejudices, or stereotypical thinking. One of the intrinsic goals of intercultural education is to help the student avoid making premature judgments about other people or peoples. It seeks to make clear the necessity for judging other people on their individual merits, on the evidence, rather than on vague impressions or hearsay. Since intercultural education is mutual education, that is, reciprocal and not unilateral, it implies an openness and willingness on both sides to change attitudes. While intercultural education seeks to bring about a change of attitudes between and among people, it does not assume that there will never be any antagonisms, sharply divergent opinions, or justified anger; it does assume that there are ways in which these differences can be worked out rationally and in a friendly manner, rather than emotionally and destructively.

Intercultural education seeks to help students develop the kinds of skills necessary to intercultural understanding and appreciation and to successful functioning within another culture. There are at least three sets of such skills.

The first is language. A large part of intercultural education is connected with the learning of a second or a third language. Language skills and facility are crucial to the understanding of any culture, especially if the student hopes to know the culture from within. This is not to deny that much can be learned about a culture by reading its major works in translation, by observing carefully its many nonverbal communication signals—its art and architecture for example—and even by working through an interpreter. But language learning is invaluable because there is an intimate and inevitable relationship between the language structure of a culture and the modes in which the people think and act, and because language is the ordinary and most distinctively human way in which people communicate their concepts and state their judgments.

People of any culture can think only the thoughts their language permits them to think, and their language in turn helps them construct their universe. The Japanese language, for example, uses different words for counting depending on what is being counted—people, birds, fish, and so forth. It also makes many more distinctions in terms of address, according to age, social status, and degree of intimacy, than do the Indo-European languages. But perhaps an even more telling example is this one from Khin Maung Win: "The fact that the Burmese people live in a radically empirical world is revealed also by the structure of the Burmese language. . . . The absence of the 'I' suggests that the person is conceived not as a realistic ontological substance, but as the sequence of immediately experienced events. . . . The Burmese language, therefore, reveals nothing more than the Buddhist conception of time and space."[1]

Although there are any number of ways that people can and do communicate with one another, the one way that gives the greatest range to expression and provides the greatest accuracy and precision is language. This is especially true at the more advanced levels of communication. On the one hand, language can be used to mislead and obscure what a person is really thinking, but on the other, it is the shortest and surest way of sharing ideas honestly held. When it is said that to know another language is to live another life, what is meant is that another language often opens the door to a wholly new set of perceptions and a different structuring of the real.

Language learning is so basic to intercultural education and communication and there are so many languages in the world that the need for a universal language has recently gained much attention. Two approaches to this complex problem have been emphasized. A common language would have to be either one now widely used or an artificially constructed language. Those who favor the universal adoption of an existing language maintain that this approach would be more natural and more readily acceptable. People for whom the adopted language is not native would learn their own and the universal language. Those who favor the adoption of an artificially constructed language insist that it could be more easily learned and would be free of all cultural overtones and implications.

Either of those approaches could work if an agreement to do so were reached. It is not inconceivable that in a generation or two all the people of the world could communicate directly with one another. The new techniques which have come to the fore in language learning, including electronic media, make such an idea much more feasible and realistic than would have been the case just a few years ago.

Second, intercultural education also hopes to enable the student to develop those analytic skills and mental capabilities or qualities that will help him more accurately and surely understand another culture. The skills in question here are not just those involved in interviewing, drawing up a questionnaire, sampling validity, and programing a computer. These skills are important, but the analytic or discriminatory skills are more fundamental and of greater scope. Coming to know what to look for in a culture, knowing where to look, how to look, what methodology to use, and establishing the hypotheses and determining the criteria of evaluation—these skills are a direct objective of intercultural education. How does one, for example, discriminate between the seeming and the real, the spurious and the genuine, in a given culture? What value scale does one use in reporting whether the people of a culture view something, human freedom for example, as important, indifferent, or unimportant? Or what are the best sources of insight into the meaning of a particular myth in a given culture?

Just as each culture has its own language, so too does it have its own logic. This logic must be understood before the culture can be understood, and yet each investigator or student tends to bring to his study of another culture his own logic or that with which he is most familiar. To analyze the system of logic itself and to know about knowing—intercultural education must seek to instill these skills as well as those of how to gather data and validate impressions. Leibnitz is credited with having said of the theory of knowledge, the understanding of the knowing process, that of all researches, there is none of greater importance, since this is the key to all the others.

Two key quotations will help to show the vast difference between the premises of two systems of logic in two major world cultures and will help to highlight the importance of the developing of analytical skills as one of the goals of intercultural education. The first deals with Buddhism.

> Anyone who is well acquainted with Buddhism knows that it has three cornerstones. They are: *Anisa, Dukkha,* and *Anata. Anisa* means that everything determinate is changing. *Dukkha* means that life in this world is full of suffering. *Anata* means that there is no determinate self. These three philosophical ideas are accepted by all Buddhists, regardless of the particular philosophical school to which they belong.[2]

The second is from the holy Quran.

> Mankind was one single nation,
> And God sent Messengers
> With glad tidings and warnings;
> And with them He sent

> The Book in truth,
> To judge between people
> In matters wherein
> They differed;
> But the People of the Book,
> After the Clear Signs
> Came to them, did not differ
> Among themselves
> Except through selfish contumacy.[3]

Anyone interested in understanding those parts of Asia in which Buddhism has had a dominating influence would have to understand the above-mentioned three cornerstones, *Anisa, Dukkha,* and *Anata.* To attempt to understand Buddhism, using either traditional Aristotelian or modern symbolic logic, is bound to miss the point. In the same way, anyone from a Buddhist culture, which holds that there is no determinate self, must use a different system of logic to understand the People of the Book. Those who follow the Quran are instructed to look to the Book, a determinate writing, to find the Clear Signs about how to settle matters wherein people differ.

Third, the learning and teaching of interpersonal skills is an important objective of intercultural education. The ability to work with people of other cultures does not come naturally. It is an acquired or learned art, as is true of the ability to relax together and to create bonds of friendship.

Perhaps the most basic interpersonal skill at which intercultural education aims, however, is the skill of intercultural dialog, discussion and the exchange of ideas, that is, the skill of engaging effectively and openly in the great human conversation. Listening and reading intelligently are as much a part of the conversation as are speaking and writing with clarity, precision and insight. Intercultural education is taking place, of course, whenever a person hears or reads anything about another culture. Information is being exchanged. For an Easterner to read Aristotle or Plato, for example, or for a Westerner to read the Upanishads or the Bhagavadgita is a big step toward intercultural understanding. But it is really in person-to-person dialog, with ample opportunity for friendly challenge and refutation, that ideas are sharpened, modified, and clarified. The skill of thoughtful and imaginative inquiry, in dialog and in mutual search with a person of another culture, is not simply an abstract intellectual skill. It is a crucial interpersonal skill as well. To articulate well the ideas of one's own culture and to create the setting or mood in which another can communicate his might be called intercultural education at its finest whether or not any kind of agreement is reached. Such dialog is fundamentally an intercultural pursuit of the truth and the mutual understanding which is intercultural education's most important proximate objective. Theodore Brameld stresses interpersonal skills in this way:

> By the "problem pivot" I mean that human relations are a field of knowledge and action constructed for the purpose of coping with areas of misunderstanding, tension, prejudice, hatred, and conflict. Throughout the world human beings are suffering from their inability thus far to associate together in such ways as to produce individual and social harmony, appreciation of one another, group cooperation, and the pervasive feeling of well-being that stems from sound, healthful interpersonal and intergroup relations.[4]

ULTIMATE GOALS

There is much more agreement among theorists of intercultural education on its proximate goals than on its ultimate goals. Construction of a satisfactory, comprehensive theory of intercultural education has long been greatly impeded by the lack of clear insight into its ultimate aims and purposes. Theorists take one of two basic positions on the question of its ultimate goals. The first holds that the ultimate goal is that each person come to know at least two cultures, namely his own and another. The second position also holds that the ultimate goal of intercultural education is that each person come to know at least two cultures, of which one would be his own, but the other, a universal or world culture. As the term *intercultural* explicitly denotes, at least two cultures must be involved. There is wide agreement that one cannot know his own culture well unless he is at the same time coming to know another culture.

Though these two basic positions are not necessarily contradictory nor mutually exclusive, the answer to the question is far from being merely academic. It is even possible that the learning of two or more cultures could be conceived of as a proximate goal and the creation of a universal culture as an ultimate goal. In any event, the question lies at the heart of any theory of intercultural education, and the answer to it will determine the fundamental directions and movements of intercultural education in the coming era.

The majority of theorists of intercultural education hold the rather traditional position that, at this stage of human development, the learning of at least two cultures, one's own and another, is all that is theoretically necessary and practically possible. According to this view a person born in the United States, for example, should learn as much as possible about the cultures of one or another Latin American, African, or Asian country. A person born in Japan ought to learn the culture, for example, of Russia or China or Canada. This is as much as one is likely to have time for; it is also sufficient for achieving all the essential goals and purposes of intercultural education. The theory is that each person would be coming to know well another culture and in that very process he would come to know both his own culture and that other culture.

It is suggested that in learning one culture other than his own, each person would come to realize how culture itself works and what it means in the thoughts and actions of all men. He would gain a culture awareness and a facility for understanding other cultures that would permit him to make at least tentative generalizations about the culture process, if not about the actual content of various cultures systems. At the same time that a specific student in one culture was learning about one other culture, all other students in all parts of the world would be doing the same thing. In that way, although it would be clearly impossible for any one student to know every other culture, all students would know one other culture, and all cultures everywhere would be understood and appreciated by some students other than those who are members of that culture.

Most advocates of this two-culture approach also specify that insofar as possible the other culture studied ought to be radically different from one's own. For a Western student, the study of his own culture would not be as beneficial as the study of Eastern culture. Similarly, a white ought to study black culture, and an urbanite ought to study an agrarian culture. The purpose here is not culture shock but the dramatic impact and vital learning brought about through the confrontation of opposites. If a student is to learn only one other culture, it should be the one from which he will gain the most culture exposure and the deepest understanding. Nor is it the thought that the student will inevitably change or modify his own cultural insights and values; the opposite might well be the case. After thoroughly studying a culture different from his own, the student might well be more convinced than ever that the values of his own culture are greatly to be preferred to those of the other. In most cases, however, the student at least takes a new view of his cultural values after studying those of another. He comes to the important recognition that other and intelligent people have arrived at answers very different from his.

There is a small but growing group of theorists of intercultural education, however, which holds that intercultural education should aim directly, explicity, and ultimately at producing a universal culture, a *culture of cultures,* a culture of man. It is essentially a new theory of intercultural education; it is both theoretically possible and demanded by the times as a basis for the human community. Because it is new and much less well known, the universal cultural position will be more fully explored than the traditional one.

A UNIVERSAL CULTURE

The movement toward creating a universal culture does not mean a call for the eventual disappearance of all individual cultures, or their amalgamation into some uniform world culture. Instead, those who see intercultural education as pointing toward the emergence of a universal or human culture have a profound respect for individual cultures, and feel that each contributes something vital and unique to any world culture. A universal culture would be an organic, consistent, and integral drawing together of those universal ideas and values that all men share.

The vision of a universal culture is even now seen more clearly in the East than it is in other parts of the world. Gandhi, for example, never thought of cutting India off from the world community by gaining India's independence, but only of giving India a chance to participate in that community in its own distinctive way, and of contributing something of its spirit to it. "Gandhi had the faith that the world is one in its deepest roots and highest aspirations. He knew that the purpose of historical humanity was to develop a world-civilization, a world-culture, a world-community. We can get out of the misery of this world only be exposing the darkness which is strongly entrenched in men's hearts and replacing it by understanding and tolerance."[5]

And Hajime Nakamura states the polarity between universal culture and individual cultures: "Our sense of belonging to one world has never been keener than at present. Yet the emphasis today on this evident fact itself implies that while every individual is affected by the quickening flow of world events, he is still strongly influenced by the ways of living and thinking in his own nation and culture."[6]

If a clear and ultimate goal of intercultural education were the creation of a universal culture, then each person would come to understand his own culture better, through realizing how the two interacted. Sharing in a universal language would be as much an integral part of a universal culture as is the sharing in scientific and technical knowledge that even now takes place. Scientific and technical knowledge is the same for all men everywhere regardless of culture and regardless of how they adapt it and use it. But a universal culture, at least in the beginning, would probably be based more on process than on content. How it would be started and moved forward would be almost as important as the content or the substantive achievement. There is no general feeling that a universal human culture is inevitable, but those who see it as a genuine possibility base their thinking on any of four principles which they see as its intellectual warrant: the creative synthesis principle, the human nature principle, the epistemological principle, and the natural evolution principle.

In its most elementary form the creative synthesis theory holds that a universal culture will come to be through an as-yet-unknown synthesis of the common elements in the presently existing cultures. As has been true in the history of science, so too in the development of a universal culture, certain broad ideas or key concepts emerge from time to time which explain or interpret the data in a deeper, more intellectually satisfying, and even in a more terse and esthetically beautiful way. A universal culture would transcend all presently existing cultures, but would incorporate in some creative way all that the peoples of the various cultures now hold most true and valuable. Whether a set of universal culture principles, uniting all men, would someday emerge or whether the universal culture would consist mainly in the widest possible search for such a synthesis is not yet clear. The synthesis might consist mainly of a community of outlook rather than a consensus on specific conclusions.

John U. Nef is a leading proponent of the creative synthesis principle, which he summarizes in this way:

If I am right, then the habitual ways of approaching books and other peoples, of which I have spoken, are most often than not a handicap to the community of outlook which we seek. . . . Much of the knowledge we take for granted about social and other historical processes, while often valuable in connection with the special inquiries that led men to obtain it, is irrelevant and dull when, as with us, it is the universal goals of existence to which we aim to give body.

This is especially true when . . . the creative synthesis which we are seeking can no longer depend only on western experiences, but must draw also on the very different experiences and methods of other parts of the world. This is why we should aim to transcend most of the knowledge and most of the concepts that have taken root in our minds from our associations with the ordinary channels of communication and even of education. We should try to shed those parts of our thinking, our feeling, and our behavior that this knowledge and these concepts have grafted into us.[7]

The creative synthesis principle is what Tagore, speaking for and about India, had in mind when he wrote that the man who is deeply and strongly rooted in his own culture is prepared to search for, and accept, truth from whatever source it may arise.

A second principle on which the development of a universal culture might be based is the philosophical insight that all men have a common human nature. Since human nature functions and operates in ways that can be ascertained, the problem of a universal culture is to find the ways of thinking or behaving that most closely conform with human nature. A universal culture would be the result of all men's applying right reason and good judgment to the aspects of life and thought that they share in common.

The human-nature principle is criticized because of its highly rationalistic character. Even if it were granted that all men share in a common human nature, the fact still remains that many of the most important components in any culture are not derived from reason alone. Man might be a rational animal, but in fact he does not act rationally at all times and in all ways. Many of the premises on which the peoples of various cultures function, the religious one for example, are not based on reason pure and simple. Some central culture concepts are beliefs and are accepted through the "leap of faith." Faith is not opposed to reason, but cannot be subjected to the ordinary canons of rational analysis.

Mortimer J. Adler, probably the best spokesman for the human-nature principle, writes:

This being the case, we can judge human societies or cultures as good and bad, better or worse, in spite of all the injunctions against doing so delivered by the sociologists and cultural anthropologists. The sociologists and cultural anthropologists tell us that we cannot transcend the "ethnocentric predicament" in which we find ourselves. Any judgment we make about a culture other than our own will assume the soundness or validity of the *mores* and value-system of our own society or culture. This would, of course, be true if *all* value-systems were relative and had validity—or acceptance—only for the culture in which they are inherent. However, the value-system involved in the scale of real goods that constitute a good human life is relative only to human nature, and not to societies or cultures. As such, it provides a standard that transcends the mores and the diverse value-systems that are inherent in diverse cultures. It is a universally applicable standard because it is based on what is universally present in all societies—human beings, the same in their specific natures.[8]

According to the epistemological principle, the development of a universal culture depends on the analysis of how people come to know and to know that they know. If the problem of knowing about knowing could be solved, agreement about that which is most worth knowing and that which is most surely known might be reached. Knowing how people arrive at ideas and how they test them is the work of epistemology. A universal or common culture would emerge from those ideas that have been put to some form of empirical test or verification. Ideas that met some previously established criterion would be valid. These tests would, of course, be vastly different from the kinds of tests employed by the natural and physical scientists, but they would have the same general purpose, that is, to arrive at knowledge which is publicly verifiable. The essential problem is the nature of proof in the humanities, including theology and philosophy, and the social sciences.

F. S. C. Northrop has done the most to advance this principle. His books, all thoroughly researched and using examples drawn from various cultures, have been extensively read and widely quoted. Northrop goes so far as to say that a universal human culture is possible; his basic point seems to be that it can be brought into being only through a greater understanding of what can be known and how it is known. One of his most important contributions has been to point out the difference between the natural history stage of the development of any science or discipline—primarily that of inductive data gathering—and the mature stage of deductively formulated theory. Whether this kind of analysis can be validly applied to the underlying assumptions in a culture, some of which are emotional and effective, is a question that the epistemologists are continuing to investigate.

The epistemological principle has led a number of theorists to conclude that the basic differences in the ways of human knowing, and in the actions and behavior patterns that flow from the ways of knowing, are reducible broadly to those of the East and those of the West. The various East-West philosophers' conferences, held at the University of Hawaii in 1939, 1949, 1959, and 1965 appear generally, for example, to have worked on this assumption. Although there are dozens or even hundreds of subcultures within the broad Eastern and Western cultures, many of those who hold that epistemology is the main concern in the developing of a universal culture feel justified in seeing only one major distinction in all human thought, namely, Eastern and Western. If this is true, if there are in fact only the two fundamentally and radically different ways of approaching knowledge and working with it, then a universal culture may be closer than most people think. It is much easier to comprehend and mutually discuss two clear positions, even though they may at first appear to be totally irreconcilable, than it is to deal with a large number of individual cultures and their almost endless minor variations. S. Radhakrishnan, indeed, goes much further, doubting even that there are fundamental differences between East and West. He says that

> there is no reason to believe that there are fundamental differences between the East and the West. Human beings are everywhere human and hold the same deepest values. The differences which are, no doubt, significant are related to external, temporary social conditions and are alterable with them. East and West are relative terms. They are geographical expressions and not cultural types.[9]

A similar statement of the epistemological principle is made by Clyde Kluckhohn, whose book on the Navaho Indians is a classic of cultural anthropology:

> There is much more to social and cultural phenomena than immediately meets the ear and eye. . . . The strain toward consistency which Sumner noted in the folkways and mores of all groups cannot be accounted for unless one postulates a more or less systematic pattern of reaction to experience as a characteristic property of all integrated cultures. In a certain deep sense the logic (that is, the manner of interpreting relationships between phenomena) of all members of the human species is the same. It is the premises that are different.[10]

Finally, a number of theorists feel that a universal culture will emerge in a more or less natural evolutionary way. As the peoples of the world draw closer and closer together geographically, so they will psychologically. Ideas that cannot stand up under the pressure of this new type of world will disappear except perhaps in history and anthropology texts. The "fittest" ideas will survive and become commonly or generally accepted. They will take on a new coloration brought about by the changing world environment in which they have struggled for existence and finally prevailed. Although this evolutionary principle is related to the creative synthesis principle, it is considerably different in that the universal culture that finally emerges is more the work of natural forces and of the modernization process itself than of man's creative intelligence.

The universal culture which is envisioned in the natural evolution principle does not, in fact, permit of basic culture differentiations. Whatever differences continued to exist would be minor ones resulting from such things as differences in climate, styles of dress, and eating habits. However long the process of evolution might take individual cultures will simply be absorbed in a world culture in the same way, for example, as small splinter groups are absorbed in major political parties or movements. While it would be absurd to urge the people of any culture to hold on to ideas and habits they have come to consider obsolete simply to preserve cultural differences, not all anthropologists or educators are convinced that the ultimate prospect for a universal culture, as foreseen in the natural evolution principle, is a good thing. A universal culture that might also be a uniform culture, they feel, is a mistake, and the evolutionary process should not be allowed to take that course. For them much would depend on the nature of the struggle of ideas that would take place. If the struggle is a fair and open one, fine. But if it involves some kind of cultural domination or imperialism based on military force or ideological closure, or if it involves an exaggerated regard for science and technology—in which the people pursue these twin gods without full knowledge of the consequences and surrender their own ideas and values and their own integrity in the name of modernization—the whole human race might be culturally and spiritually impoverished.

Seeing positive value in the signs they note of the growth of a common world culture, Reischauer and Fairbank, in their masterful study *East Asia, The Great Tradition,* write:

Without understanding between ourselves and the peoples of East Asia we cannot hope for harmonious relationships and fruitful coopera- tion; in fact, we may face ultimate disaster. But understanding can be based only on knowledge, and a sound knowledge of East Asia is not easily achieved. The cultural gap is too great. . . . On the other hand, there are many signs in East Asia, as elsewhere in the world, of the growth of what may be called a common world culture. In every phase of life, whether it be transportation facilities, political systems, or even ethical ideas and family relations, we and the peoples of East Asia today have much more in common than we did a century ago. Ultimately the growth of this common world culture and of the mutual interest may greatly facilitate harmonious understanding among the various parts of the world.[11]

While each of these four principles afford some insight into how a human culture might emerge and on what thinking it might be based, the creative synthesis principle seems to be the most important and persuasive. The human-nature principle is based on a metaphysical premise or postulate that human nature, as such, exists. While many philosophers agree with the premise, it is not at all universally accepted, nor is it likely to be. The epistemological principle suffers an over- emphasis on logic, reasoning, and theory of knowledge. It is immensely helpful in explaining why different people arrive at different conclu- sions, but it is remiss in not taking emotional and affective factors sufficiently into account. The natural-evolution principle, if allowed to proceed unimpaired, might result in a common standardized human culture based on science and technology or, worse yet, on an imperial- istic ideology imposed by military might.

The creative synthesis principle, on the other hand, which seeks in Professor Nef's phrase "a community of outlook" would appear to offer the best basis for a universal culture which at the same time makes due provision for genuine cultural differences. The community of outlook implies that people will learn how to live with differences, indeed how to learn from them and enjoy them, rather than regard them as ominous or threatening. A creative synthesis means an under- standing at a higher level of the way of viewing all those things which men have in common, the human experience, which acknowledges the fact that in many ways men are both alike and different.

THE DYNAMICS OF INTERCULTURAL EDUCATION

An adequate, viable theory of intercultural education must include not only a statement of the goals of such education but also a clarification of the principle means for the achieving of those goals. This section, then, attempts to analyze the major components of the intercultural educative *process*. Attention is here focused on what actually happens in intercultural education; that is, on the interaction between the learning process and that which is to be learned.

As the word *dynamics* indicates, intercultural education is a vital, changing, energy-filled process. Though its goals remain relatively constant, the learning process can be neither static nor inert. The content is always changing, either because of the greater depth of insight or because of a constantly broadening scope; its methods are open at all times to being revised and refined; its teachers and learners are at each moment growing in understanding and appreciation, in finesse and exactness. There can never be a fixed and final state of intercultural education, just as its goals can never be fully achieved. Intercultural education is to be understood here in its broadest sense. The discussion is not limited to intercultural education in a formal or in an institutionalized setting, although the same basic concepts would, of course, apply to such institutions as schools, libraries, museums, and culture centers.

Intercultural learning is clearly a part of the general learning process. One learns another culture or about another culture in the same way he learns anything else, whether religion, the law, or poetry. The unfortunate fact is that knowledge of the learning process itself is still at an early stage of its development. Although psychologists are putting intense effort into trying to understand this important process, and are making some progress, no one is yet certain as to what learning is or exactly how it takes place. How does the mind move from the particular to the general, from the concrete to the abstract; what are its powers of attention, concentration, problem-solving; what is memory, creativity, imagination; how do doing and thinking interact; what conditions are most conducive to effective learning—these and many other questions go into learning about learning.

Some generalizations about learning are reasonably well established, perhaps the most important of which is that learning is a self-activity. The student himself is the active and primary agent in learning. The teacher, the curriculum, the learning environment are at best stimulators in that they assist the student to learn; they cooperate with him in his efforts to learn and they create surroundings conducive to learning. But learning itself can take place only in accord with the talents, interests, and motivations of the learner. In these, it is most probable that no two people are exactly alike. Intercultural education, above all, must respect the learning backgrounds, the modes of learning, the needs, capacities, and aspirations of those who engage in it. As in all education, the student must want to learn, must be ready to learn, and must be capable of learning; but intercultural education involves certain sensitivities, certain inclinations or resistances, certain new experiences and opportunities, and a degree of effort and concentration that makes intercultural learning both more taxing and more rewarding than is ordinarily supposed.

One of the more recent theories of learning deserves brief mention because it seems to throw light on the special problems associated with intercultural learning: it has been called the "neurological theory" or "the natural-science theory." It calls on discoveries both in neurophysiology and in cybernetics, and it is based in part on analogies running in both directions between the human brain and the computer and other automatic-control mechanisms.

The neurological theory of learning begins with the fact that the fifteen billion or so neurons in the human nervous system are arranged in elaborate networks; these neurons are the means by which and through which all sense-perception and eventually all learning takes place. When a neuron is stimulated, it in turn discharges a small electrical current which, across a synaptic gap, stimulates another neuron and so on through the neural sequence. The nervous system traps and preserves impulses, among other ways, by means of reverberating neural loops. But the new advance in this theory is the insight into the functioning of these neural loops. Robert Rossow, Jr. explains:

> When new data presented to the system are incompatible with the ideas already trapped in it, a breaking of the original circuitry can result, which will be followed by a searching and scanning process leading eventually to the formation of a new circuitry that accommodates the new data. This may be termed the eureka process; it differs from the enculturation process . . . both of them types of learning . . . in that it results in new conceptual forms, rather than the mere transmission of old ones. It is exemplified in scientific inquiry and is the basis for man's capacity to adapt to new situations. It is the essence of human growth whereby man increases his knowledge and ultimately his mastery over his environment.[12]

The neurological theory of human learning seems, at least for the moment, to be the most exciting and practicable theory with which to work. It, too, is dynamic; it is subject to further revision and clarification as more and more data become available. This theory of learning conceives of man operationally as an information-processing communication system in a social context. It offers an explanation, at least partially demonstrable, of how man learns and how he modifies his thoughts, actions, and behavior patterns, in accordance with the goals he sets for himself. The setting of goals, goal orientation, is itself a part of learning. This theory clearly moves far away from any of the simplistic stimulus-response or connectionist theories of learning which could never account adequately for abstract ideas and human purpose.

If, as is assumed to be the case by this neurological theory, culture, that is, one's customary ways of thinking and acting, is the result of certain *sets, traps, loops,* or *programs* within the central nervous system, then to learn another culture or about another culture becomes primarily a matter of disconnecting or breaking this smoothly functioning electrical circuitry within the nervous system. Information, new data about another culture, is processed into the communication system of the learner by way of stimulation and neural impulses. What the system then does with this data depends in large part on how seriously the previous neural circuits have been disrupted. The learner may ignore the new data altogether if it comes to him in a form with which he has had absolutely no previous experience. For example, no communication takes place if the language is entirely foreign. Or, at the other extreme, the new information may be of such force and quality as to put his previous thinking into total disarray and disorganization and to change his entire way of life, that is, total conversion. In any event when he has learned something, when communication or learning of whatever form does actually take place, new neural loops are formed in his central nervous system.

Messages are communicated, of course, in a number of different ways. As Edward T. Hall, in his classic work on the subject, has so well pointed out, verbal communication is only one form of communication. However, the receiver, the learner in this case must get the message, that is, he must literally receive it, in one way or another, if there is to be any learning, any communication, at all. Each receiver, moreover, receives the message in his own way, according to his own capacities, selection, and discrimination skills. Because the human mind and nervous system can attend at any one time to only a very limited number of signals, clues, or messages—for example, no one can read several chapters of even the same book simultaneously—the communication (message) must be broken down into manageable parts. Otherwise, there is grave danger of overloading all the neural circuits with the subsequent loss of power to learn anything. Over-communication, resulting in confusion and erratic behavior, is in this sense worse than lack of communication.

In this theory of learning, the concept of feedback plays an important role. Especially in the more elaborate and sequential types of learning and communication, neither the communicator nor the communicatee will know whether genuine learning is taking place unless there is some signal to that effect. The communicator must be made aware of the fact that the message is getting through so that corrections may be made if necessary. Feedback is essential to keeping the learning process moving on course and in the direction of the goals set for it. Feedback is not something outside the learning and communication process but is an integral part of that process; some of the output of the communication system is returned as input as a way of monitoring the process.

Intercultural education takes place in many ways at many times and at many levels. However, when one asks the theoretical question "What is to be taught or what should be taught in intercultural education?" the implication is that the teaching and the correlative learning is in some way to be systematic, organized, and sustained. Intercultural education will, of course, be taking place in occasional and random ways at the same time that more formal intercultural study and learning are moving forward. The inner content of intercultural education is one of its dynamic elements; this content has a validity and integrity of its own.

A general curriculum for intercultural education would begin with the knowledge that the established disciplines have built up, particularly that knowledge which comes with social psychology and cultural anthropology.

Intercultural education might well start with the history of a given culture, although the historical approach, with its ease of chronological ordering, is not necessarily the most exciting to the student. It is always crucial to know the origins and sources of a culture and the major steps in its development. Even when history is explicitly written to be used in intercultural education, sufficient attention often is not paid to the history of ideas and to social, spiritual, and artistic development.

But to know a people or a culture, one must first learn how they came to be what they now are.

Practically all literate cultures have had their historians, but even those not literate often have an oral tradition that gives some account of their beginnings. Historians have to exercise great care in working with oral tradition because so often oral transmission of information about origins is highly subjectivized as it passes from one generation to another. Sometimes the best history of a culture is recorded by a member of that culture; sometimes, by one who is outside it. Whether there is any such thing as objective history and whether history is written primarily to glorify the culture or to view it as it really is makes little difference in this connection. The history of a culture is itself highly selective and thus helps in the understanding of how a culture viewed or views itself.

Knowledge of the history of a culture and its religious system and orientation supplies the necessary background and one integrating framework for a more detailed study of the culture. In this detailed study, there is practically no branch of knowledge that does not yield rewarding insights. In one sense, every culture, present or past, exhibits to some degree the evolution of all the arts, sciences, and technology, and can be known only through a knowledge of the present standing of these arts and sciences. The literature of a culture—its stories, songs, poems, myths, and moral tales—reveals its soul, but so do its mathematics and physics, and its temples, bridges, and roads. The culture expresses itself both in what it does and in what it does not do. What constitutes a culture is the very fact that the people in it experience the real world in their own way; the experience itself is different from any other, and different cultures put varying emphasis on differing aspects of their experience. The study of a culture therefore includes its psychology, its perceptions of beauty, its regard for people and things, its political and military organization, its cognitive and affective levels, its economic status, and its ethical patterns.

A curriculum in intercultural education necessarily includes all such knowledge, although the majority of students will not pursue it in its comprehensiveness and depth. In any culture, of course, there are key concepts, the knowledge of which is essential, since everything of value in, and of interest about, the culture follows from them.

Up to the present, little attention has been paid to that field of knowledge which is intercultural or transcultural per se in designing a curriculum for intercultural education. This field deals specifically with the nature and development of culture, the relationships among cultures, the deeper understanding of *why* peoples of various cultures arrive at different ways of seeing and doing things.

Whatever name is given this field, and *culturology, metaculture,* and the *philosophy of culture* have been used, it is important that the concept be clear. Intercultural education can never be fully effective if it stops at recognition of the fact that different cultures do have different gods, values, life-styles, and ways of perceiving and organizing thought and action. The student in the course of his education should, and inevitably will, ask why. Culture as a major phenomenon of human experience requires an explanation, and this is one of the principal tasks of intercultural education.

To take a simple, common, and relatively noncontroversial example: One of the basic differences between Eastern and Western cultures is that the Eastern are dominated by the concept of harmony; the Western by power. In the East, it is said, knowledge is for the sake of living in better and closer harmony with nature and man; in the West, knowledge is for the sake of controlling nature and man. In the East anything that disrupts harmony is bad, so that maintaining peace and order is a prime value; in the West, achieving the things that power makes possible is considered by many as a primary goal.

Whether and to what extent this distinction is accurate can be tested and is not at issue here. Intercultural education is concerned with *why* it is true, if indeed it is true. What is there in the Eastern tradition and mentality that makes harmony so important, and what is there in the Western heritage that makes power so important? Knowing the facts is very worthwhile, but it is the most elementary form of intercultural education. Knowing what is behind the facts and how indeed the facts came to be facts is intercultural education at its best. Continuing the same example: there can be little intercultural understanding between East and West if those who put primary emphasis on harmony and those who put primary emphasis on power simply realize this to be the case. To know why it is the case means stepping outside, or beyond, the culture perspective and analyzing the imperatives in culture itself that have resulted in these different positions.

The field of the philosophy of culture is just beginning to develop. It is the searching for those first and ultimate principles that apply to cultures and culture learning in general, and not just to a particular culture. Various ultimates have been advanced—usually by some form of reductionism or determinism. For example, some maintain that religion determines the culture; others that language is basic, in that a person can only think, experience, and communicate in the ways that his language structure opens up to him; others argue that geography and climate, the availability of food and water, dictate the premises on which a culture functions; still others insist that socioeconomic factors within and among cultures determine how the individual thinks, and how one culture interacts with another. This view is that economically deprived cultures tend to think in patterns oriented toward change, while economically affluent cultures think in patterns which at least subconsciously preserve the status quo. Culture has been described as the manifestation of the human mind in human behavior, and the philosophy of culture is fundamentally concerned with the ways in which life determines thought, and in which that thought determines life.

An intercultural education curriculum, then, entails both kinds of knowledge: that drawn from both the emerging and the established disciplines, and that which puts culture itself in perspective. The study of metacultural concepts is an essential, integral part of intercultural education. Because it is both an illuminating fund of knowledge in itself and a necessary tool for the study of culture, it consequently should come very early in the student's educational program.

A second essential element in the general curriculum for intercultural education is the study of the principles and the functioning of one's own culture, a better understanding and appreciation of which is one of the goals of intercultural education. By definition one's own culture is that life pattern within which one feels secure. Ordinarily one comes to accept his own culture's principles and premises almost unconsciously, to take them for granted. At some point in his education the student must be helped to stand apart, to take a wider view, so that if he then decides his culture principles are adequate and appropriate for him, he will come to know them well and more reflectively. If he decides a change is necessary, it will be because he has arrived at that conclusion with full knowledge and mature judgment.

Coming to know one's own culture is an extremely complex matter. Since culture is a way of life that is affective and emotional as well as a system of intellectual principles, knowing that culture involves knowing both its principles or ideals, and how these principles function in practice. Further, a culture does not exist in a completely homogeneous way nor, in modern times, in isolation. Not only are the underlying unifying principles of a culture being constantly modified in the clash of ideas and interchange with other cultures, but also within any culture there are bound to be great tensions among the various subcultures and countercultures. In practically every culture, for example, traditional groups will seek to preserve their position and privileges, while progressive groups will strive to bring about change. Similarly, the younger members of a culture will often *see* things quite differently from the older members.

Nonetheless, there must be a sharing of fundamental principles within a culture; otherwise it would not constitute nor be identifiable as a culture. The people of a culture share, in varying degrees, a common history, a common language, a common theological or religious outlook, a common geographical area, a common moral or value system, a common juridical and political system, a common educational system and literature, and often a common skin coloring or physiological appearance. In general the people of a culture share the same system of ideas and interpret their life experience in the same ways. It is coming to know these shared ideas and values in an explicit and articulate way which is coming to know a culture, whether one's own or another's.

One of the main difficulties in coming to know one's own culture is in trying to determine who are its authentic spokesmen. Who within a culture best sees what it means and where it is and ought to be going? Within every culture there is a big difference between its ideals and its realities, and there are often strange contradictions and anomalies between them. If one knows only the ideals of a culture, he misses the immense strains and shortcomings of the daily living out of these ideals. On the other hand, if one concentrates on the day-to-day thoughts and habits of the people of the culture, he might miss its noblest hopes and aspirations. One might either miss altogether or mistrust the best flowering of the culture's ideals in the lives of those who most clearly represent it and who most fully inspire it. No one person ever completely embodies a culture, but not to know Gandhi, for example, is to misread the culture of India.

One comes to know his own culture simply by being a part of it, by being born into it. One has no choice. In the process of growing up, of living, one becomes almost automatically enculturated. He learns what things and what persons are esteemed, valued, and respected. He learns at his mother's knee, and in some cultures in front of the television set, which gods are his gods, and which family and flag are his. He comes to know quickly which actions are rewarded and which meet with disapproval. The language of the culture becomes his simply by his hearing and speaking it—naturally, that is, in ways not yet fully understood. He absorbs the manners, customs, rituals, mores, folkways, games, and sports by participating in them and by imitating what his parents and peers do and enjoy. Regrettably, he also learns the fears, prejudices, superstitions, animosities, and hatreds of the culture to which he is first exposed by observing those he necessarily regards at the time as his models and heroes. Throughout his life in the culture these earliest impressions will be reenforced, modified, or completely changed, depending on the experiences he has and the alternatives opened to him.

Coming to know one's own culture, however, in a reflective way is a much different matter. Rightly understood and properly organized, the curriculum of the formal school aims to bring the student to a much fuller realization of his cultural background and heritage. What the student had earlier just accepted, he now studies and examines in depth. The philosophers speak of this kind of knowledge as that by second intention. One not only knows, but knows that he knows, and why. The student becomes aware in a systematic way of his culture's origin and his own through the history he reads, the catechism he studies, the classical documents he analyzes, and through the language, literature, and the social and natural sciences to which his teachers introduce him. Through his program of studies he learns how to evaluate and criticize, to reason discursively, to make judgments and draw conclusions, and to use his imagination in arriving at new ideas and creating new things.

Depending on the design of the curriculum and the quality of the instruction, the student either becomes more and more convinced of the value and beauty of his culture heritage, or he begins to draw further away from it. Traditionally in most cultures the schools have aimed to develop deep loyalties to the culture even when they have held its principles up to the light of intellectual scrutiny. They have sought to reenforce cultural attachments through suggesting ways in which the culture might be improved, but they have worked on the assumption, in turn reenforced by the feelings of the larger society, that the culture itself is sound and worth preserving. The schools have been looked on as a way of strengthening the culture rather than leading to basic change. Detached intellectuals and culturally displaced or marginal men have long been regarded with suspicion.

A modern view of intercultural education and its dynamics, particularly with reference to curriculum design, must include provision for developing a universal human culture. The first step is to attempt to delineate what the concept means. If culture is the manifestation of human thought in human behavior, is it possible that that thought and that behavior could be directed toward establishing a universal culture, to which all men could subscribe and of which all men would be part? Is the "ethnocentric predicament" so inescapable that the concept of a universal culture implies a contradiction in terms? It would not seem so. By definition a culture is composed of those ideas, values, and habits which people share in common. A universal culture would simply mean a broader base than the word culture ordinarily implies, so broad a base in fact that it would include all men.

Many theorists think that a universal culture is not necessarily impossible in theory, but that it could never be achieved in practice. They maintain that man at present is incapable of identifying with any idea as remote and comprehensive as all mankind. They suggest, further, that those major world religions which speak of the unity of mankind and the solidarity of the human race do so in a mystical or metaphorical sense that has little relation to reality. Certainly, the history of mankind up to this time would warrant great caution in proposing that intercultural education aim at creating a universal culture; if anything, there is ample evidence that men are becoming more nationalistic and culture centered now than ever before.

On the contrary, those who favor striving toward the creation of a universal culture maintain that never before in the history of man have the conditions for effectively thinking about a universal culture been so conducive to it. The nature of the world and of man's relation to it and to his fellows have changed radically with the growth of new forms of communication and transportation, with technology and modernization generally, and man's outlook must change with it. A world or universal culture is now not only possible, it is also imperative for both human progress and survival.

All culture is, of course, learned. One is not born possessing a particular culture or even innate ideas which will predetermine his accepting the ways of one culture rather than another. For example, a child born in one culture but immediately placed in another and brought up in it will take as his the ways of the new culture. He has no real choice since his experience and learning are all within the new culture. To be sure, the child begins learning as soon as he is born, perhaps even before, and he quickly learns to learn in the ways possible to him, that is, the ways of the culture of which he is in fact a member. Clearly, if he learns to learn in ways which are culture centered and limited, he will develop modes and habits of thought which reflect this fact.

However, the human mind is not per se limited to learning only the thoughts and behaviors of a particular culture. As philosophers have pointed out, the proper object of the human mind is everything knowable, that is, capable of being known by the human intellect—all being, all that is, everywhere. Thus it is that learning is coextensive with being rather than with culture. To come to know a universal culture would require only that its principles, ways, and interpretations were available to be learned, which, of course, is not presently the case, but need not always be so. Developing a universal culture would mean new experiences, new ideas, and new viewpoints, but it would not mean creating a new kind of human mind or intellectual being. In short, the development of a universal culture does not, in theory, have to await another stage in human evolution, in which man would presumably develop a higher type brain.

The idea of a viable, organic, universal culture, for the foreseeable future, would seek to avoid the pitfalls of extremes. On the one hand, a universal culture does not imply that one of the existing cultures would win universal acceptance. (This outcome cannot be rationally excluded but seems so unlikely as to be nearly impossible.) Most certainly a universal culture does not involve any one culture's forcing itself on others in any form of cultural imperialism. On the other hand, a universal culture, in order to be integrated, must avoid the danger of an artificial synthesis in which values are arbitrarily put together with the hope of pleasing everyone, or of balancing ideas of one culture against those of another. Finally, a culture of man does not mean uniformity. A culture can be universal without being uniform or so standardized that all cultural differences disappear.

It is not the intention here to attempt to lay out the specifics of a curriculum which might lead to a universal culture. There is probably no one clear or necessary way of designing an actual curriculum; a variety of approaches might prove to be required. But there are certain underlying principles on which such a curriculum would have to be based, and it is to these that attention must be given.

The first is that the purpose of all education is the training of intelligence. The word *training* is used in a completely honorific sense, realizing that the training of human intelligence, unlike the training of other forms of animals, means strengthening, sharpening, deepening, and perfecting an intelligence which is vastly superior, if not altogether different in kind, to that possessed by other animals. However one conceives the nature and functioning of the human mind in a philosophical sense, a common sense fact of human experience is that all people use intelligence and reason and each observes others doing the same. Man is defined as *Homo sapiens* because he is intelligent, capable not merely of instinct and sense experience but also of conceptualization, of imagination and creativity, and of problem solving. Different people, of course, have different degrees of intelligence and they use their intelligence differently; but man living, man at work or at play, is an intelligent being. Mistakes are frequent and erroneous judgments, resulting from incorrect or insufficient knowledge or faulty reasoning, have plagued mankind since its beginning, but these are sometimes the result of lack of training rather than of intelligence. The fact is that human intelligence in general is limited in its nature and potentiality.

Many people will argue, of course, that misunderstanding and conflict do not arise out of intelligence and reason but out of emotion. It would be relatively easy, it is said, to develop a world culture if men were strictly rational and reasonable, and if they defined intelligence, rationality, and reasonableness in the same way. But there are vast dark areas of the individual and the collective subconscious, including likes and dislikes, loves and fears, which go into the shaping of man's thoughts and actions and of which he is not always aware.

This is precisely the purpose of *training* intelligence and of all education, including especially intercultural education. The person whose intelligence has not been trained tends to rely heavily, perhaps exclusively, on emotion and feeling; his reactions tend to be instinctive, compulsive, and sometimes aggressive; natural rather than cultivated or civilized. The very process of training the intelligence leads it to see more clearly and fully alternatives and consequences, to weigh evidence more carefully, and to use imagination as a way of opening up new options. Up to this point, most educational systems have trained intelligence in ways narrowly circumscribed by cultural boundaries. Intercultural education, as it moves toward a universal culture, seeks to introduce intercultural and transcultural ideas and methods into the training of intelligence.

A curriculum in intercultural education thus would have to be based on trained intelligence and reason. Weak in some ways, vastly powerful in others, the human intellect is all in the natural order that man has with which to try to achieve objectivity, knowledge, and consensus. Emotions are, indeed, an important part of human life and no one would want to deny or underestimate them, but the effort must be constantly made to bring the emotions more and more under the control of reason. To do so is the essence of the training of intelligence. Reason, in the past, has sometimes been thought to be coldly calculating, purely logical, and scientific. But this is a limited view; the proper exercise and display of emotion can be completely reasonable. The heart is said to have reasons which the mind knows nothing of. Rather than eliminating those reasons, intercultural education seeks to encompass them and bring them into open examination and consideration.

The building of a universal culture and the curriculum designed to achieve it, must be guided by the assumption that man ultimately will be directed by reason and intelligence. Unless there is initial understanding and agreement on this point, a universal culture is impossible. Since intelligence and reason are universal phenomena, not confined to a particular culture, all men might come to accept a reliance on trained intelligence and reason as a first principle in curriculum building, at the same time realizing that each culture has something to learn from every other.

Second, a program of studies aimed at the development of a universal culture would also accentuate those ideas or values which are common to all cultures. Though the differences among cultures are many, and at some levels apparently irreconcilable, the similarities are also great. It is probably accurate to say that all men and cultures have much more in common than they have which separates and divides them. Since neither the similarities in cultures nor the differences give the whole picture, both would have to find a place in the curriculum, but the accent would be on the similarities. Once people realize how much they have in common, they find it much easier to work, talk, and think together. There is one school of thought which maintains that the differences hold the key to the understanding of different people and cultures in that they are dramatic and interesting while similarities tend to be routine, but in fact it is through knowing the similarities that one realizes that man is already on the way to a universal culture.

To say that the curriculum would accent the similarities means that more attention would be devoted to pointing out the nature and sources of these similarities than of the differences. Intercultural education in the past has emphasized differences. In their desire to establish the validity of the concept of culture and to illustrate it, anthropologists have tended to stress cultural differences in their descriptions. Perhaps because differences are more obvious and recognizable, the average layman in viewing a foreign culture also tends to notice the differences more than the similarities. The seemingly new and strange always make for good intellectual exchange. All too often, for example, historians have written of countries and cultures in ways which point out the superiority of their own country or culture over others, and so have magnified differences. And courses in comparative religion or literature have, by and large, accentuated the differences even more than they do the fact that in both cases it is the same phenomenon, namely, religion or literature, that is being studied.

Similarities among cultures arise from two principal sources: first, that man has a body as well as a mind, and second, that he has an intelligence and is a philosophizing animal.

As part of the biological world, men experience similar needs for food, clothing, shelter, and procreation, and in each culture there are organized ways of providing these basic necessities. Not only are the needs themselves similar, but frequently the ways of satisfying them are also strikingly similar. There are, for example, only a limited number of known ways of procuring food from the land and the sea. Nature itself is limited and generally orderly and recurrent. The methods of agriculture, for example, may be more or less efficient, but they all involve the same fundamental processes—cultivating, sowing, harvesting—and it is only natural that men everywhere would find similar, though not necessarily identical, ways of carrying on these processes. Whether a man works a small plot of land by himself or whether he uses a combine to work thousands of acres, he is concerned with a basic human process. An intercultural curriculum and a universal culture would stress the worldwide nature of the food problem in its quantitative and qualitative aspects. There is remarkable similarity in the ways in which different cultures handle the search for food and in the rituals and mythologies connected with its consumption.

Man is not only a biological species; he is a special and unique case in that he also philosophizes. Once he has provided for his basic biological necessities, he turns to the questions of how to interpret himself, his fellow men, his world and nature's, and of how to organize his life so that he can find the greatest possible realization and happiness as a human. He begins to develop a higher, more spiritual, and more humane culture.

The philosophizing process is universal and similar in all cultures. The premises, or starting points, differ greatly from one culture to another, and consequently the conclusions become dissimilar. But the process is generally the same and includes, among other things, the search for explanatory principles, the quest for reasons and answers, the thrust toward consistency and integration, the communication and sharing of ideas, the development of symbols and rituals, the mechanisms and logic of acceptance and rejection, the incorporation of beauty into daily life, and the assignment of priorities among goals and goods. If all men started with the same premises and followed the same lines of reasoning, there would, of course, be only minor cultural differences flowing from such accidentals as climate and geography. But since this is not the case, the similarities in the philosophizing process itself provide the best basis for emphasis in a curriculum for intercultural education.

The question is rightly asked, of course, why do people of various cultures start from different premises in their philosophizing process? Apart from the simplistic answer that different cultures have different histories, experiences, problems, and religious and philosophical insights, and that at present they have different interests and purposes that greatly affect their thinking, the best answer seems to be that different cultures find different premises sufficient to account for the phenomena of life, and that very often the premises are so subtle and ingrained they go unquestioned. The fact that people do see things differently, is immediately observable as a fact. That they will always do so in the sense that seeing things differently is a natural rather than a cultural phenomenon is not at all clear. Much will depend on the intercultural educational processes of the future.

A third principle on which a curriculum aimed at a universal culture would be based is that cooperation among the peoples of the world is, in the final analysis, much more beneficial to all than is competition and conflict.

Here, the overall historical record and much current thinking seem to be somewhat at odds. History seems to make clear that when those within a culture cooperate among themselves and when peoples of different cultures cooperate across cultural lines, the greatest possible advantages, both short and long run, accrue to all concerned. On the other hand, competition invariably leads to conflict, to animosity, to rivalry, and threats of war. Yet there is a significant intellectual tradition which insists that human progress results more from competition than from cooperation.

The point made by those who hold that competition is not only inevitable but good is threefold: (1) People naturally seek their own self-interest and most often what they regard as their interests are in conflict with what others regard as theirs. (2) People tend to cooperate only when they are compelled to do so by outside force. People will join ranks to protect themselves, but not to help one another, particularly if this means surrendering some of their independence, privilege, or advantage. (3) The clash of ideas, of systems, or even of weapons leads to new and better ideas. A culture is like an individual, it is said; unless it is competing for something, it stagnates and too readily settles for things as they are. Out of competition comes greater initiative, sharper thinking and clarification of issues, and new inventions.

It is precisely because the argument favoring competition is so strong in the modern world that a new type of intercultural education and intercultural person must come into existence. Competition may well have its place in sports and games, in the dialog of ideas, and to an extent in business, but when it becomes the kind of competition that leads to military force, it can result only in waste and destruction and, if carried far enough, to ruin for the human race.

A necessary corollary of the principle that cooperation among cultures is to be preferred to competition is that it must be voluntary. Cooperation cannot be imposed; it has to be reciprocal and understood as leading to greater benefits for more people. Domination and exploitation are the exact antitheses of cooperation and the respect it implies. Since cooperation does indeed imply the surrender of some autonomy in the interests of the common good, it rests on an awareness of other people and a concern for them as well as for one's self. Cooperativeness is a learned phenomenon, depending very much for its development on seeing its benefits and on a willingness to give as well as to receive.

Finally, an intercultural curriculum pointing toward creating a universal culture would have to be open, flexible, responsive, and inclusive. All ideas honestly and responsibly held by persons of all cultures would be considered appropriate for the curriculum. None would be rejected out of hand and none would be considered so sacrosanct as to be outside the regular processes of examination and criticism. Insofar as possible all ideas would be approached with objectivity and given an impartial hearing. Not only are new ideas constantly emerging within all cultures, but also older ideas are continually either being more fully verified and accepted or are being replaced by other ideas.

Openness to new ideas does not mean that those who design the curriculum would never make their minds up about anything or that the students would come out of the program without any definite ideas. On the contrary: openness means that the curriculum is not so rigid that all conclusions are foregone ones. It also means that all ideas are judged on the basis of the evidence and the force with which they present themselves, whether to the minds of those who are responsible for drawing up the curriculum or to the students who pursue it. An idea is not good merely because it is old nor because it is new. It is not good because it is an Eastern idea or a Western idea, nor just because it is *ours*. Ideas are good because they indicate a correspondence between what is judged to be true and what is in fact true. An open curriculum is one which seeks and accepts what is true from whatever source, no matter what changes the acceptance of the new and valid idea might imply.

Each student will eventually have to judge for himself whether the curriculum has been successful and whether by means of it he has come to know and understand universal culture and participate in it. The individual, drawing on all the help he can get from wiser minds, has to be the final judge of the truth and value in his own culture and of human culture itself.

4

Culture Learning
Through Literature

People who try to understand what culture learning means and who actually undertake the study of another culture are sometimes dismayed at the enormity of the task. Realizing how difficult it is to know well and understand a single individual even in one's own culture, particularly if that person is of a different age, sex, race, or religion, the attempt to arrive at valid generalizations about an entire culture seems almost hopeless. The study is further complicated by the fact that just as each individual constantly changes as he grows in age and knowledge, so too each culture constantly changes in many ways. Finally, there is the question of delimiting or defining the culture which one wants to learn. Does one, for example, attempt to learn Western culture as a whole and American or English culture as subdivisions of it, or Muslim culture as a whole and Pakistani or Egyptian culture as subdivisions thereof. Or, more generally, what delimits a culture: language, race, nationality, religion, history? Or all these together?

As is true in all learning, there is a certain arbitrariness in setting out to learn a culture. There are no specific objective guidelines for determining the degree of generality or specialization in any intellectual inquiry. In the broadest sense all knowledge is interrelated since it is the product of the human mind, although some fields are more sharply differentiated than others. Whether, for example, a man is going to study Oriental culture, or Chinese culture, or the culture of the Sung dynasty is a question the individual must decide for himself. The only stricture imposed is that his conclusions be open to examination by the intellectual community. And his conclusions will depend on how well

94

and how deeply and clearly he has demarcated his field, how appropriate his methodology is, and how competently he has amassed and interpreted his data. If he has arrived at convincing generalizations concerning a culture, they will be accepted by his colleagues and by the knowing public; in some cases his conclusions will be tested for their validity by seeing whether they lead to further possibilities for predicting behavior and changes in behavior patterns of the people of that culture, or at least to a better understanding of why such predictability is impossible in given situations.

Culture learning, like learning in general, is concerned with fundamental principles and ideas; it is thus the coming to know the structure of the culture to be learned. As Jerome Bruner has pointed out, "To understand something as a specific instance of a more general case— which is what understanding a more fundamental principle or structure means—is to have learned not only a specific thing but also a model for understanding other things like it that one may encounter."[1] The object of culture learning is to know a culture in its basic unifying ideas and structuring rather than in its details, because only in this way can the learner guard against overgeneralization, and at the same time realize which details are truly significant and revealing. What Bruner has found to be true of learning as a whole applies especially to a field as complex as culture learning. He writes that "mastery of the fundamental ideas of a field involves not only the grasping of general principles, but also the development of an attitude toward learning and inquiry, toward guessing and hunches, toward the possibility of solving problems on one's own."[2]

At every level of culture learning it is the individual, the one doing the learning, who is the subject of the learning process. This is of course true of learning in every and all fields. But it is especially important to keep it in mind in discussing culture learning because, unlike some of the more objective disciplines, culture learning involves the individual's own cultural background and perceptions. The understanding of one's own culture and of any other is a deeply personal and ever-changing matter. The ultimate aim of culture learning, namely understanding, is the same for all people, but it is not at all likely that a Chinese or a Japanese, for example, would ever understand Indian culture in precisely the same way an American would. He is either closer to it or further away from it, more friendly or more hostile toward it, better or less able to understand it well. In any case he brings an altogether different frame of reference, a different system of attitudes, concepts, and values to the study.

Ortega y Gasset has written that the way to understand an individual, a people, or an age is to begin with an ordered inventory of its system of convictions and to establish which were the more fundamental and sustaining convictions. While this has to be true in theory, setting up the inventory and validating it through experience and observation, and in the light of a conceptual framework, will always depend on the individual learner. Ortega's ordered inventory of the convictions of modern China, for example, would be considerably different from that of a less perceptive man of his own culture, and much different from that of a man from an altogether different culture. Not only might they not observe the same phenomena but even if they did they would most likely see them and order them differently. What one sees is often what one is expecting to see rather than something objectively given. The concurring reports of a number of skilled observers tend to give greater reliability to such an inventory, but in the final analysis it is the individual who determines what he sees and accepts, and what he learns about the culture.

But the individual is not only the subject of culture learning, he is also the one paradoxically enough, who is the object of culture learning, that which is to be learned. At first this may seem strange, since culture is structured according to that which individual persons have in common. It might appear more logical and consistent if culture learning were directed toward learning what people share rather than studying individual members of the culture. Although the result of culture learning, to be sure, is a knowledge of the ways of thinking and behaving that people have in common, this result can be achieved only by beginning with the study of individuals.

No culture exists in the abstract; it does not have a life of its own above or apart from those individuals who comprise it. On the one hand, the particular persons who most influenced a given culture and gave it form may, of course, be long since deceased; they are known only through their writings, their accomplishments, and the traditions and legends still current about them. On the other hand, the culture, existing as it does only in individuals, is nothing other than what the individuals assume or perceive it to be and how they accept it and incorporate it into their daily lives. If one who wants to learn another culture attempts to start elsewhere than with individuals, he is likely to construct an idealized version that has little relation to reality. The culture does not manifest itself in exactly the same way in any two individuals, although there is sufficient similarity to make generalization possible; otherwise it would not make sense to speak of a culture at all. Some cultures are more stable and standardized than others, but within any culture there will be, for example, those individuals who lead the forces of change and those who insist on maintaining things as they are.

There has been in the past a great temptation for those desiring to learn another culture to reason a priori, or out of some vast system, or some philosophy of history. Thus, for example, the investigator might start with the assumption that a given culture is Hindu, or Buddhist, or Christian and draw conclusions about thoughts, attitudes, and values with very little regard for whether the individuals in the culture were in fact what he had assumed them to be, or whether their heritage actually influenced their thinking and living to the extent he had at first thought. It is now much clearer that the only way to get at an understanding of a culture, to determine where it is and what it means at any moment, is to learn what the people in fact think and feel and how they interpret the world in which they live. Though it is a reciprocal process, the people make the culture and live it as it is, rather than the culture as abstractly outlined making the people. The living, dynamic culture expresses itself through individuals and not through formal documents or master ideas which may ideally or traditionally have identified the culture. Knowing the culture means knowing the people who are members of it, what they think and do and value, and why they do so. But it is obviously impossible for any one person to know all the members, with their immense diversity, of a particular culture.

An important distinction must be introduced here. To *understand* a culture is one thing; *to be understanding of* another culture or other cultures is quite different. Neither necessarily implies intellectual agreement with fundamental cultural principles, but to understand implies that the learner sees how it is intellectually possible for the people of a culture to have arrived at its ways of thinking and its system of values. He sees not only that they think and value as they do but also *why* they do so. To be understanding of another culture is much more a matter of attitude than of insight. To be understanding of a culture implies openness, friendliness, receptivity and sensitivity, but also indicates that the learner does not himself regard the principles of the other culture as valid or persuasive. Both types of understanding are involved in culture learning.

Intercultural education in the modern era needs desperately to be directed away from two countervailing tendencies.

At one extreme there is the possibility that cultural differences would continue to be so highlighted that man would be identified as *culture man,* completely dominated and controlled by his culture. This has been the leading mistake of the past and of most education aimed at enabling a person to become a participating and productive member of his own culture only. The overwhelming majority of people knew their own culture exclusively; they were culture bound, limited in their thinking and seeing to that which their own culture had taught them. The accentuation of cultural differences throughout history has led to immense misunderstandings and often even to that final human folly, all-out war.

At the other extreme, there is the possibility in the highly technological and scientific contemporary world, in the age of development, that cultural differences would be so minimized or glossed over that man the world over would become part of a common, standardized technological culture. Man would no longer be culture man, but would become *technological man,* one and the same everywhere. His language, literature, philosophy, religion, art, and even his history would be that taught him, not by his culture, but by that great standardizing force, technology, and by the kind of urbanized, industrialized, and cognitive society needed to sustain it. Evidence of a move toward a common technological culture is already seen on every side as the developed countries come more to think of technology as their highest value and as the developing countries come to regard technology as their most needed import. Technology tends to carry with it a way of seeing the world as well as a way of living.

Both these tendencies are stated in their extreme forms in order to emphasize the problem. The reality is not quite so extreme. There have always been some intercultural persons, those who have broken a cultural mold, just as there are now many people who understand the limitations of technology. Nonetheless the tendencies are real ones and they ought to be recognized. The new era of intercultural education must seek ways of preserving genuine, legitimate, and enriching culture differences at the same time that it seeks a culture which would be unifying, upgrading, and open to all mankind.

The new concept of culture learning and intercultural education sees the cultures of the world existing *alongside* one another and each contributing in its own way to the overarching culture which is that of man himself. The cultures of the world are man's experience of life up to this point and should not be taken lightly. But the older notion that world cultures were each interested only in the well-being and common good of their own members, and that it was inevitable that cultures be considered as existing on a scale running from higher to lower, superior to inferior, or advanced to primitive, must be replaced. Newer world conditions clearly reveal that at present no culture can think only of itself, only of its people; enlightened self-interest sees the good of the culture itself as forcing it to extend its range of concern and cooperation far beyond the limits of its own cultural influence and, in fact, to all people. Similarly, newer culture analysis and criticism makes clear that cultures cannot be qualitatively ranked in any serial order. Some are strong in one way; others in other ways. Some emphasize this value or that insight; others emphasize different, though equally important, aspects of life. What appeals to the European or American mind does not necessarily appeal to the Oriental or African mind and neither do they necessarily have the same ordering of values or the same attitudes toward life.

While conceived of as existing alongside one another, rather than above or below one another, the cultures of the world would, of course, continue to be in close contact, and each would continue to seek a better understanding of the others. Simply because modern technology makes it possible, if for no other reason, there will be much more intercultural communication and exchange in the future than there has ever been in the past. Changes of thinking and attitudes within individuals and cultures will take place at a greatly accelerated rate as intercultural education is extended and improved. In the exchange of ideas and in the new understandings generated, whole cultures or major concepts within them may well undergo drastic revision, each culture learning from the others and each being dramatically influenced by the others.

Technology can and should serve the purposes of all men in helping to provide the economic necessities of life and in making it possible for all to enjoy more of the goods of this world and more leisure. But that is only the beginning of culture and not the end of it—nor even the most important part of it. A common culture of man dominated by technology, one in which man became literally a servant of production and a necessary means for consuming that which was produced, one in which men came to think alike because they all lived in the same way with the same values and feelings, would not only not be a culture, it would be a tragedy. A human culture, if it is to be human in the truest sense, must be one in which each person can be creative, free, imaginative, thoughtful, and loving—one in which he is able to express himself in all of his spiritual fullness. This, given the limited nature of man's knowing and seeing, always implies diversity. It implies that no one person and no one culture has seen or experienced in all possible ways of seeing and experiencing.

A world culture, a culture of cultures, from the viewpoint of content or substance, would have to take some form of higher synthesis including the facts that men of different cultures see and value things differently and that even logically incompatible culture principles can coexist peacefully, provided that one of the culture principles is not the violent subversion of the principles and functioning of other cultures. All cultures would be known, represented, and understood as fully as possible, and each would contribute to the synthesis, that is, to the total human experience of seeing the world, interpreting it, and reacting to it. Each individual, as is even now the case in the free societies and cultures, would decide for himself which culture principles held the richest meaning for him and how to integrate them into his own system of thinking. From the viewpoint of process, a human culture implies freedom of access to information and freedom to think for oneself; it does not imply agreeing on all things or even on basic things, but does imply using reason, persuasion, and negotiation in resolving disputes instead of using brute force.

CULTURE AND LITERATURE

All great literature is a statement about life, about how humans think and feel in the concrete and specific circumstances of the real daily world they encounter. It speaks to, and about, all humans and every human because it is successful only to the extent that it sees the universal in the particular. It differs from logical analysis or sociological treatise in that the author is invested with the freedom to set the stage as he wants it and literally to step inside the minds and spirits of the dramatis personae about whom he is writing. In doing so, the author not only reveals, for all the world to see, the characters he is depicting but also says much about his own values and meanings through the words and actions of the people he creates.

Literature—the novels, dramas, poems, ballads of a culture—is perhaps the surest and most illuminating source of insight into a culture. What its most creative spokesmen say, and what its people think is important enough to read and remember, is a distillation of what the culture believes and holds most dear, what it deplores, and what it honors and glorifies. Even more than its theological discourses, its philosophical tracts, and its legal codes, its literature lays bare the soul of the culture. It is in its great literature that one sees, with immediacy and power, what a person is in a culture, what his problems are, and what he and his fellows strive to be. If one understands its literature, one is well on his way to understanding the culture and its people. Literature reveals clearly how it is possible to conceive of a universal human culture at the same time that individual cultural differences are nourished and treasured.

The following discussion is in two sections. The first is a general consideration of the nature and meaning of literature. The second is a series of specific examples drawn from the world of literature, of the power of literature to disclose a culture and lead to a greater understanding and appreciation of it.

So much has been written about literature that to some it would hardly seem necessary to say anything more about it. Strangely enough, however, very little has been written about literature as a source and a means of intercultural education, and most of what has been written tends to view literature as didactic and pedagogical, as based on cognition and analysis and *teaching-a-lesson* rather than on intuition and emotion, an experience, a *feeling-with* or a *feeling-through*. In order to understand the role literature can play in intercultural education it is necessary first to understand literature in and of itself. There are three important aspects of the question: one historical, one psychological, and one philosophical.

No specific mention is made of the religious dimension or perspective in literature. The assumption, however, is that all great literature is essentially religious in the same sense that all education, as A. N. Whitehead points out, is essentially religious:

The essence of education is that it be religious. . . . A religious education is an education which inculcates duty and reverence. Duty arises
from our potential control over the course of events. Where attainable
knowledge could have changed the issue, ignorance has the guilt of
vice. And the foundation of reverence is this perception, that the
present holds within itself the complete sum of existence, backwards
and forwards, that whole amplitude of time, which is eternity.[3]

There is in fact no distinguishable religious dimension in literature;
it is either religious, in the sense in which Whitehead uses the word, or
it is not worthy of the name literature. There is, of course, education
in a specific theology or religion—its creed, its traditions and laws, its
structure, and its rituals—and there is also great literature dealing
explicitly with religious themes—Dante's *Divine Comedy,* for example.
Religious education in the narrow sense is good education, and not
indoctrination, only if it is also religious education in the broader sense.
Similarly, religious literature is good literature, and not propaganda,
only if it is primarily true to itself as literature, that is, if it is saying
something genuine and real about man and his life as it relates to man's
ultimate concerns. Not to speak explicitly of religion in literature is
not to imply that it is therefore unimportant; on the contrary it is to
say that religion is so important to literature that the two cannot be
separated.

Throughout human history, literature, in the broadest meaning of
that word, has recounted man's reflections and feelings as he encountered the universe in which he lives. Long before man could
write he had an oral literature, often enough put forth in song form,
in which he told of the beginnings of things, of heroic feats in war, of
the violence of nature and the ferocity of animals, of gay things and
of sad, of the joy of love, and the sorrow and tragedy of death. This
literature was a source of enjoyment and relaxation at times, but it
was also a form of education. That which was regarded as most important was committed to memory and one generation told the next.

Man's earliest literature, a mixture of myths and fairy tales but
containing the wisdom of the time, shows both a powerful imagination
and a blending of fact and fiction, a ready merging of the real and the
fanciful. Man's world was one in which the gods spoke casually and
as a matter of course with man, and one in which man spoke freely
with the animals and all the forces of nature. His stories, moreover,
indicated where man's thoughts were and what his feelings were, and

the storyteller told just as much about himself and his times by what he left out of his stories as by what he included. Earlier storytellers were often good mimics and pantomimists; the man who could tell a good story, either his own or another's, was a man of prominence and stature among primitive peoples, even as he is among the more sophisticated peoples of later civilizations. Many of the stories were told over and over again for succeeding generations, but each new generation of storytellers felt free to embellish a story as they saw fit in order to bring it up to date or to make a point that did not need making earlier.

The invention of the alphabet and of writing made it possible to put the best stories in permanent form, but since most people could neither read nor write, the tradition and art of oral storytelling continued throughout the centuries. By Homer's time, storytelling had reached epic proportions and had become an art of the highest order in both the East and the West. Much of what is now known, for example, about ancient Greece and ancient India is revealed in such books as the *Odyssey* and the *Bhagavadgita*. Adults were eager to hear about the exploits and adventures of their heroes, their triumphs and their defeats, and about why they were victorious or why they were brought to ruin. Children were introduced to the culture by hearing the stories of its great men and their achievements in doing battle with the gods, with nature, or with their human enemies. As is always the case, the society or culture, through inspiring its storytellers and accepting or rejecting the stories they tell, gives form and substance to the stories that are told, but it in turn, is then shaped by these very stories.

Within the genre of story telling and reading special mention must be made of the parable. Its primary purpose is to instruct, to convey a message, but it does so by way of allegory, analogy, or comparison. The parable has been used by the world's greatest teachers, as a means of making lessons, especially moral lessons, more vivid and realistic and easier to remember and apply. Every culture has its parables— sometimes called folktales or fables—which in a simple and beautiful way instruct the young and the uneducated in the ways of the culture, and at the same time give anyone interested in the culture a ready and valuable source of information about its basic views and values. It is, of course, interesting to note the similarities as well as the dissimilarities in theme and expression in the parables of the different cultures of the world. Some parables become highly elaborate and complex, as for example *Alice in Wonderland*—which is required reading for any student of English culture, or Western culture in general.

The invention of the printing press and the extension of education both vertically and horizontally made it possible to distribute a culture's literature widely among the people within a culture; they also made that literature available to other world peoples. There is no way of measuring exactly the educative and formative influence of great literature, but it is known to be immense. Not only do readers, which for the most part are collections of stories, become a principal source of ideas and attitudes for the very young in their school days, but also certain literature courses are required in nearly all colleges and universities. It is most unlikely, for example, that anyone educated in either England or the United States has not studied a number of Shakespeare's plays, and it is highly likely that a large number of people in other cultures will be familiar with at least one of his major works. A good novel, to say nothing of a classic, will sell hundreds of thousands of copies and be translated into a number of languages. Generation after generation of students grow up reading such books, to mention only a few of the more famous, as the *Iliad* and the *Odyssey*, *The Tale of Genji*, *The Canterbury Tales*, and *The Arabian Nights' Entertainments*.

PSYCHOLOGICAL ASPECTS OF LITERATURE

In considering the implications of literature for intercultural education and in attempting to understand exactly why it has such powerful educative value, it is necessary to see literature from the reader's viewpoint. What happens inside the mind and the total being of a person when he reads a great literary work?

The basis of reader participation in literature is ease of identification. The reader sees himself or others that he knows well in the characters as they take shape and substance in the book. He becomes directly and immediately involved with them; he literally likes and dislikes them as much as, and often more than, he does the people with whom he associates every day. He is transported outside himself as he becomes engrossed in the people and events about which he is reading. The characters come to life for him, not vaguely, indistinctly, or even scientifically, but as real persons. The reader feels, thinks, fears, loves, and hates with them; he cries or laughs with them, admires or despises them as the story moves along. The better the book is, the more the reader is sorry to see it end because, in it and through it, he has met friends with whom he can sympathize and with whom he can feel at one.

Even further. The reader of great literature identifies not only with the persons but also with their problems. He sees real people as they wrestle with real problems and challenges that are also real to him. As he reads he is anxious to see how they resolve their conflicts, and although he is aware that these are people in a book, and not on the street, and that he cannot help them, he so identifies with them that he wants to help, if only he were able to do so. He sees the drama unfolding and knows that he has been, could be, or will be sometime in a similar situation. He continually asks himself, perhaps even unwittingly, "What would I do and what ought I to do if I were in those same circumstances?" The reader does not know all the conditions or background of any problem in the book—he knows only the essential details that the author has selected for him to know. Yet he feels he knows the principal characters well enough to understand why they have acted as they have, and he also knows that the onrush of life in the everyday world does not slow down so that one can take all the time he would like to learn all the antecedents and possible consequences of a course of action he might take.

As he reads a great novel by an author of another culture, the reader finds himself identifying as well with those personages as he would if the book had been written by an author of his own culture. He soon realizes that the people of other cultures, their problems and their answers to them, are different, and interestingly so, but have an essential similarity. People are wise or vicious, lofty or ignoble, heroic or weak-willed in all cultures, and their literature reveals these and similar qualities in about the same proportions as the literature of one's own culture does.

Although literature is not intended to be primarily didactic—even so-called historical novels take great liberty with the facts of history—the reader inevitably learns much, often more than he is aware of, from his reading of a first-rate novel, poem, or play. He learns not only with his mind but with his whole being, depending on the intensity of his own feelings and his ability to identify with the thoughts, motivations, and actions of those persons around whom the book centers. He learns at several different levels of both conscious and unconscious learning, not just because he is enjoying something in which he is deeply interested but because he is observing how other humans react to the problems they face. If the piece of literature is truly good, it becomes a part of the reader; the book and the reader become united in a unique experience, basically different from the experience of anyone else who reads the same book. The reader learns something of life, and what it means to be human, from participating in life as lived by others. His is a vicarious experience, controlled and orchestrated by the author to be sure, but a gripping and imaginative one. His attention is concentrated on what he is reading in a way quite different from that with which he reads other kinds of writing. He is the final judge of any literature he reads and in the end he cannot escape passing judgment. Some authors are not trying to convince him or persuade him, but merely trying to let him in on something that has happened: an episode, an event, a scene, some person or persons that the writer suspects the reader might find interesting or worthy of attention. The reader learns more and more about himself as he discovers which persons in literature attract his love and his anger, which appeal to his sense of decency and honor, which he finds of no concern, and which incite him to action and to imitation.

A PHILOSOPHICAL CONSIDERATION

Among all the forms of art, literature has a special place and value in recalling to mind the essential interrelatedness of things, specifically the interdependence of all men. This it does in its use of imagery, and through movement, action, impression, and suggestion. Literature tends to unite men rather than to divide and separate them, as abstract logical systems of thought sometimes do, in that it constantly seeks the universal, the unifying element in the particular. In fact, literature is regarded as great or classic only to the extent that it succeeds in depicting something of universal significance, something of the essence of things, through the particular story, poem, or drama. In literature, the universal idea or concept, the universal feeling or emotion is given a local habitation and a name and is expressed in humanistic ways rather than in logical syllogisms or mathematical formulae. The question of the universal in and through the particular is one aspect of the ancient and continuing philosophical problem of the one and the many.

In the modern age it is both essential and possible to develop a worldwide culture, in which all can participate and to which all can contribute, without destroying the culture differences which now add so much beauty, strength, opportunity, freedom, and richness to human life. Variety within an overarching unity, *from many, one,* would have to be the keystone of a viable world culture. Literature is a fundamental expression of every culture and a basic ingredient in it, whatever its stage of advancement. In fact, great literature is likely to do as much, if not more, in shaping a world culture as would any abstract statement of human rights or any formal political constitution. Interestingly enough, it is in the field of literature that the world seems to have advanced the farthest toward the goal of a culture of cultures. There is already wide agreement on which writings constitute a part of world literature—books that everyone in the world would be interested in reading and with which everyone could identify. The Nobel prizes for literature are generally awarded to those who have said something of significance for all mankind and not just for members of the culture within which the particular author happens to have written. At the same time, the Nobel prize winners have usually said something about their own culture that leads others to understand it better and appreciate it more. Excellent literature has always been regarded as revealing the particular culture—its values and goals—and the particular author, as well as revealing something about the spirit of man as man.

It is of exceptionally great importance, then, that the idea of discovering the universal through the particular in literature—what this means and how it is done—be explored further. Literature might well be seen as one model for developing a world culture, as well as a profound and pervading part of it, and as a means of bringing it about.

Something is said to be universal when it applies to all members of a certain class or category. There is some identifiable sameness about all the individuals to whom the concept applies; otherwise they would be excluded from the category. The concept of universality in literature implies that there is something in a given literary work which speaks to all mankind, though not necessarily, or even likely, in precisely the same way—since individuals are always individual and each brings his own background and personality to whatever he reads. The truly universal in literature appeals to something in man regardless of his historical period, race, religion, socioeconomic background, age, or even of his level of formal education. Universality in literature is achieved, of course, in varying degrees, and only the recognized literary critics and the testimony of history—as indicated by whether the work survives and is widely read—can judge whether and to what extent a work has universal quality and value. For example: Joseph K. Yanagiwa says of *The Tale of Genji,* written by Murasaki Shikibu sometime between A.D. 1002 and 1019 and still read and studied both in Japan and the rest of the world, that "this great work is distinguished not only as the masterpiece of classical Japanese fiction, but as perhaps the earliest 'novel' of world literature."[4]

Achieving universality in literature depends on two reciprocal and continually interacting elements: on the one hand, the universality of the theme and the literary form in which it is cast, and, on the other, the universality of the thoughts and emotions that it evokes in the reader.

All great and lasting literature embodies some theme of universal importance. The height of literary art is attained when the theme and the form in which it is presented are so appropriate to one another that they cannot be disengaged without destroying the integrity of the work. But whatever form is used, the underlying theme must be something of such significance that it transcends the local and the specific. The theme need not be monumental nor epochal, but it must be genuine and honest, even if it is a work of sheer imagination. Such themes are almost limitless, of course, but they include man's search for God or for gods; man's relationships with nature and its forces; the conflicts of war and the efforts for peace; man's simple loves as well as his great ones; man's conquest of himself; his being born, growing up, maturing and dying; his joys and his inner torments; his relationships with his fellows; the changing times, and his yearning for a just and civilized social order. Such themes, and many others, are universal in that all men, in every period of history, find themselves deeply concerned with them, and each man knows that his fellows, each in his own way and degree, are confronting the same broad questions as part of their human experience.

That one finds universal themes in all great world literature is well known. What is not so well known at present is that anthropologists also report similar universal themes in their studies of different cultures. That works of literature should express these themes is only natural, and the fact that anthropology corroborates such expression, and vice versa, gives further validity and realism to them. Theodore

Brameld refers to the works of the anthropologist Ralph Linton and states that

> Linton does not deny that a great deal of comparative research is demanded by this task. Yet he is prepared to state that the differences among cultures, which hitherto have been the principal interest of anthropologists, are already known to be less than the similarities. Among the similarities with value implications are: marriage as a life-long ideal; responsibility of parents to children and vice versa; personal property and eminent domain; charity; economic obligations involving goods and services; opposition to murder and sex violence; and psychic as well as physical security. Thus he concludes, "The resemblances in ethical concepts so far outweigh the differences that a sound basis for mutual understanding between groups of different cultures is already in existence."[5]

But universality in literature derives not just from the theme with which the work is concerned. It also presumes and entails a universality of thought and emotion among the readers of the work. It appeals to, and responds to, the basic loves, fears, drives, anguishes, perceptions, sensitivities, and sympathies in all humans. The reader feels a rapport with the writer, to be sure, but he also feels some degree of rapport with fellow readers of the same book; he intuits, if he cannot actually prove, that most men are going to feel the same way he does about the point and theme of the work and about the persons in it. It is only the distorted mind, for example, that wants to see other people suffer or that does not want to see love, goodness, honesty, or bravery prevail; even if all men do not define virtue in the same way, they seem to want to be virtuous in their own way and according to the standards of their conscience.

Great literature strikes a responsive chord among all men throughout the world, that is, it is universal in both its emotional appeal and its thought content. It challenges man's mind at the same time that it opens his heart. The reader finds himself agreeing or disagreeing with what the author sees as true and valuable, or at least questioning whether he agrees or not and if not, why not. He realizes that the author wants to share an idea or an insight as it is incorporated in a specific and immediate human experience, not as it might be stated in a theological or philosophical treatise. He comes to a deeper understanding of people and the way people live in a setting which combines emotion and reason and makes it possible for the emotions to temper reason and for reason to restrain and direct the emotions.

Finally, there is beauty in literature, and the human soul in every culture and civilization awakens and becomes aware under the influence of beauty. Beauty is in the beholding, in the eye of the beholder, but a great literary work makes it possible for the reader to see a whole new world through the eye of the writer. Esthetic pleasure or delight cannot be separated from the total experience of writing worthy of the name literature. This perception of beauty in literature—of harmony and balance, of form and integrity, of coloring, shading, nuance and suggestion, and of sureness of hand—is in part a recognition that something excellent, something intensely human and satisfying to the sense of proportion, ordering and control, has been made or created by the writer-artist. There is as much, if not more, beauty in Dante's *Divine Comedy* as there is in the most magnificent of the Gothic cathedrals— and this comparison has often been made. There is beauty in the economy and choice of language, in the use of imagery and the play of imagination, in the movement of the plot and the building of suspense, in the unfolding of the characterizations, and in the often subtle creating of moods. But beauty is also in part in the "seeing" with the bright clarity of the mind's eye the fuller meanings of such things as love, passion, sorrow and suffering, joy, and even tragedy. Beauty also resides in the sudden discovery of one's spiritual kinship with both the author and the people and things about which he writes.

The crucial point in understanding how, in literature, the universal is arrived at through the particular is the analysis of the material with which the writer-artist works, the world with which he deals. It is not the actual world of minute-by-minute or day-by-day experience. Rather it is a world of imagination—selected, focused, and concentrated, and designed by the writer to achieve the effect he has more or less consciously in mind. Even those works which purport to show life as it really is do not include all details as they would in fact be lived, but only those that are essential to the purposes of the book. Literature is a form of art. Wilbur Schramm points out that "the true function of the mind in making art is to perceive and shape a reality which the artist believes to be more real than the actual." He goes on to say: "The artist brings his antecedent experience and his world view to bear on a special problem, to enrich the stimulus; the lightning flash of intuition helps to fuse the core of his thinking, to make diamonds out of carbon; the final lucubration polishes and cuts the diamonds to the utmost concentration of beauty and genuineness."[6]

The world of the writer-artist is, at least in one sense, more real than the actual world precisely because it transcends the actual world through showing that which is universal in the particular. Not that the particular is unimportant in and of itself; the actual world is a world of particulars, though not unrelated and not fully independent. It is rather that the particular becomes much more significant, literally a much higher, newer, more human reality, when it is seen as a manifestation of something universal. The particular then represents or symbolizes the whole and is in very fact a part of the whole. Northrop Frye puts it this way:

> But the poet, Aristotle says, never makes any real statements at all, certainly not particular or specific ones. The poet's job is not to tell you what happened, but what happens: not what took place, but the kind of thing that always does take place. He gives you the typical, recurring, or what Aristotle calls universal event. You wouldn't go to *Macbeth* to learn about the history of Scotland—you go to it to learn what a man feels like after he's gained a kingdom and lost his soul. When you meet such a character as Micawber in Dickens, you don't feel that there must have been a man Dickens knew who was exactly like this: you feel that there's a bit of Micawber in almost everybody you know, including yourself. Our impressions of human life are picked up one by one, and remain for most of us loose and disorganized. But we constantly find things in literature that suddenly co-ordinate and bring into focus a great many such impressions, and this is part of what Aristotle means by the typical or universal event.[7]

The classic argument among literary critics as to whether a piece of literature should be considered in the light of the author's background —his culture and times; his education, philosophy, and religion; and his status in society—or whether the work should be read simply for what it is without reference to anything external to it, has almost certainly been overdrawn. Though the purists on either side of this argument would not agree, there is something of value in reading literature in either or both ways. Every author necessarily reflects in his writings the thoughts, values, preoccupations, and confusions of his time. Even Robinson Crusoe, all alone on his island, could not throw off the influences of the society and culture of which he had been a member. Neither can any writer, no matter how much he tries to isolate or divorce himself from his own culture, become so universal that his work completely escapes human space and time. The past, and his past, continually rise up to haunt him if he tries to write directly for some abstract universal audience. On the other hand, literature does have an objective existence, an intrinsic meaning altogether apart from the author, once his work has been made public, once it belongs to the public—however universal that public may be. One can, for example, read *King Lear,* which many regard unsurpassed as drama, or *Oedipus Rex,* another supreme instance of the dramatic form, without reference at all to Shakespeare or to Sophocles.

The story, poem, or play has to be read for what it is, for what it tries to do, and not for any grand idea, explicit message, moral, or statement about life. It should certainly not be read as some kind of veiled sociological or anthropological treatise. Yet one cannot read *King Lear* or *Oedipus Rex,* or any other great work, without learning in that very reading much about the society and culture which gave rise to them. They reveal the culture out of which they took shape without in any way being limited to it, and without either intending or not intending to do so. Neither Shakespeare nor Sophocles was writing just for Elizabethan England or for the Golden Age of Greece. Each was simply writing about what he knew and what he felt was important enough to write about. It is to be assumed that each was writing for all mankind, however clearly he recognized that fact; each will endure as long as man endures precisely because in touching the mind and heart of man he achieved universality and, through it, immortality.

ILLUSTRATIONS OF CULTURE LEARNING THROUGH LITERATURE

Literature both illustrates the finding of the universal in the particular and shows one way in which a world culture that preserves and enhances the values of individual cultural differences might develop. Literature would be a vital element in any world culture; it says something of universal significance even though the author is a member of a particular culture and draws his inspiration in part from the life and meaning of that culture. Although almost any great literary work could be used to illustrate, three novels, one autobiography, and one play have been selected. They represent a number of different cultures; all are very well known; four of the works are relatively contemporary and one, the play, was written five hundred years before Christ; each touches on a different theme of central human importance. The novel predominates because it has often been described as the richest mode of personal communication ever devised: a mode of communication in which the author frequently reveals himself in ways he would not even to his closest friends.

DOCTOR ZHIVAGO

Doctor Zhivago is, to be sure, one of the most magnificent love stories ever written. The love between Zhivago and Lara, doomed, as the author Boris Pasternak makes clear from the very beginning, to lead in an immediate sense only to separation, heartbreak, and anguish, but in a more spiritual and symbolic sense to endure for all time, reaches such intensity of emotion and such height of honest communication that even if the novel were nothing more than a love story it would be unforgettable. Anyone anywhere who has ever loved feels the love of Yurii Zhivago and Lara and shares in it. Pasternak summarizes this love as Lara stands at the side of Yurii's coffin:

> She neither spoke nor thought. Sequences of ideas, notions, insights, truths drifted and sailed freely through her mind, like clouds in the sky, as happened so often before during their nighttime conversations. It was such things that had brought them happiness and liberation in those days. A spontaneous mutual understanding, warm, instinctive, immediate. . . .
> Oh, what a love it was, utterly free, unique, like nothing else on earth! Their thoughts were like other people's songs.
> . . . They loved each other because everything around them willed it, the trees and the clouds and the sky over their heads and the earth under their feet. Perhaps their surrounding world, the strangers they met in the street, the wide expanses they saw on their walks, the rooms in which they lived or met, took more delight in their love than they themselves did.
> Ah, that was just what had united them and had made them so akin! Never, never, even in their moments of richest and wildest happiness, were they unaware of a sublime joy in the total design of the universe, a feeling that they themselves were part of that whole, an element in the beauty of the cosmos.
> This unity with the whole was the breath of life to them.[8]

Important as is the love of Yurii and Lara, it is in the final analysis only the occasion for drawing a much larger picture of life in Russia during the years preceding the revolution and during the revolution itself. Zhivago's life spans some forty years. The story centers on the lives of a small number of people, but they are caught up in significant movements and great events. In following Zhivago's life the reader comes to understand what large numbers of people thought and felt, how they lived and what they went through during that period of cataclysmic change.

Zhivago is a humanist and litterateur as well as a man of science, combining in his education and in his life the best of both sides of the two-culture gap which perplexed the Russia of his day, and still perplexes modern societies the world over. He writes poetry with the same skill and concern that he shows in the practice of medicine. Sensitive and intelligent, he thinks deeply about his times and he cares much about what's happening to it and to the individual people in it, some sick in body and many more sick in heart and soul as the new society takes shape. The country is vast and it seems that an escape to the Ural Mountains might give Zhivago a chance, far from the chaos and uncertainty of the city, to find himself and to live freely, fully, and happily, farming and writing, rather than pursuing his medical profession. But in fact there is no escape. In the end he finds himself, drawn through some inner compulsion, back in Moscow, where he is lonely, dispirited, looking only half-seriously for his wife and family, and suffering from heart trouble. He feels that the city is "the only source of inspiration for a new, truly modern art" and that "the living language of our time, born spontaneously and naturally in accord with its spirit, is the language of urbanism."[9]

Zhivago, discussing his sclerosis with friends of earlier years, diagnoses his own case with dispassion and objectivity. He does not consider himself a symbol but rather an individual particular person of flesh and blood, body and soul. The reader, however, sees that in diagnosing his own case, Zhivago is speaking of a universal sickness. He says:

> Microscopic forms of cardiac hemorrhages have become very frequent in recent years. They are not always fatal. Some people get over them. It's a typical modern disease. I think its causes are of the moral order. The great majority of us are required to live a life of constant, systematic duplicity. Your health is bound to be affected if, day after day, you say the opposite of what you feel, if you grovel before what you dislike and rejoice at what brings you nothing but misfortune. Our nervous system isn't just a fiction, it's a part of our physical body, and our soul exists in space and is inside us, like the teeth in our mouth. It can't be forever violated with impunity.[10]

As a medical doctor and as a human being living through a time of war and revolution when hundreds of thousands of people died either from starvation or from bullets, Zhivago had seen much of suffering and death. He knew that anyone facing death is likely to ask the question: What happens next? The author confronts this universal question and gives his answer as honestly as he can through the words of Zhivago. Zhivago himself dies suddenly in the middle of a bustling crowd on a busy street in Moscow without anyone to comfort him or even to know who he is, but when he was earlier tending Anna Ivanovna in her illness, and she asked Zhivago to comfort her by telling her what death meant, what would happen next to her, Zhivago replied:

> However far back you go in your memory, it is always in some external, active manifestation of yourself that you come across your identity—in the work of your hands, in your family, in other people. And now listen carefully. You in others—this is your soul. This is what you are. This is what your consciousness has breathed and lived on and enjoyed throughout your life—your soul, your immortality, your life in others. And what now? You have always been in others and you will remain in others. And what does it matter to you if later on that is called your memory? This will be you—the you that enters the future and becomes a part of it.[11]

It is not to be expected that everyone will agree completely with the answers Zhivago gives. For example, many will disagree with his answer to Anna Ivanovna, saying that it is inaccurate, insufficient, and not scriptural nor traditional. But no one will disagree with the fact that it is beautiful, honest, and inspiring. Many will hold that it is the best possible answer to a question which has tormented man throughout the centuries. Clearly *Doctor Zhivago* asks some of the most fundamental questions about man's personal and social life and about how to live and how to die. Zhivago's answers reveal what his thinking and his experience, his culture in other words, lead him to conclude. People in other cultures might well answer the same questions differently, and they will live in accord with their own answers and conclusions. This too is good. Zhivago presents his ideas and values so that other people can consider them openly and publicly, so that they can know them and come to understand and respect them. Though Zhivago, as a thinking and feeling person, arises out of the spirit and soul of Russia and reflects that great country in the very essence of his being, he also rises above Russia as a particular culture to join in the community of man, universal throughout the world.

REPORT TO GRECO

"Mankind's struggle is truly an uninterrupted sacrament." This insight is only one of many such memorable and quotable comments that make Nikos Kazantzakis' autobiography *Report to Greco*[12] a major work of contemporary world literature, and an extraordinary example of autobiography as a literary genre. Kazantzakis, a man of immense soul, had a full and exciting life. And he knew how to write.

Most men feel it difficult to write about themselves, and even more difficult to evaluate themselves and their work. Men tend to be either too hard or too easy on themselves. Kazantzakis is an exception for the very reason that he regards his life as an ascent, a search, not an accomplishment. He feels that to a greater or lesser degree each man spends his life reaching for something he never quite attains, and that the essence of life is in the struggle, the search, the desire, and the effort to be something fuller and better than he is at any one moment. "The self-respecting soul, as soon as he reaches his goal, places it still further away. Not to attain it, but never to halt in the ascent. Only thus does life acquire nobility and oneness."[13]

Kazantzakis said of himself that his entire soul, his entire life, was a cry; the cry yes to the command, springing from his Greek heritage, to "reach what you cannot." Perhaps more self-consciously and explicitly than any other contemporary work, *Report to Greco* explores modern Greek culture and asks what it is in itself, what it means for the rest of the world, and how it influenced one particular man, Kazantzakis himself. Perhaps Kazantzakis overstates the case for Greek culture; perhaps he understates it. These are his words:

> All things in Greece—mountains, rivers, seas, valleys—become "humanized": they speak to man in a language which is almost human. They do not torment him or crushingly overwhelm him; they become his friends and fellow workers. The turbid, unsettled cry of the Orient grows pellucid when it passes through the light of Greece; humanized, it is transformed into *logos*—reason. Greece is the filter which, with great struggle, refines brute into man, eastern servitude into liberty, barbaric intoxication into sober rationality. To give features to the featureless and measure the measureless, balancing the blind clashing forces, such is the mission of the much-buffeted sea and land known as Greece.[14]

Report to Greco ranges over large themes and small, over great events and minor ones. The author writes of Christ, Buddha, Lenin,

Nietzsche, of life and death, of love and hate, of uncertainty and struggle. He delights in nature, in art, and most of all in the soul of man.
But even his observation about sports puts them in a new, Olympian,
and magnificent light:

> No other people had comprehended sport's hidden and manifest value
> so perfectly. When life has succeeded by dint of daily effort in conquer-
> ing the enemies around it—natural forces, wild beasts, hunger, thirst,
> sickness—sometimes it is lucky enough to have abundant strength left
> over. This strength it seeks to squander in sport. Civilization begins at
> the moment sport begins. As long as life struggles for preservation—
> to protect itself from enemies, maintain itself upon the surface of the
> earth—civilization cannot be born.[15]

But as much as Kazantzakis loved Greece—the title of his autobiography derives from the fact that at the end of his life he is reporting
on that life to his Greek grandfather, and through him to the people
of Greece—he was also constantly aware of the fact that he was first
a human being, or at least that being human and being Greek were
so inextricably intertwined that priority could be given to neither. As
a member of the human family, he realized with great clarity that to
be fully Greek and proud of it made him at the same time more
human, and that to share a common humanity made him more intensely and consciously Greek. Two very different kinds of reflections
make this point clear: one is a philosophical but deeply personal
consideration; the other is a passing vignette that Kazantzakis would
recall some fifty years later so profoundly did it impress itself on his
soul. The first speaks directly of man's universal oneness:

> There have been two supreme days in my life. . . . On both of
> those days I felt that human partitions—bodies, brains, and souls—
> were capable of being demolished, and that humanity might return
> again, after frightfully bloody wandering, to its primeval, divine one-
> ness. In this condition there is no such thing as "me," "you," and
> "he"; everything is a unity and this unity is a profound mystic intoxica-
> tion in which death loses its scythe and ceases to exist. Separately, we
> die one by one, but all together we are immortal. Like prodigal sons,
> after so much hunger, thirst, and rebellion we spread our arms and
> embrace our two parents: heaven and earth.[16]

The second illustrates man's common humanity in a simple episode,
rich and warm in its meaning:

> I was surrounded by olive trees and vineyards. The vintage still had

not begun; the grapes drooped heavily and touched the soil. The air smelled of fig leaves. A little old lady came along. She halted. Lifting the two or three fig leaves which covered the basket she carried on her arm, she picked out two figs and presented them to me.

"Do you know me, old lady?" I asked.

She glanced at me in amazement. "No, my boy. Do I have to know you to give you something? You're a human being, aren't you? So am I. Isn't that enough?"

The two figs were dripping with honey; I believe they were the most delicious I ever tasted. The old lady's words refreshed me as I ate. You are a human being. So am I. That's enough![17]

On another occasion Kazantzakis visited Knossos in the company of a Catholic priest.

We stopped at a square column of glazed plaster, at the top of which was incised the sacred sign: the double-edged axe. The abbe joined his hands, bent his knee for a moment, and moved his lips as though in prayer.

I was astonished. "What—are you praying?" I asked him.

"Of course I am praying, my young friend. Every race and every age gives God its own mask. But behind all the masks, in every age and race, is always the same never-changing God."

He fell silent, but after a moment: "We have the cross as our sacred sign; your most ancient ancestors had the double-edged axe. But I push aside the ephemeral symbols and discern the same God behind both the cross and the double-edged axe, discern Him and do obeisance."[18]

ANTIGONE

Antigone is relatively short—one of the so-called Oedipus plays of Sophocles, who died two thousand three hundred and seventy-six years ago in Greece. The play has been a favorite throughout the centuries; but it is now probably enjoying greater popularity and closer study than ever before. It deals with two fundamental problems—perennial human problems that are even more on the minds of thinking men today than they were on the minds of those who first viewed the play in Athens. The two problems are not of the same scope and profundity, yet each is of vital importance as the men of the modern world seek for a new theory of human development, move toward greater democracy and individual freedom, and attempt to fashion a world culture or civilization. The first has to do with the role of women in society. The second concerns the individual conscience as it faces the law of the land, and the question of how the higher law relates to the law of man, and which is to be obeyed when they conflict. By opening up these two questions, the play takes on a universal significance at the same time that it is thoroughly rooted in ancient Greek life and culture.

Antigone is a young woman, about to be married to Haemon, son of Creon, king of Thebes. Creon has ordered that the body of Antigone's brother Polyneices, who had died in the insurrection, is not to be given the burial rites considered necessary by the Greeks if the departed is to have peace in the next world. Antigone, who if she were alive today might well be a leader in the women's liberation movement, decides that she must, in obedience to a higher law of love and loyalty, bury Polyneices even though the penalty for doing so, as decreed by Creon, is death. She asks her sister, Ismene, to join with her in the burial rituals. To this request, Ismene, as a woman and a law-abiding citizen, replies:

> Think how much worse our end will be than all
> The rest, if we defy our sovereign's edict
> And his power. Remind ourselves that we
> Are women, and as such not made to fight
> With men. For might unfortunately is right
> And makes us bow to things like this and worse.
> Therefore shall I beg the saints below
> To judge me leniently as one who kneeled
> To force. I bend before authority.
> It does not do to meddle.[19]

Antigone proceeds on her own to bury Polyneices. She is apprehended and brought before Creon who is enraged that anyone should have disobeyed his order; he finds it even worse that the criminal is a woman. He says, "No woman while I live shall govern me,"[20] and

> . . . If yield
> We must, then better yield to a man, than have
> It said that we were worsted by a woman.[21]

The question of the role, the rights and responsibilities of women is only briefly touched on in any direct way in *Antigone*. Yet Antigone is one of the most famous women in all of world literature precisely because of her womanliness. It is not an accident that Sophocles chose a woman to violate the law and to withstand Creon; the whole play is imbued with her spirit, her thinking and feeling, her courage, and her character as a woman. Whether a man might have or could have reacted in the same way Antigone did does not matter. What is important is that men and women of all ages can see in Antigone the personification of selflessness, otherness, love, the passionate concern for justice which is the universal name for women.

The work, life-style, self-respect, and self-identity of women vary from culture to culture. Some anthropologists go so far as to say that within each culture there are really two cultures: the man's and the woman's. It is beyond doubt, however, that in the world now taking shape the influence and power of women will extend far beyond their roles with the home, the children, and the church, important as these are. A world culture or civilization will have to be built with men and women working together in mutual respect, love and understanding; each sex contributing in its own way to the fuller development of a common humanity. The very idea of a world civilization implies that all human beings would treat all other human beings with dignity and honor and that neither man nor woman would be oppressed or subjugated, either by custom or by law.

The larger question for every civilized society opened up by *Antigone,* whether a particular culture or a world culture, is the question of justice, specifically in those cases in which the conscience of the individual conflicts with the law of the land. Creon, a legitimate and lawful ruler, had made a law which he felt was for the good of the whole society. Even when he begins to waver about whether the law was wise, he has no doubt that it must be obeyed. He says:

> . . . But one who breaks the laws and flouts
> Authority, I never will allow.
> For, whom the state appoints to govern, *he*
> Must be listened to in little things,
> In just things, in things their opposite.
>
> And I am confident that one who thus
> Obeys, would make a perfect subject or
> A perfect king; who even in the thick
> Of flying spears will not desert his post
> But staunchly stands at his comrade's side.
> O Anarchy! there is no greater curse
> Than anarchy. It topples cities down,
> It crumbles homes. It shatters allied ranks
> In broken flight, which discipline kept whole—
> For discipline preserves and orders well.[22]

Antigone, however, feels that Creon has no right to make such a

law, since for her to obey it is to disobey what she regards as a far
higher, more noble, and transcendent law; in this case it is the positive
command of the gods that all men should be decently and ritualistically
buried. The duty to bury the dead devolves most heavily on those who
are related both by blood and by love. Antigone concludes that she
has no choice but to follow her conscience. She explains it this way:

> Creon: So you chose flagrantly to disobey my law?
> Antigone: Naturally! Since Zeus never promulgated
> Such a law. Nor will you find
> That Justice publishes such laws to man below.
> I never thought your edicts had such force
> They nullified the laws of heaven, which,
> Unwritten, not proclaimed, can boast
> A currency that everlastingly is valid;
> An origin beyond the birth of man.[23]

Man's history shows clearly that whatever the nature of his society,
he must have laws. The common good of all men in a particular society
or in the world at large cannot be attained and preserved unless the
laws of that society are reasonable, well known, and enforced. However, when the laws themselves are unjust, inhuman, or contrary to
God's law or the universal laws of duty and charity, the individual
person, following the dictates of his own conscience, must assume the
responsibility for changing the laws. Open, democratic societies, aware
that law is an evolving and changing thing which must be responsive
to the needs of the people and to changes in thinking and social conditions, make provision for changing the laws when it is necessary to do
so, within the very procedures established by the law itself. However,
not all societies are open societies and any established order is very
difficult to change. The individual who senses injustice must be willing
to accept the consequences of stepping outside the law to bring about
those changes which even the demands of justice call for. Antigone
says:

> Burial of my brother? Not a man
> Here would deny it, if his tongue
> Were not locked in fear. Unfortunately
> Dictatorship (blessed in so much else besides)
> Can lay the law down any way it wants.[24]

Dictatorship is not just a twentieth-century phenomenon. It is as
ancient as man. But it may breed the kind of repression of the indi-

vidual, the kind of national or personal self-serving, that stands squarely in the way of achieving justice and freedom either in an individual culture or on a worldwide basis.

DREAM OF THE RED CHAMBER

There are many similarities between *Dream of the Red Chamber,* by Tsao Hsueh-chin, who died in 1764, and *The Family* by Pa Chin, of which the first edition in English appeared in 1958. Both are exceptionally good novels and both are centrally concerned with the same basic theme: the complex or extended family, which has long been the basis of social life and order in China. *Dream of the Red Chamber* is filled with mythology, fantasy, and superstition; *The Family* is written with the harsher social realism characteristic of much of the literature of the modern People's Republic of China. Both novels portray vividly the advantages and disadvantages of the Chinese-type family organization in times of good fortune and bad, but especially in times when that family system is being challenged and changed by new social conditions. Both are replete with maxims, aphorisms, and quotations from the sages which encapsulate and throw so much light on the Chinese mind and manners.

Wang Chi-chen, who translated *Dream of the Red Chamber* in a version published in 1958, says that " . . . judged as a whole there can be no quarrel with the general if not universal opinion in China that *Dream of the Red Chamber* is the greatest of all Chinese novels."[25] For that reason a closer analysis will be given to it than to *The Family.*

Dream of the Red Chamber is a series of stories or episodes, all loosely joined by the fact that they involve five generations of Chinese living together in one large family compound. This particular family is dominated by the matriarch who, in one of the stories, celebrates her eightieth birthday, although earlier she was not above lying about her age—a delightful human touch even in a society in which age itself commands respect.

Against this particular background—that of a wealthy extended Chinese family of the eighteenth century—the reader gets an excellent view of the customs, the qualities of mind and soul, the views and values of one of the world's greatest and most enduring civilizations. A close reading of the book makes it possible all the better to understand and appreciate the Chinese response to some of man's most universal and persistent problems and concerns: loyalty to family, devotion to ancestors, saving of face, search for higher wisdom, structure of a hierarchical social and political system, and even methods of driving a bargain.

On one occasion Chin-shih, one of the sons of the family, summarizes for his already married daughter, Phoenix, what is to be expected and what is to be done to make sure the family continues to prosper. In doing so he reveals much Chinese wisdom, which is also human or universal wisdom, and much about his own set of priorities —the family always coming first in any consideration:

> "You are a very unusual woman, Shen-shen," Chin-shih said. "In many ways you have more intelligence and foresight than many men who wear caps and gowns. So surely you know the meaning of the saying that the moon waxes only to wane and the cup fills only to overflow, or the saying that the higher the climb the harder the fall. Our family has prospered for over a hundred years. If one day misfortune should overtake us, would it not be laughable if we were as unprepared for it as the proverbial monkeys when their tree home falls from under them?"
>
> Phoenix shuddered at the ominous words. "What can we do to prevent possible reverses?" she asked.
>
> "How naive you are, Shen-shen," Chin-shih answered a little sadly. "Reverses follow prosperity, and disgrace comes after honor. One cannot prevent it; one can only provide for famine in times of plenty. There are two things that should be done." When Phoenix asked him what they were, Chin-shih answered, "We must first make provision for perpetuating ancestral offerings and then for the family school. We should buy large tracts of land around the cemetery. The rental will take care of the offerings and the maintenance of the school. In this way the future will be assured; for even in case of Imperial disfavor and confiscation, this consecrated land will be exempted. Just now the family fortune is in the ascendency—an event is to occur that will bring new honors to the family—but reverses always come when least expected."[26]

That among the Chinese, ancestors are regarded as somehow still living, somehow still part of the family in the sense that they can be honored or humiliated by actions of the members of the family living in the flesh, is brought out in *Dream of the Red Chamber*. In this regard, Chinese thought is part of the broader thinking in the East about the connections between the living and the dead. But men the world over honor their dead in ways they think appropriate, so that the Chinese devotion to and even worship of their ancestors is part of a universal human respect. Three examples from *Dream of the Red Chamber* will illustrate how much stress the Chinese place on duty to ancestors.

When one of the servants, living with the family and thus looked on as part of it, is dishonest, Chia Cheng says: "Such a thing has never happened in this house. Since the time of our ancestors we have always treated our servants with kindness. Because of my negligence in recent years, those in charge of affairs must have been persecuting the more helpless of the servants. What a disgrace to the memory of our ancestors!"[27]

And on more than one occasion Pao-yu is advised "to give his thoughts to the Examinations, the only road whereby one could fulfill one's duty to one's parents, one's ancestors, and one's Prince."[28]

Pao-yu, considering what his vocation ought to be, comments: "Have you not heard the saying that when one son abjures the Red Dust (that is, the things of this world) seven generations of his ancestors are elevated to Paradise?"[29]

Finally, an example to illustrate the Chinese search for the higher wisdom, and the conflict between following one's own path and subservience to the family dictates and ways. In one episode Shih-yen meets a Taoist priest. They talk together about such things as how short life is, how many people mistake the illusory for the real, how uncertain fate and fortune are, and what the meaning of existence is. The Taoist priest says to Shih-yen: "For if you are free, you'll forget, and if you forget, you'll be free. In other words, to forget is to be free and to be free is to forget. That's why I call my song 'Forget and be Free.' "[30] Shih-yen is so impressed with this thought that he goes off with the priest, freeing himself and forgetting about his wife and family in so doing.

NECTAR IN A SIEVE

Kamala Markandaya is an Indian novelist who writes in English. She understands the problems and the promise of India not only with her mind but deeply with her heart as well; she writes with immense feeling and authority. In *Nectar in a Sieve*[31] she tells the story of one Indian family as it faces the changes brought to India by technology and modernization, and what these mean for a people who have lived for centuries close to the land and nature, and closely with their gods and with their own inner patience, forebearance, and resignation.

Nectar in a Sieve is not exactly a story of human triumph over the tragedies and debasements arising from poverty, although there is something of this in it. Rather, Ruku, the mother of the family, emerges as a splendid woman more because of the great love she has for her husband and their children, and because of the hope—which is the nectar in the sieve—she continues to entertain that the changes that are occurring throughout India will make a better life possible for her children and grandchildren. Loving the land dearly and knowing that her husband has no skill other than farming, she also sees that change is going to bring great difficulties.

Nectar in a Sieve is a story about poverty—what it is, what it leads to, what it does to and for man's soul. To that extent it is of universal interest, although the setting for this particular story is that of a couple with six children living in a mud hut, with a thatched roof, near a small rice paddy in India. Poverty, the struggle for food and for a little money to buy the other necessities of life, is the overriding concern of their existence. The family is poor, direfully poor—a poverty they share with millions of others in India and the world.

One year the always meager rice crop on which they subsist failed completely. Ruku who, before marrying a tenant farmer, had been used to a somewhat better way of life and who, unlike most of her friends and acquaintances, could read and write, describes the hunger and the poverty:

> Early and late my sons roamed the countryside, returning with a few bamboo shoots, a stick of sugar cane left in some deserted field, or a piece of coconut picked from the gutter in the town. For these they must have ranged widely, for other farmers and their families, in like plight to ourselves, were also out searching for food; and for every edible plant or root there was a struggle . . . a desperate competition that made enemies of friends and put an end to humanity.[32]

Later, in a much more philosophical vein, she formulates her thoughts this way:

> To those who live by the land there must always come times of hardship, of fear and of hunger, even as there are years of plenty. This is one of the truths of our existence as those who live by the land know: that sometimes we eat and sometimes we starve. We live by our labours from one harvest to the next, there is no certain telling whether we shall be able to feed ourselves and our children, and if bad times are prolonged we know we must see the weak surrender their

lives and this fact, too, is within our experience. In our lives there is no margin for misfortune.[33]

And in a third place she puts the same pervading thought in a more poetic but equally poignant way:

Hope and fear. Twin forces that tugged at us first in one direction and then in another, and which was the stronger no one could say. Of the latter we never spoke, but it was always with us. Fear, constant companion of the peasant. Hunger, ever at hand to jog his elbow should he relax. Despair, ready to engulf him should he falter. Fear; fear of the dark future; fear of the sharpness of hunger; fear of the blackness of death.[34]

But running throughout *Nectar in a Sieve* is the haunting question: Can nothing be done to break this endless cycle of poverty? Is the problem so vast that nothing can or should be done other than to accept one's place and lot in life as predetermined by fate or by the deities, benign or malicious? It is clear that one small paddy can hardly feed eight people—especially when rent has to be paid for the field itself—to say nothing of provision for proper health care or for educating the children. True, two of the sons in the story leave India altogether to go to work in the tea fields of Ceylon, but this means for them permanent separation from the family and the land they love so much. True too, a tannery comes to the nearby village, a town grows up around it, and some of the men go to work in it. But standing in the way of economic progress and clearly revealed in numerous ways in the novel as the root of the psychological conflict is the ancient Indian tradition of detachment from material things and of resistance to change—a stolid and complacent acquiescence in things as they are, the too ready agreement with the thought that what has to be, has to be.

This conflict between the need for material things and the desire to rise above them is most clearly shown in the interchange between Ruku and Kenny, a foreign medical doctor who has come to build a hospital in the town. Kenny remarks, "Never mind what is said or what you have been told. There is no grandeur in want . . . or in endurance." Ruku makes no reply but tells what she is thinking.

Privately I thought. Well, and what if we gave in to our troubles at every step! We would be pitiable creatures indeed to be so weak, for is not a man's spirit given to him to rise above his misfortunes? As for our wants, they are many and unfilled, for who is so rich or compassionate as to supply them? Want is our companion from birth to death, familiar as the seasons or the earth, varying only in degree. What profit to bewail that which has always been and cannot change?

. . . do you think spiritual grace comes from being in want, or from suffering? What thoughts have you when your belly is empty or your body is sick? Tell me they are noble ones and I will call you a liar.

Yet our priests fast and inflict on themselves severe punishments, and we are taught to bear our sorrows in silence, and all this is so that the soul may be cleansed.[35]

One leaves this beautiful novel with the thought that India will perdure and that in time, with the help of many of the other nations of the world, having overcome her grievous economic difficulties, she will make a spiritual contribution to human culture and world civilization that will greatly benefit all mankind.

A principal aim of all culture learning and intercultural education is deeper and clearer cultural and human understanding. The study of the literature of other cultures is only one of the keys to mutual respect and understanding, but, as is seen in these illustrations, it is an essential and powerful one. To know another culture means much more than knowing its literature; all disciplines and all sources of genuine knowledge are part of intercultural education, in that each contributes to the dispelling of fears, suspicions, and mistrust born of ignorance or misinformation. Literature, however, is particularly important in that through it people of all cultures come to realize they are learning about other real people, specific individual people, with names, families, flesh and blood, loves and sorrows. They learn they have much in common, that they share the same humanity, even with those who think and act in ways vastly different from their own. They learn that they can work together, cooperating, sharing, and helping one another, and that the world is large enough to embrace many different cultures at the same time.

No discussion of intercultural education through literature would be complete without reference to the excellent work being done by the UNESCO translation program. Some two hundred titles have already been published in a number of languages, and more are in preparation. George L. Anderson, who edited the review of each of the some one hundred works published in English under the title *Great Literature East and West,* wrote that the purpose of the series is to bring insights into the various cultures of the world by making available their literature.

5

Intercultural Education and the Schooling of the Future

In his testimony before the Committee on Foreign Relations, United States Senate, in 1967, Dr. Edwin Reischauer stated:

> But I have a very strong feeling that we are going to have to do something more than bring Asian studies to our universities and colleges. In the long run, we are going to have to bring . . . [these studies] down even to the intermediate and elementary level, because our education today in its main lines, is clearly a Western-oriented education, and insofar as non-Western things come in, it is only peripheral and emphasizes the oddities of the non-Western world. I think we will have to do more thinking about education for our young people so that they are prepared to live in the unitary world in which we now do reside.[1]

And the final sentence of John McHale's book *The Future of the Future,* reads: "As for the larger communication and understanding implied in a shared planetary culture, it is more than obvious today that we must understand and cooperate on a truly global scale, or we perish."[2]

Taken together, these two quotations indicate certain of the key weaknesses of the schools of the past and present, and clearly point out the challenges that must be met and the changes that must be made if the schools of the future are to serve well the persons and the society of which they are a part. In its most basic form the problem is that the unitary world and the planetary culture are even now in the process of coming into being—an interdependence brought about by common necessities if not by higher feelings—and that for the most part those who direct and manage the schools have not clearly enough under-

128

stood the nature of the world in which the schools now function, or the reasons or purposes for which they might best function for the future. At this point it is essential to work toward the development of a new theory of the nature of the schools and their role in the world society which is so rapidly emerging. It is a question of whether the schools will help in the formation of a world culture or whether they will be a hindrance to it. There seems to be little doubt that the world culture will develop with them and through them or, if need be, in spite of them.

THE SCHOOLS AND CULTURE

In any society, the schools are those institutions whose primary purpose it is to transmit to the young those knowledges, skills, attitudes and values which will best prepare them to encounter fully and effectively the world in which they live, and to contribute, each person in his own way, toward its improvement. The term *schools* is limited here to those formal educational institutions which serve the young of the society. It includes, but is not limited to, nursery schools, kindergartens, elementary or primary schools, and secondary schools. In the American system of education the first two years of the liberal arts college might properly be classified as secondary schooling since they are concerned in most colleges with general rather than with specialized education. Higher education, the university, is a distinctly different kind of institution.

In seeking a new theory for the schools or for schooling, particularly as the theory relates to intercultural education, a distinction must be made between the schools in the so-called developed countries and those in the developing or underdeveloped countries.

As late as 1962 UNESCO reported that: "measures to promote among youth the ideals of peace, mutual respect and understanding between peoples must take account of the fact that most of the world's young people do not go to school. They must be reached through community action, youth movements and organizations and media of mass communications."[3] It is to be hoped that a new theory of schooling, as it might be accepted and applied universally, would help the underdeveloped countries to advance much more rapidly, to become fully participating members of the community of man, without repeating the mistakes that the developed countries have made and now find great difficulty in correcting. In some of the underdeveloped countries there is still virtually no systematic schooling. In one sense such countries have an educational advantage in that a modern theory of schooling does not, for all practical purposes, so much entail replacing existing ideas and structures as it does starting afresh. On the other hand, where schools do now exist, to whatever level in the developing countries, they tend, by and large, to be traditional, rigid, one-culture centered, backward looking, imitative, lacking in financial resources, and frequently are open only to the children of the relatively well-to-do.

To understand the need for a new theory of the schools and schooling, it is necessary to review briefly the general historical principles which have been at work in the growth of the schools in those societies in which they now exist.

Systematic schooling tends to develop in any culture as soon as that culture has acquired enough control over the physical environment so that the full time of young and old alike does not have to be devoted to concern for material subsistence. Even in the most primitive societies and in those in which the daily struggle for existence commands uppermost attention, however, the young learn many things by imitation, observation, and through their own experience, including the language of the culture, in informal, natural, and direct ways. Schooling emerges when the culture has sufficient knowledge, leisure, reflective awareness and sophistication to want to introduce its young people more surely and more quickly into the ways, customs, values, and ideas of the culture. Most often, the teachers in those cultures in which formal schooling is just beginning are those who have other primary roles in the society, that is, religious leaders, medicine men, and military leaders. Often too, the earliest types of schools are those in which the religious ideas, the myths or the mysteries of the culture, which must be carefully guarded and transmitted precisely as given, are the central subject matters. Schooling, whether on a group or an individual tutorial basis, is fitted in around the other activities, the hunting and fishing, the sowing and harvesting, and the making of tools and other handicrafts in which the members of the culture engage.

As societies advance and knowledge becomes more extensive, schooling comes more and more to be regarded as an important responsibility of the culture. Schools are established in specific places, and definite times are set for attendance; ordinarily the privilege of attending school is at first reserved to a small percentage of those of school age—

usually an elite of the nobility or the wealthy—and only rarely to the poor but talented. Those who are to do the teaching have to spend more and more time in preparation, and teaching in turn becomes a full-time profession. Later in the development of the society, schooling is expanded vertically so that it occupies a greater number of years of each student completing the course, and horizontally so that it is open to more and more young people.

Systematic schooling tends to grow in two separate but overlapping phases. First, the introduction to the culture and preparation for leadership in its more highly regarded political or professional roles through a study of its language, symbols, and rituals, its religion, philosophy, and literature. Second, a preparation for specific vocations, careers, occupations, crafts, and trades. Traditionally, the formal schools have emphasized the importance of the first phase on the assumption that everyone, regardless of whatever career he might later follow, should share with all others in the culture the ability to read, write, and calculate, and a knowledge of those elements in the culture that are its common heritage. As the society or culture becomes more diversified and specialized, and as it becomes clear that many students have neither an interest in, nor an ability for, abstract academic learning, the schools establish separate programs for those who will be going directly from school into one or the other kind of specialized job. One of the continuing objections to schools as they now exist is that those who are pursuing the more academic subjects do not get enough education through the use of their hands, through doing, and those who are pursuing the more practical subjects do not get enough understanding of theory or fundamental principles.

Schools, since they are created and maintained by the society, inevitably reflect the society and are responsive to its needs. If the society happens to be a democracy in which all the citizens above a certain age have the right to vote, it is important that all those citizens be well informed so that they can judge candidates for political office and vote intelligently. At this stage, schooling becomes compulsory. It is no longer a privilege of the elite but a necessity for all. The society regards the schools as a way of making sure that its members share certain experiences and loyalties and have a body of common knowledge that unites the society and gives it its distinctive quality. In other words, the society looks to the schools to insure its identity and continuity.

The administration of schools has also reflected the society or culture in which they exist. In those countries in which the government has been highly centralized, the control of the schools, as one of the functions of government, has also been highly centralized. In those countries in which the central government does not exert such tight control, the schools have been close to the people. In the former case the schools are thought to serve the needs of the culture directly and as a whole; the curriculum is centrally determined, uniformly taught, and success or failure is determined by state examinations. In the latter case, the local school board, the local principal, and to some extent even the individual teacher, has a degree of authority over what is taught and how it is taught. The local school, while conscious of the need for coordination with other schools in the system and the culture, is thought to serve the needs as well of the community which supports it. For example, a school in a farming community might be designed to serve its specific needs which, at least in part, are different from the needs of an urban or suburban community.

In either case, however—whether school administration is centralized or decentralized—in the modern world the curriculum tends to vary little from place to place within a culture or country. At least in the more developed countries, and increasingly in the developing ones, there is little, if any, difference between the literature or mathematics taught in a farm community and that taught in an urban area. Extracurricular activities will vary more widely and the use of the school building as a community facility depends to a large extent on the nature of the community. The assumption that the student for the rest of his lifetime will be a member of the same community in which he went to school is proving to be less and less valid. The newest and best textbooks and educational methods are recognized as such and are used in all the good schools regardless of their locality. Decentralized school administration is a great safeguard against the intrusion into education of purely political controls, but one disadvantage is that the individual school or school district frequently lacks the tax base from which to gain sufficient revenue to provide a high quality education; as a result, great inequities and imbalances arise in the different parts of the country or culture. The centralized school system, as all the great dictators and totalitarian leaders unfortunately have clearly recognized, makes it easily possible to subvert the schools for ideological or purely political reasons.

Historically, the colonial powers took their ideas about schooling with them whenever they took possession of a colony in whatever part of the world. Some of the school systems in Asia, Africa, and Latin America still mirror the theories of education and the educational practices of the colonizing mother country, although the former colony has now gained its political independence. India, for example, still suffers under an educational system that is fundamentally British in design and was intended to serve altogether different purposes than those of modern, independent India. Even if it is assumed that the colonizing powers brought their systems of schooling with them out of the best of intentions, the fact remains that a system of schooling, however appropriate and successful it may be in one country, cannot easily be transferred to and imposed on another culture. In one sense good schooling is good schooling anywhere in the world, since young people have so much in common and since knowledge is knowledge, but in another equally important sense the school system of a culture should grow organically out of the concerns, values, priorities, and thought patterns of the culture itself. No one knows, for example, what kind of a school system would have evolved in India if it had been left on its own, but whatever the system, it would surely have been more natural, more fitting, and would probably have been much more workable than the present system. Strangely enough, however, when countries become independent of those powers that have colonized them, they ordinarily retain the educational theories and practices of the colonizer. Whether this is the result of reasoned choice and decision or results simply from the difficulty in changing a system once it is set in motion is difficult to determine and varies from country to country.

In every culture the schools always have faced, and probably will always have to face, a number of ambiguities and tensions. Though the schools are the culture's formal and systematic means of education, they are by no means the only educators in the culture. The relationship between the parents in the home and the teachers in the schools is a delicate one. At one extreme some parents do not place high value on formal schooling, and may either sabotage or neutralize whatever the school tries to do. At the other, some parents who see high value in schooling feel they have a right to monitor and even to direct the educational programs in which their children participate. Further, a number of studies indicate that the student's peer group and older siblings have as much educative influence on him as do either his parents or teachers. Another ambiguity stems from the question of whether the school should stress *information,* that is, knowledge, principles, and ideas, or *formation,* that is, personality, citizenship, and socialization. That information and formation are in practice inseparable is evident enough but exactly what the relationship is between them and to what extent one can rightly be sacrificed for the other is not quite clear. The private or nontax-supported, schools have a somewhat freer hand to pursue the purposes they designate for themselves than do the tax-supported schools. And the residential or boarding schools in which the young person spends all of his time during the periods of the year when the schools are in session clearly assume obligations and responsibilities that the nonresidential schools do not have.

The history of the schools reveals that up to this time they have been conservative rather than innovative forces in most societies. They have tended to preserve and protect the ideas and values of the culture that brought them into existence. Rather than looking forward to what society should be like in future, and seeking to prepare students to live with change and to influence the directions of that change, they have for the most part taken the safe and secure pathways. The schools tend to be stabilizing elements in society, placing more weight on conformity than on creativity. As depositories of the traditional beliefs, customs, habits, and usages of the culture, they are inclined to be more accepting than critical, more a part of society as it is than part of what it could or should be, more conventional than experimental. Both administrators and teachers are selected more on the basis of how they fit in than on the basis of new ideas they have or changes they would like to make. This is not to say that the schools, taken as a whole and given all the circumstances, have not achieved much for society. That they have done so is without doubt; culture and civilization would have made little progress without them. It is only to say that the schools, as well as society itself, have reached a new historical stage in which a new theory of their purposes and the best means for achieving these purposes is now essential. The schools will have missed a magnificent opportunity if they continue to function in a unitary world as if individual cultures were still the only determining and driving forces in human affairs.

A new theory of intercultural education would, to be sure, have to include and encompass the contribution that the schools can be expected to make to intercultural education and to the formation of the intercultural or universal person. It would have to be assumed that those who are administering the schools and teaching in them feel that intercultural education is an important opportunity and responsibility of the schools.

The theory would also assume that the basic concepts of intercultural education would apply to all schools, as defined earlier, everywhere in the world and not just to certain cultures or regions. In theory, isolated provincial one-culture education can no longer be considered good education since it does not prepare a person for life in the modern world, which is now seen as diverse in many ways but also as unitary in a planetary sense. In the practical order, however, there are certain cultures that are actively opposed to intercultural education on ideological grounds, either because they are dominated by reactionary regimes or because they seem to fear the free exchange of ideas. In a deeper sense, however, intercultural education should extend to everyone. The people in the closed societies should, even for their own purposes, want to know more about the people in the free societies, and vice versa. Intercultural education is crucial even if peaceful coexistence should prove to be the only workable idea in international affairs. The art of coexistence in a small world is dependent on a deep knowledge of those with whom coexistence is necessary.

There is at present an immense amount of thinking going on about what, in general, the schools of the future should look like and what they should do. The full impact of educational television has not yet been felt; for example, there are some theorists who maintain that television, the new cognitive, urbanized, and computerized society, and the changing home life and work patterns of society call for a major and drastic reform of the older forms and methods of schooling. In any event much greater flexibility and much greater attention to individual students and their needs are sure to be features of the new schools, whether they are schools with or without walls. Whatever judgments are to be made about the way the schools have succeeded in teaching the traditional subject matters for which they have felt responsible, the schools of the future will be called on to play a much greater role in intercultural education and in the creating of international and intercultural understanding.

The new theory that the schools can make an integral and important contribution to the development of the intercultural and universal person is based on the premise that in the modern world it is both necessary and possible to view man as man, and at the same time to view him as a member of a particular culture. This is not to say that it is easy to do so because such thinking runs directly counter to what has been up to now the customary and ordinary way of viewing him. Presumably it would always have been better educational theory and practice if students had been taught to regard themselves first and essentially as members of the widest community of man, but now there is no choice. However drastic the change in thinking and however difficult the educational planning is, a new outlook is necessary. The schools can and should play a large part in clarifying it and in promoting it.

C. A. O. Van Nieuwenhuijze states this new emphasis in this way:

> Present generations are witnesses to the process of shrinking sociocultural world space, due to which the starting point for interrelations between the several parts of mankind is bound to be fundamentally revised. Thus far these interrelations have always had secondary status, whereas the way of life to which one belonged was the number one datum. By now the interrelations are due to achieve at least equal rank, if not primary importance. We cannot afford to omit shifting focus; we must reason, starting from mankind as a whole, towards its component parts, or at any rate no longer the other way around. Whether we like or not, the accent has been shifted.[4]

And Ketty A. Stassinopoulou puts it even more strongly when she writes:

> Can we deny that if our curiosity of mind, our vision of the world and humanity, have taken this ecumenical route, this is certainly due to the extension of communication—not only physical and material communication, but also communication of ideas and feelings and faiths? Can we possibly minimize the effect upon our lives of the facilities of travel, of meeting, of taking and receiving messages, of mass media of every sort, of exploring land, sea, and sky? Can we not see what all this means for us, as we try to know, understand, and interpret human beings and the different situations in which they are involved? And our understanding need not be in parts and fractions: It can be as a whole. For it is an undeniable fact that if we truly want to know anything, we must learn to see it whole—not necessarily in all its minutiae, but in its main lines and character.[5]

THE SCHOOL AND THE HOME

It has long been recognized in educational theory, and sometimes in practice, that the school, or any particular grade in the school system, must start with the student where it finds him. There is little point in any school's or in any teacher's assuming that a student already has such and such knowledge, attitudes and skills, and proceeding to build on what might not be there in the first place. This is true, to be sure, of all subjects but it is particularly true of those involving intercultural education and understanding. The student spends far more hours each day, week, and year outside school, or at least outside the classroom, than he does in it. Schooling is part of the entire process of living, not something separated and sealed off from it, and one of the most important parts of the living and learning process is the home and its environment. In one sense the student brings his home background with him to school each day and, with regard to intercultural understanding, this home background says much about where the teacher finds the student. Those in the schools can do many things in intercultural education but here, even more than in most other areas, it is essential to know where to start and how to proceed.

Because schools, generally speaking, are located where the students will have relatively easy access to them, they take on the characteristics of the neighborhoods in which they are situated. The students come to schools, which themselves reflect the culture concerns and priorities of the persons in the various neighborhoods, and the students, even before coming to school, have also acquired, to a greater or lesser extent, the biases, prejudices, attitudes, ways of thinking, and styles of life they have found in their homes and neighborhoods. Improved means of transportation and the general mobility of the population in some countries, as well as the feeling that all children should meet children of other cultures and races, have done much to change the thinking about whether the concept of the neighborhood school is any longer viable. The central school complex or school park is one plan suggested for the future. In their pioneering classic William E. Vickery and Stewart G. Cole have shown, however, what kinds of things can be done in the neighborhood schools to help ameliorate individual and group conflicts that arise in the United States because of differences in race, religion, national background, and socioeconomic status.[6]

The primary distinction to be made, however, in considering the relationship between the home and the school with reference to intercultural education is whether the student comes to the school with a home background that includes a positive prejudice against some or all other cultures, or whether he is simply ignorant of or indifferent toward them. Prejudice, or prejudging, in this sense, can be either positive or negative, favorable or unfavorable. On the one hand ancient fears and hostilities do not die easily and parents and the family group pass theirs on to their children, both knowingly and unknowingly. On the other, the memory of friendly relationships and warm feelings toward another grouping or culture quickly becomes a part of the student's intellectual and emotional heritage. Children, having no basis of comparison, tend to take for granted whatever they hear and experience at home; they are thus very easily prejudiced in one direction or another, but these are learned prejudices and not instinctive or natural ones.

Those who come to school with negative prejudices against the people of another culture constitute the greatest challenge to those school authorities who are genuinely interested in intercultural understanding. In some few cases, these negative prejudices are so strong in the parents, and subsequently have been so deeply embedded in the student, that it is difficult, if not impossible, to correct them in the school setting. The set of predispositions that the student brings to school, which he has learned readily from his parents' attitudes, words, and actions—and of which he is probably not even consciously aware —filters everything he hears about another culture, and is the basis on which he interprets whatever he experiences of other cultures. In some cases these negative prejudices approach xenophobia, in which the child fears or distrusts all strangers, including the teachers themselves if they happen to be of another race, religion, or cultural background. Negative prejudices are especially pronounced where racial or religious feelings run high, where one country has suffered greatly in a hot war, or where ideologies are in sharp and open conflict in a cold war.

In the vast majority of cases however, even negative prejudices can be made less intense or diffused altogether in the right setting and with affirmative experiences and explanations. One of the principal aims of intercultural education, in fact, is to make it possible for students with good motivation, guidance, and assistance to overcome negative prejudices. The schools are an ideal place in which to work toward this end—to put the matter in its worst form, the school should be the last place in which negative prejudices are heightened or reinforced. The schools are primarily concerned with the students but there have been good intercultural results in those cases in which the schools have worked with both students and parents in striving to overcome negative prejudices. In their best and most rational moments most parents do not want their children to be negatively prejudiced, just as they do not want them discriminated against, and they realize that intercultural respect and understanding is the only hope for a peaceful and harmonious future for their children.

The relationship between ignorance or little knowledge and negative prejudices needs to be studied much more fully. The assumption has always been that the more one knows about the people of another culture the less likely he is to be negatively prejudiced against them. If he knows them, he is likely to see more clearly why they think and act as they do, to respect their customs and ways, and to tolerate more broadly the differences which separate them even to the extent of looking for historical or psychological excusing causes. More knowledge about a culture and its peoples, rather than ignorance of them, will lead to more intellectualized and more rational judgments about them even if those judgments should turn out to be negative in some respects. At least the judgment would not have been made in advance of getting the facts and weighing the evidence. Conversely, however, it seems to be a psychological phenomenon that the least well informed persons also appear to have the most negative prejudices, so that there is a high correlation between ignorance or little knowledge of a culture and its peoples and negative prejudices toward them. Perhaps it is the case that a little knowledge is just sufficient to highlight those aspects of the other culture that lead to feelings of strangeness, difference, unexpectedness, and threat.

The fact is that the majority of students coming to school in any culture will have little, if any, knowledge of cultures other than their own, and because of their very youth will have only a limited knowledge of even their own culture. There are some few international schools attended by students of different cultures or nations, but these are so few as to have little effect on the whole problem. Intercultural education in the schools, then, is most often not so much a question of overcoming prejudice (except for example in those cases in which the newly independent countries still feel a strong antagonism toward the colonial powers) as it is fundamentally a matter of dispelling ignorance. When they are very young, most students do not even realize there are other peoples and other cultures; their world, the one they see and experience, is *the* world. They often have neither positive nor negative attitudes toward other cultures because they are literally unaware even of their existence. In some cultures and countries this situation is already changing rapidly, and will continue to do so as more young people have an early exposure to other cultures through travel, through movies and television, or through the new intercultural toys and games for the young. As a rule, it is in the school that the student has the first systematic opportunity to learn about people and places other than those in his own culture.

It is almost inconceivable in the modern world that the home alone could give the school age young the knowledge and the vision necessary to comprehend mankind as a whole, and to see the unitary nature of a human culture. But the schools can, and it is hoped that they can count on the cooperation and support of the homes in this effort. In this area, more perhaps than in any other, parents and schools are partners or correlative agencies in the education of the young.

INTERCULTURAL POTENTIALITY OF THE STUDENT

It has been a standard assumption of the schools of most cultures that the student naturally does and should learn first about the culture of which he is a part. Though schooling is becoming more and more widespread in all cultures, it should be remembered that there are now throughout the world a number of developing countries—some very large—in which less than 50 percent of the population is literate, and in which less than 50 percent of those between 5 and 19 years of age are in school. However, as Adams and Bjork point out, perhaps with undue caution,

> One basic innovation in the early process of development is likely to be an increase in the number of people who are exposed to formal schooling. This tends to shift functions from the family and church to a growing educational complex. The question, for those with some control over this trend in the beginning phases of development, is how rapid the extension of formal education should be and which level should receive emphasis.[7]

Theory, as well as practice, has stressed the idea that the student learns most quickly those things which are near at hand, which enter immediately into his direct experience, and which in some way appear to his consciousness as a problem or a challenge. He is best able to see meanings and establish relationships among things insofar as he identifies with them and is sensitive to them. In general, it is thought that, since the student directly experiences his own culture, primary emphasis, if not exclusive attention, should be put on it. Further, the schools have always regarded themselves as institutions in which basic loyalties to the culture should be taught and encouraged, and the best way to do this is to concentrate on the knowledge, skills, and values proper to the culture itself. As a rule, the teachers in the schools of practically all cultures have been one-culture persons.

In spite of this very formidable tradition of one-culture teaching, students themselves have great potentiality for intercultural learning and education. More potentiality, perhaps, than those persons who are older and more settled in their ways of thinking and acting! Just as the young, even the very young, can acquire a second language more quickly and easily than older people can, so too can a young person be brought more quickly to understand and appreciate the beauty, values, and truths of other cultures. The student has a capacity or potentiality for thinking interculturally that has not yet been oblit-erated by constant and complete thinking along one-culture lines.

Though certain school-age youngsters may have brought some negative prejudices against this or that culture or country from their home background, these prejudices are not yet at this early stage full blown and ineradicable. The children have taken on such prejudices emotionally rather than rationally, superficially rather than profoundly; the potentiality for changing attitudes and outlooks, preferences and viewpoints, among the young is vast. For those youngsters who do not arrive at school with predispositions regarding other cultures, learning about other peoples and cultures at the same time that they learn more about their own—one excellent way of learning more about their own—can be a thrilling part of the educational program, and one to which they respond enthusiastically.

The program in intercultural education, in schools in which it is now offered, is constantly being revised and expanded. In most schools incorporating a program in intercultural education will mean intro-ducing something entirely new. In any event, the concept that students are not interested in intercultural education or that they do not have a potentiality for it is no longer tenable. That they should be deliberately and systematically deprived of the opportunity for intercultural learning is a concept to which only the most closed, totalitarian, and backward-looking societies could subscribe.

The psychological world of the young person is one of imagination. As he grows older, of course, his imagination comes more under the control of reason and the harsher realities of time and space, but while he is still young the dictinctions between reality and phantasy are not clear-cut. He *peoples* his imagination not only with persons close by, but also with those in physically remote regions; they have a reality for him which leads him to empathize with them as if they were in fact his geographical neighbors. He steps lightly over the barriers that age will later impose on him and sees things as part of a whole rather than as isolated segments. He is not conscious of man as black, white, red, or brown, but simply of man as man. In imagination's eye the reality of *all men everywhere* is not at all as incomprehensible as it might appear to those whose range of imagination has been sharply curtailed by the rigidities of the ordinary educational program. Youth roams in imagination over the face of the planet, and beyond, and it finds it filled with wonder. In a good program of intercultural education the student's fertile imagination helps make up for the lack of experience with peoples of other cultures. And in all teaching, it is the imaginative way of presenting ideas that captures the attention of the students.

In the same way, the young person is almost inherently curious. He enjoys discovering what is beyond, below, above, and around. Whatever is new and different arouses his curiosity and his interest. He cannot help wondering about how other young people, and other adults as well, eat, dress, play, think, and work. While he is curious about things nearby, he is also curious about those things which are more remote and which are not necessarily part of his direct live-a-day world. He is curious about his role in life and the order of things, and about how other people regard themselves and their roles. At first impressionable and eager to know and experience as much as possible, it is only as he matures that he finds his curiosity narrowing to those areas that particularly fascinate him and move him to more specialized inquiry. Intercultural education, here too, builds on the student's native curiosity; as a person himself, his curiosity about other people is basic, vivid, and human. Intercultural education offers all the excitement of a genuine and authentic personal adventure.

Most students come to school with an openness toward learning whatever it has to teach them. They are open to all forms of existence and intelligence, as they discover them or are presented them. They accept as valid and important those things which the schools so regard. If the schools offer programs in cross-cultural learning, the students will come to accept it as important as well as interesting.

THE SCHOOL IN THE NEW AGE

Much has been written about schools of the future, and about what they must do to prepare students for the new age in which they are and will be living. And although much has also been written about intercultural education, as yet there has been little attention paid to the fact that the primary and central characteristic of the new age is precisely that it is and will be intercultural. The schools obviously exist for the students and, if schools are to be successful in achieving their purposes, they must understand the kind of world the student lives in now and will live in in future. The world context in which the schools function has changed in the last three or four decades and will change much more in future. The school must see the world and itself from a fundamentally different perspective than it has in the past. In its clearest possible form this means that the schools must change from educating a student exclusively for life in a particular culture, and must instead educate him for life in the world as a whole, that is, educate him to be, in very fact, a citizen of the world. This perspective is fundamentally new and will require much new thinking and re-structuring on the part of the schools, but the forces and movements which have brought the new age into existence are already clearly recognizable.

There are certain general characteristics of the new age of which educational planners and those who operate the schools must be constantly aware.

First, the new world in which the student lives and will live has grown closely interdependent. This is a central fact that dominates everything from questions of peace and war to the exchange of goods and services, and to the newly developing life-styles and aspirations. The statement that no man is an island might just a short time ago have been considered a bit of poetry or mysticism; now it is a specific and clear dictum of the modern world. No man, no nation, no culture can claim to be an independent island, looking out only for its own interests and welfare. A correlative truth of the new age is that each man's welfare is intimately tied up with the welfare of all other men in all other nations. Even those nations which set out to be as self-contained and independent as possible soon find it necessary to win the goodwill and the cooperation of other nations.

Within his own culture the individual is increasingly dependent on other people, as the functions and roles of persons within a society become more highly specialized. Just as the idea of the independent person or family, providing for itself everything necessary for a self-sufficient unit has all but disappeared, so likewise has the idea of an independent nation, able to isolate itself from the rest of the world and provide for everything it needs. Even if it could do so, it would be a lesser culture for so doing; it would miss the challenge and the vitality that comes from intercultural communication and interchange. Whether the interdependence of cultures and countries has been caused by the great developments in technology, industrialization, democratic thinking, transportation and communication, or is merely concomitant with them is beside the point. The fact is that the developed nations depend just as much on the underdeveloped nations as the reverse. Pollution of the earth's atmosphere or of its rivers and oceans, for example, affects the lives of all who live on earth; it makes no difference whether the pollution comes from the rich and developed nations or from the developing ones. An important scientific advance or the discovery of a cure for a certain disease benefits all people, regardless of their culture. Gunnar Myrdal illustrates the interdependence of the moden world in the area of agricultural development, as one important area out of many, when he writes:

> . . . FAO has just published its voluminous *Provisional Indicative World Plan for Agricultural Development.* It is prefaced by many reservations, but without any doubt this work of both fact-gathering and analysis will be a basic source for the discussion of agricultural problems in the years to come. The authors attach particular significance to the term *indicative* in the title, yet this first global attempt to present orders of magnitude and to show how the different targets are related in quantitative terms constitutes an important step in the right direction.[8]

So many of the problems facing modern man—whether of monetary policy, food supply, population control, international law, airway or publication rights, or of general cultural diffusion—transcend national or regional boundaries that a general policy of consultation with the others involved, rather than of unilateral action, has become a keynote of political and social action. Consultation is the recognition in practice of interdependence. Decisions and actions in an interdependent world have far-reaching consequences. The schools need to be aware that worldwide interdependence is already a fact, and will be much more so in the future, so that they can prepare their students to live in an interdependent world at the very same time that they preserve the independence of thought and action that is most commensurate with this new kind of world.

Ritchie Calder writes:

> . . . The generation which was born into the atomic age, had their [*sic*] birth registered by computer and had Sputnik as their zodiacal sign—take for granted the marvels which still bewilder their elders. They [*sic*] are also more aware that most of the arguments of what we call international politics are irrelevant—mankind has become an entity, interdependent through our common necessities. The post atomic generation senses all this: their [*sic*] elders are still schizophrenic —recognizing the facts of a shrunken world but rejecting the implications which upset outworn creeds. . . .[9]

A second evident characteristic of the current age in which the students now in school live and will live is that it is increasingly cognitive rather than manipulative. This means simply that less of the work of the world will be done by hand and more of it will be done by highly complex machines, tools, and instruments that require advanced levels of intellectual skill to construct, operate, and maintain. Mechanization and automation demand the use of more cognitive power and less physical force. The cognitive society lifts the burden of the world's work from man's back and puts it, through a rigorous and precise cognitive process, at his fingertips. In so doing it gives man much more leisure time for the possible enjoyment of the good things of life, spiritual, intellectual, social, and material. Human beings do not cease having emotions and sensitivities in a cognitive society; the affections are recognized as important, even to the growth of knowledge, but they enrich the life of the individual and society rather than dominate it.

What the cognitive society implies is that more people are both producers and users of knowledge. In more primitive, manipulative societies, what knowledge there is exists in the minds of a few, while all the others share in it only in a limited way. In a cognitive society all the people have need of knowledge all the time. Because of the ways knowledge is now so rapidly and vastly disseminated, all societies and cultures are becoming increasingly cognitive, though at different rates of speed, so that world society can now be called cognitive. Knowledge, of course, creates a thirst for more knowledge and since a cognitive society is one in which knowledge is honored and rewarded, the growth rate of knowledge available accelerates very rapidly. Basic and applied research and experimentation go on continuously in a cognitive society and an increasingly higher percentage of people devote their full time and attention to these activities.

The schools, to be sure, face the difficult task, in a cognitive society in which knowledge is so diverse and of such great magnitude, of determining what is to be taught and how best to do so. Although students in a cognitive society tend to spend more time in schooling than do those in manipulative societies, the amount of knowledge to be assimilated is so vast that that which is important must be selected out from that which is less important. At the same time the more cognitive the society, the more crucial the work of the school. Since society functions and moves forward on the basis of what the citizens know, the schools have the responsibility of making sure the students are intellectually equipped to perform effectively and creatively in the society. The schools cannot hope to impart all existing knowledge in depth and detail, but they can aim to make clear the essential principles, ideas, and concepts of the major fields of knowledge. They can make sure that the student has acquired a love of learning and of knowledge, and that he has learned how to learn.

Another feature of a cognitive society is that it opens up far greater numbers of options to each citizen, not only as they relate to the citizen's personal life, but also as they relate to the goals of the whole society. Decisions are made on the basis of the best knowledge and thinking available at the time, not on the basis of custom and tradition alone. If the decisions are to be good, the knowledge and information on which they are based must be accurate and comprehensive. While an increased number of options in decision-making for the individual and for society are evidence of freedom and maturity, the citizen can easily be overwhelmed by the different options facing him if he is not confident that his education has been a good one. A cognitive society offers many advantages for man but it also imposes heavy obligations, and exacts its toll in psychiatric disorders from those who are not prepared for it.

A third generalization about the current age that educational planners must keep in mind is that it has within itself the possibilities of a new and profound humanism and that students now in the schools will have more time to devote to strictly human concerns. Humanism in this sense encompasses all those activities which distinguish man from all other animals and which are aimed at perfecting and fulfilling man's potentialities as a human. The word carries much more meaning than that given to it during the Renaissance when it was used to signify the movement which rediscovered the glories of ancient Greek learning. Far from being necessarily opposed to theology and religion, humanism as a basic outlook or world view understands that religion has always been one of the principal concerns of man as man. Put somewhat differently, humanism is concerned with much more than simply seeing to it that all men have sufficient food, clothing, and shelter, and reasonable access to the comforts and conveniences the modern world has to offer. A broad and integral humanism seeks to incorporate everything, including religion, that might contribute to the happiness, welfare, and advancement of man, and to make these ideas and things available to as many men as possible.

A new humanism would imply a heightened awareness of the common problems, common energies, and common aspirations of all mankind. Whether inspired by religious motivation or derived from simple recognition of man's common plight—his misery, his grandeur, and his opportunities—such a humanism would seek to improve the spiritual and material lot of all men on earth. Within individual countries and among nations there is a growing perception of the need either to provide, for example, for the sick, the handicapped, the poor, the elderly, and the unemployed, or to make it possible for them to provide for themselves. Education is more and more regarded as a right of the individual, and supplying it, as a responsibility of society. More humane attitudes are rapidly developing in all cultures about the working conditions of all persons and about the mutual responsibilities of management and labor.

The 1962 UNESCO report stresses the social responsibility implicit in the new humanism when it states:

[The objectives of action] . . . are to increase among youth a knowledge of the world and its peoples; to engender sympathetic attitudes which will enable young people to view other cultures without prejudice and to react to differences with friendship rather than hostility; to develop understanding of the need for international co-operation in the solution of world problems; and to encourage respect for human rights, a sense of moral and social responsibility for others, and a desire to act in the common good.[10]

The new humanism requires a greater political awareness as well as a new social consciousness.

In the introduction to *Democracy in America,* Alexis de Tocqueville wrote,

It is evident to all alike that a great democratic revolution is going on amongst us; but there are two opinions as to its nature and consequences. To some it appears to be a novel accident, which as such may still be checked; to others, it seems irresistible, because it is the most uniform, the most ancient, and the most permanent tendency which is to be found in history.

And in a later page he indicates which opinion he favors:

But the scene is now changed; and gradually the two ranks mingle; the divisions which once severed mankind are lowered; property is divided, power is held in common, the light of intelligence spreads, and the capacities of all classes are cultivated; the State becomes democratic, and the empire of democracy is slowly and peaceably introduced into the institutions and the manners of the nation.[11]

De Tocqueville died in 1859. The irresistible tendency toward democratization of which he wrote has flowered in the modern age more than he could possibly have foreseen. It needs to become much more vital and widespread.

Democracy, in theory and practice, is a most direct expression of the regard for the dignity and worth of the individual person. It assumes that each person has a right to a vote and a voice simply because he is a free and responsible human being and, as such, democracy is a natural concomitant of humanistic thinking. The ideal of self-government and government in the interests of all the people emphasizes the human spiritual and intellectual quality of all and of the individual. Humanism and democracy stress that the individual is important, important enough to participate in the making of decisions that will shape his life. Whatever the precise future of the world, the different stages of democratic thinking and the humanism it represents will be important factors in it.

These social movements and forces, and the growing realization that a new and more human age may be a real possibility, have lead to profound changes of thinking about the schools. They, too, must become far more human and humane both to reflect the new humanistic concerns and to engender them. The training of intelligence will become more important, not less so. But there will also be much more regard for the student as an individual, his total moral and emotional person, and the quality of his interrelationships with his fellow humans in his own and the world culture. The aim will be to assist the student to develop his distinctive critical and creative powers as he learns the perspectives and principles that will dominate the new age. Human relations and interactions will become more important than economic, technological, or even legal relationships.

This resurgence of interest in humanistic study is by no means in opposition to the development and expansion of science and technology; it is corollary with them. It is now recognized that the greater and deeper the reaches of science, the more necessary it is that humanistic studies—for example, theology, philosophy, history and literature—be strengthened to make sure that man has a balanced and integrated view of the world. Neither, of course, are humanistic studies in opposition to social sciences or fine arts. Humanistic studies are concerned with man as man in all of his activities, relationships, and expressions.

One aspect of the new humanism that is gaining prominence, and is to some extent responsible for the resurgence of interest in humanistic study, is the realization that all cultures, not just those of the more developed countries, have something of truth and beauty to say about man. The East and the West are, in fact, meeting and learning more about each other and about man himself in the process.

The resurgence of interest in humanistic studies can be measured in a variety of ways: in the number of books in these areas published and read each year, in the popularity of humanistic courses in both lower schools and universities, in increased viewing of important movies and television shows, and in the attendance records at symphonies, art galleries, and museums. But it is probably best accounted for or explained by the *crisis of values* which has swept the modern world. Interest in humanistic studies, which are admittedly, but not blindly, value oriented, stems largely from the search of the modern world either for new values or for finding contemporary meaning and significance in the older systems of values. The humanities speak to the heart as well as to the mind of man. It is clear that the high development of both science and the humanities is essential to a modern civilization or culture: the former reveals what is, how it works, and is somewhat value neutral; the latter seeks out what ought to be, what ought to be done, and which things in life are the most to be valued, and are the most worthy of human pursuit and endeavor.

INTERCULTURAL ENCOUNTER IN THE SCHOOLS

Most schools are so designed and situated that direct intercultural encounter is limited, if not impossible. Especially at the younger levels, there is little opportunity for a student even to meet, to say nothing of coming to know, peoples of other cultures. Exchange programs, in which students from one country spend a year or a summer in another country and live in the homes of the students with whom they exchange, are more common now, but they still affect a small percentage of all students. At the time in the life of a student that intercultural learning through direct encounter would be the most influential, it is the most difficult to arrange. For the most part, students meet only other people, adults and students, who speak the same language and generally share the same backgrounds, ideas, and values.

While it is true that no one person or small group embodies the totality of a culture—since even within a culture the individual's range of experience and understanding is limited—nonetheless, the best single way to learn about another culture is to meet it directly in the people who are part of it. This is also true of a subculture, as for example the black culture in predominantly white America, or the youth culture in the colleges and universities. To encounter a culture as it is actually lived and as exemplified in human beings is much more effective than, for example, reading about it. Yet most of the schools of the world make little, if any, effort to provide the student with any direct encounter with another culture. This is naturally difficult where distances are great, but in the world of modern technology, imaginative ways of achieving some measure of direct encounter with other cultures might be worked out if the schools were in fact deeply interested in doing so. For one example, *confervisions* in which students of one culture might talk with students of another, seeing them on a television monitor as they do so, in much the same way as some businessmen now have meetings via confervision, may soon be a possibility. It is still fairly common, for example, to hear an American adult say that he has never met anyone who is not an American. Such a statement reflects poorly on American schools and the American life-style in the modern unitary age.

The educative advantage of personal intercultural encounter, of course, is that it opens the door to a sensitive, explicit understanding rather than to an abstract, generalized one. Personal encounter creates a sense of immediacy and reality rather than of remoteness, of a real human being, not just a symbol or shadowy figure. In personal encounter an exchange of impressions as well as of ideas can take place, and through the nuances of interaction—even in the very young through immediate liking or disliking—a person becomes aware of how those of other cultures feel, and of whether they display their feelings or hide them. Having directly encountered a person of another culture, and especially having worked, talked, joked, or experienced good things together, a person can much more easily put himself in the other person's position. He can almost literally see what the other sees and feel what he feels.

Since direct encounter with another culture in school is still minimal, the next best thing is vicarious encounter. Here the schools can do much more than they are now doing without any great difficulty or expense.

Vicarious encounter with the people of another culture can be informative, interesting, vital, and profound. Instead of directly experiencing other cultures through person-to-person contact, the student encounters ideas and feelings through hearing and reading about them, seeing exhibits, pictures, movies, dramas, and television shows about them, and even through simulations and animations. Vicarious encounter, to be sure, like direct encounter, depends on the degree of sensitivity and receptivity of the one experiencing and on the quality and the attractiveness of what is presented. It is seeing the people of another culture through the eyes of an intermediary, such as a teacher, a book, or a camera man, but it is at least seeing something of the other culture. If the teacher, book, or camera man is good, the student will see that other culture with accuracy and vividness; if the intermediary is excellent it could well happen that the vicarious encounter because of its focus and structure might be more educative than a fleeting or superficial direct encounter.

In 1959 UNESCO published an excellent booklet entitled *Education for International Understanding,* subtitled *Examples and Suggestions for Class-room Use.* A second printing was issued in 1964, indicating wide demand for the booklet. It should be updated; much has happened in the fields of educational media and intercultural education since 1959. Nonetheless, it still remains a rich supply of practical suggestions for effectuating intercultural education programs that any teacher could use to good advantage, either in or outside the classroom. The booklet tends to overemphasize human *rights*—the whole of chapter three is devoted to "Teaching about Human Rights." Young people respond much more readily to challenges, opportunities, adventures, and to ideals and aspirations than to abstract legal and technical matters. The authors apparently wanted to make sure they were on solid ground by stressing the "Universal Declaration of Human Rights," proclaimed by the General Assembly of the United Nations on 10 December 1948. The booklet, however, makes the important and valid point that "no programme to develop international understanding is complete without reference to the United Nations as an example of international cooperation on a worldwide scale, and no attempt to teach about the United Nations can fail to convey some sense of the interdependence of different countries, of the urgency of world problems and the need to solve them through co-operation and peaceful means."[12]

In planning the schools of the future the thought should be kept in mind that intercultural learning and experience are an essential part of modern education. This thought should influence the location and design of the school buildings, the types of classrooms, the selection of teachers, and the nature of the curricula. The student must come to know his own culture, of course, but he should also come to know himself as an individual human being, and he must be given the opportunity to know other cultures. A one-culture education was always incomplete because it set limits on the ideas and values open to the student, and foreshortened his possibilities for human fulfillment, but it is especially so in the modern world of greatly increased contact and communication between peoples and cultures.

The student will more and more be experiencing an intercultural world in his out-of-school life. He should also experience that world in the school so that life and school are much more closely interrelated. As Carl Rogers has pointed out:

> I believe that this picture of the individual, with values mostly intro-jected, held as fixed concepts, rarely examined or tested, is the picture of most of us. By taking over the conceptions of others as our own, we lose contact with the potential wisdom of our own functioning, and lose confidence in ourselves. Since these value constructs are often sharply at variance with what is going on in our experiencing, we have in a very basic way divorced ourselves from ourselves, and this accounts for much of the modern strain and insecurity.[13]

Beginning even in the schools the student must be helped to find the potential wisdom of his own functioning and his own values and concepts in this intercultural and unitary age.

Intercultural Education
and the Universities

The International Association of Universities selected "International University Cooperation" as the major theme of the Fifth General Conference in Montreal, Canada, 1970. In so doing it stressed a tradition of the universities which extends from their earliest beginnings. The theme also emphasized the need of the present era to enlarge and expand the concept and practice of international university cooperation on a truly worldwide scale.

Just as in theory the university has always been a place in which knowledge from all sources is examined, and wisdom and understanding are pursued, so too has it been a place in which scholars from many cultures and all over the world have been welcomed. In the medieval universities in the West it was common practice for faculty and students from a given nation to establish a house or a college at one of the central universities. There was clearly much intercultural education taking place as the scholars from the many nations met to discuss ideas of mutual interest and followed lectures together. It was only much later that the university came to be regarded as a national institution and in some places in fact became an instrument of national policy and pride. To be sure, for a number of reasons nationalism itself had not yet become prominent, and Latin was still the common language of the educated classes.

Even in more nationalistic times the universities in most countries remained open to faculty and students from other nations and indeed welcomed them. It is a rare university today which does not have an international center, or which does not at least encourage qualified foreign students to enroll, often doing whatever is possible to provide scholarships and other financial assistance. The direction of the flow of students and faculty members from one nation to another is relatively consistent: those from the developing countries go to the developed countries to learn science and technology and those from the developed countries go to the developing countries to learn more about the humanities and the arts. (This generalization does not include those who go from one country to others as members of educational or technical assistance teams.) Agreements have had to be worked out to make sure that students who study abroad return to their native lands when their studies are completed to prevent the so-called brain drain.

The percentage of university students from all countries who study abroad, though still small, is constantly increasing. The same is true of the exchange of professors. Impressive as the absolute numbers of professors and students involved are, even more important is the growing recognition that programs to exchange professors and to study abroad are important in intercultural education, and contribute much, both to the spirit and the fact of intercultural understanding.

In very recent times, as William W. Marvel points out, the universities of the world are becoming increasingly similar. Marvel insists that universities in various countries will always continue to reflect the national, cultural, and historical traditions that give a distinctive personality to each, but that what is taking shape is a truly international intellectual community, based on fundamental matters of purpose, role, structure, and functioning. He says that

Essentially, that community exists among men of learning, who seek after new knowledge, who are at home in the realm of ideas—and who feel the responsibility to transmit their learning, knowledge, and ideas to their own contemporaries and to the generations that follow. It is to be found among men who are drawn together by bonds of common interest and pursuit, who communicate across national boundaries and language barriers.[1]

The first major way in which the universities have contributed to intercultural education up to the present time is through the various area studies programs. Most universities and many colleges have now developed specializations in one or the other, and in some cases practically all, of the culture areas of the world. The area studies programs tend to be fairly broad in nature—Asian studies, African studies, Middle Eastern studies, American studies—though it is commonly the case that a faculty member or student will specialize still further in a specific region or even a country within the broad area: China in Asian studies or sub-Sahara Africa in African studies.

Area studies programs are by their very nature interdisciplinary since that which is studied is the total life of the people of a given geographical area. Consequently, in most universities they have grown up outside the regular departmental or disciplinary structure of the university. In the United States, the International Education Act of 1966 made clear that the program included both undergraduates and graduate students. It provided for "the establishment, strengthening, and operation . . . of *graduate centers* which will be national and international resources for research and study in international studies and the international aspects of professional and other fields of study" and for grants to institutions of higher education "to assist them in planning, developing, and carrying out a comprehensive program to strengthen and improve undergraduate instruction in international studies."[2]

Area studies programs usually include attempts to get at an understanding of the history, religion and philosophy, literature, art, social structure, and psychology of the region under study as well as of the economy and the status of technology. Often the faculty members in the area studies programs have some formal affiliation with one of the regular departments of the university. A faculty member who teaches African Literature, for example, may also be a member of the literature or English department. This arrangement is not simply an administative convenience but is intended to help make sure that the faculty and students keep informed about the general development of the discipline, apart from the way its insights are manifested in a certain geographical region. Most of the good programs require, as well, that the student spend some time in the geographical area he is studying and, if at all possible, that he do his research on problems that demand a firsthand use of the resources of the area. That area studies programs are a vital and essential part of modern university intercultural education goes almost without saying.

Learning at least one foreign language has long been regarded as a basic component of any program of general or humanistic education. The educational theory has been that, regardless of whether the student ever used the language, the very fact of his having learned it would broaden his mind and alert him to the nature and function of language and to the culture of the people whose language it is. At some point in his education, everyone should be required to demonstrate a minimum proficiency in one foreign language even though, when carried to an extreme, to do so means giving college credit for elementary language courses. Whatever humane value learning a foreign language might have had in earlier times, because intercultural contact is so much more frequent in the modern world, a second language is no longer regarded as an educational adornment, but more as a practical and necessary means of communication. The problem is that there is no guarantee that the second language will be the one the student needs in a given circumstance.

Language learning in connection with area studies programs is also a key to culture learning; for without the language one can never really understand the culture. Naturally, area studies programs emphasize speaking and reading and have been responsible for many improved techniques in teaching languages. The language student usually knows he is going to use it in further studies and is thus highly motivated. Knowledge of the area language is a prerequisite of most area studies programs, for a sophisticated language facility is as essential to learning another culture as it is to learning one's own culture, not only because it opens the door to direct communication but also because the language in which people think determines, in no small part, what and how they think.

Area studies programs and language-learning programs are a major step forward in intercultural education. The fact that they are attracting faculty and students in relatively large numbers indicates a strong contemporary realization that people within the different major regions of the world have many common ideas, interests, and problems. Area studies programs are established so that they correspond in fact to natural groupings of people, not only by reason of a shared geography but also because of cultural similarities. They are sometimes challenged as superficial, since the amount of material to be learned is so vast. For a man to be called an "Orientalist," for example, implies not only that he is an expert in at least one of the Oriental languages but also that he has studied deeply all that goes into the ways of thinking and living of the peoples in the Orient. A question frequently raised is whether anyone can sufficiently master knowledge of an entire area to be called an expert in it. The answer, of course, is that in any field there are different levels of generality and of specialization; levels about an area as a whole just as, on the opposite end of the scale, there are about any one country or culture.

The problem with area studies, at least from one point of view, is not that they are too broad and general, but, on the contrary, that in part they are too narrow and too regional. They make it possible for the student to see a given area as a whole, that is, to see that the people in the given area form a unity linguistically, culturally, and even economically. But all too frequently area studies stop there. Asians or Africans, for example, come to be regarded basically as members of an area or regional culture system rather than as human beings, sharing in a common, emerging world culture. The concept of area study is a middle-range abstraction that looks not so much at the individual person or at all men, but at men grouped together according to certain common characteristics. The abstraction is used to make analysis somewhat easier and more comprehensible, and to make it possible to discover interrelationships and state generalizations that a narrower focus would not permit. Such abstractions have their place and are valid; there are vast and important differences among world areas, and regional and cultural diversity do much to make this world more interesting and exciting. But the total human world in which each man shares cannot be ignored; in the modern age the force of circumstances is such that the unity of man, a much broader and equally valid abstraction, must also be studied in all its possible dimensions. Area studies grew up, in large part, as a reaction to some of the "philosophies of history," or armchair studies of civilizations, which, in the last century especially, were much too common and general to be very informative. Area studies programs and the concept of a world culture based on a true understanding of the solidarity of mankind are not at all incompatible. Just the opposite! Mario Pei says that

> perhaps we should learn to regard culture as something worldwide rather than as a mosaic of different parts, and begin to realize that it is precisely this worldwide aspect of culture and civilization that lends itself to the proposition that mankind is fundamentally one. No civilization has grown to truly great stature without copious contributions and admixtures from countless foreign sources.[3]

A second major contribution of the universities to intercultural education has been the fact that, over the last decade or two, many of the universities in the more developed countries have carried on extensive technical assistance programs in the less developed countries. Sometimes the technical assistance programs are closely related to the area studies programs; sometimes they are quite independent. Further, some technical assistance programs are cooperative arrangements worked out by a consortium of universities in conjunction with the host country—frequently, as in the United States, in collaboration with a government agency, such as the Agency for International Development, which supplies the funding and helps with some of the initial planning but which turns the management and the operation of the technical assistance programs themselves over to the universities. Other programs are direct technical assistance programs worked out between one university in a developed country and a university or similar agency or authority in an underdeveloped country. Technical assistance programs are of many different kinds and range all the way from helping to plan and build a power plant to creating a new school of public administration. The persons assisting give their time and expertise to getting a specific job done or a specific project under way. Frequently those who go on technical assistance programs to another country spend relatively extended periods of time in the country or culture they are assisting. Technical assistance, however, is ordinarily regarded as temporary assistance, lasting only as long as is necessary to make it possible for those in the country itself to develop the skills and resources for doing the work, whatever it might be, themselves.

The intercultural value of technical assistance programs consists mainly in the fact that those who assist have to get to know the people of the country in which they work. This itself is an educative experience of highest intercultural value. No matter how particularized or how broad a technical assistance program is, it must be seen as part of the overall culture, pattern and development plan of the area concerned, if it is to be successful. Technical assistance, then, should be seen as having mutual, long-range benefits; through its educative influence both in the sense of sharing ideas and in the sense of the psychological rewards of working together on worthwhile projects, it helps the country assisting almost as much as it does the university or country being assisted.

Technical assistance and educational assistance are, of course, very closely related; so much so that the term *technical assistance* is often used to include the many forms of educational assistance that one university may give another university or culture. The term technical assistance is generally used to indicate that the assistance being given is politically and ideologically neutral. Often enough a university or country is willing to accept badly needed assistance only if it is clear that such assistance does not carry with it any threat of interference with its internal political affairs. In many ways it would be clearer to differentiate sharply between technical assistance and educational assistance, although technical assistance is almost always educational in some way, since it involves both knowledge and exemplification. R. Freeman Butts is correct when he writes that "for peoples who need help in improving or modernizing themselves, the most rewarding assistance that can be given is that of educational assistance."[4] All assistance, whether technical in the strict sense, or both technical and educational, is intended to help other peoples help themselves.

THE UNIVERSITIES AND WORLD SOCIETY

The universities, while often charged with being conservative rather than innovative forces in society, are nonetheless responsive to the needs of society and reflective of its major concerns. The idea that the university stood apart and functioned in lofty and ivory-towered distance and disdain from the society of which it was a part, and according to some clear archetypal blueprint of what a university should and should not be, long ago disappeared in most cultures. Newer countries, in establishing their universities, are taking as models the universities that are complex and multipurposed, and are calling on them to help meet the needs of society, both short- and long-range. In turn, the society calls on the university to help it set its goals and priorities. The university itself, then, is almost constantly in flux and transition as the needs of society change and as these changes require new university programs.

As world society becomes more unitary and intercultural, it is to be expected that universities will reflect greater interest in intercultural education and that they will devise new programs by which their students and faculty will be able both to function well in an intercultural world and to lead it in desired directions. Though the very word university, from *ūniversitās*, implies that both scholars and ideas come to the university from all sources, that is from all the world, not just from local sources, the university, since the rise of the modern nation-state, has not been particularly attentive to its international and intercultural role. (It has been said, for example, that the English universities regarded the rest of the world as simply a problem in management.) This fact is now rapidly changing as society itself changes and as the universities respond to a clear need of the new age—a world society.

The universities have always had an intercultural dimension, and there has always been some intercultural interest, activity, and programming. But in the new world that has now come into being the universities, often with both moral encouragement and financial support from government, began to take intercultural and international education seriously. The universities become aware that "every aspect of modern life is becoming world oriented, and as people everywhere become more and more interdependent, national boundaries become, in a sense, less and less significant. . . . The world is made up, therefore, of nations politically independent but otherwise deeply interdependent, increasingly forced to seek a world context rather than a strictly national one."[5]

The universities had begun to realize, as well, as Senator J. W. Fulbright has said, that

> the purpose of international education transcends the conventional aims of foreign policy. This purpose is nothing less than an effort to expand the scope of human moral and intellectual capacity to the extent necessary to close the fateful gap between human needs and human capacity in the nuclear age. We must try, therefore, through education to realize something new in the world, a new concept of the nation and a new concept of the human community. Far from being a means of gaining national advantage in the traditional game of power politics, international education should try to change the nature of the game, to civilize and humanize it in this nuclear age.[6]

If the need of the age is for a new concept of the nation and a new concept of the human community, these new concepts are going to have to take shape in the universities, in which work at the outermost frontiers of knowledge has been a commonly accepted responsibility.

By and large the intercultural education programs of the universities of the past, even the fairly recent past, have not fully and clearly understood what is demanded of them by the unitary and nuclear age that is the twentieth century. University intercultural education programs have suffered greatly from at least two different kinds of narrow vision. On the one hand they have all too often assumed that intercultural education is mostly a matter of telling people of other cultures about one's own; on the other, they have tended to assume that the purpose of intercultural education is to get the peoples of different cultures talking together and that this will automatically result in general goodwill and friendship among peoples. Neither of these assumptions is accurate; the first can be positively harmful in intercultural encounters; the second, while not entirely false, is wishful thinking. The new intercultural education in which the universities will inevitably more and more engage, and which they will help to fashion, will have to start from different premises and take on a different orientation.

The first such premise is that all intercultural education implies mutuality and reciprocity. Much intercultural education in the past, when it took place at all, even at the university level, has been one-way. It appeared in part to be missionary inspired or doctrinaire, since its aim was to make sure that the people of one culture were well informed about another culture. Intercultural education was commonly carried on as if its purpose were selling, persuading, or convincing. In the process, spokesmen of one culture talked *at* representatives of the other culture, each taking for granted that what he was saying was the better and preferred way of looking at things. Intercultural education also has often been passive and inert because of the assumption that people of other cultures were not really interested in learning anything from different cultures that might require them to change their own ways of thinking. As a result, what passed for intercultural education was actually one directional: two one-way conversations with very little communication or education. Neither party would seriously confront, engage with, or respond to the truth or value content of the other culture. Even this one-directional intercultural exchange is a major advance over historical periods when the people of one culture lived in complete intellectual isolation from other cultures. But frequently people still assume that the other cultures have nothing to offer, and that to show a serious interest in the ideas and values of other cultures somehow indicates a disloyalty to one's own, and a kind of basic treason against it. Intercultural education, even when it leads beyond mere information to a certain appreciation of the other culture, results in a standoff. Many students have made an a priori decision against the possibility of any real assent to the cultural principles of cultures other than their own.

At its best, however, and especially at the university level, intercultural education is a mutual process, a two-way relationship and communication, a genuine and open interaction in which the possibility of rethinking one's own positions is not foreclosed. As is true of the pursuit of knowledge and wisdom generally, the openness to new truths as perceived and comprehended must be a part of intercultural education. The person whose mind is already made up, whose mind is so set and closed that he refuses to listen to anything during the intercultural encounter, does not engage in genuine intercultural education. If the university is truly a place where all ideas are welcomed and weighed, the university scholars in any culture ought to be willing to examine the system of another culture openly and fully without prejudice and preconception. The assumption has to be that both cultures have something to say, not that one or the other should only listen.

Because intercultural education is mutual and reciprocal, it is even more difficult than other forms of education. No one person speaks for any culture in its entirety. Then how does an outsider find out what a particular culture is when, as is the situation throughout the modern world, the rate of change within all cultures is rapid and when an individual representative of a culture is himself constantly coming to new levels of understanding and appreciation of it? Does a willingness to engage in intercultural education already imply some degree of detachment from the culture that one represents?

Mutuality in intercultural education at the university level implies that at one and the same time each person is both teacher and learner; each culture has something to teach as well as something to learn. This is, of course, true of all good education, but in the case of intercultural education it takes on exceptional importance. As is also true of all education, mutuality in intercultural education suggests an honest effort to find the best possible teachers and to create the best possible learning environment. Each person presents his views and interpretations, in writing or in personal dialog as clearly as he can, with the feeling that his views will not only be heard but also will be honestly considered and evaluated. Intercultural education deals with such subtle and elusive things as what people feel and think and why they feel and think as they do, and the danger of misunderstanding is great. To take just one example: if it is said that one of the basic principles of American culture is *equal opportunity* for everyone, it is essential that a non-American trying to understand

American culture know what equal opportunity means to Americans, where the idea came from, and how the principle is applied in practice. Do Americans on the whole really believe in equal opportunity, or do they only say that they do? Different Americans in an intercultural-education setting will explain the principle differently; those non-Americans who are learning about this principle of American culture will interpret the concept in the light of what they see and hear, and in the light of their own backgrounds. In intercultural education, then, a correction factor must be built into the process so that both teachers and learners will have enough mutual trust and concern to check all data and all impressions to make sure that interpretations are as accurate as possible.

C. A. O. Van Nieuwenhuijze takes the argument a step further. For him mutuality in intercultural education requires what he calls "transculturation" of the subject-matter of intercultural or cross-cultural education. He writes:

> Even if cultural diversity is not misrepresented, it yet needs careful attention. It is not at all impossible that further research would yield the conclusion that, regardless of the subject-matter, attention must be paid, in any cross-cultural education project, to what is, in the given project, the actual meaning of cultural diversity. After all, many of the factors that can be ascribed to this diversity are like icebergs. For the major part they are invisible and unknown. I am not usually conscious of the peculiarities of the cultural atmosphere in which I have been born and bred. Yet I must become conscious of them if I am to make a success out of the cross-cultural education project in which I participate.
>
> This remark leads to the heart of the matter. Once one recognizes the diversity of culture patterns, one must admit its logical consequence as to cross-cultural education. The subject-matter of such education must undergo two processes instead of the usual one. Naturally and as always, it must be transferred from teacher to pupil. But, besides, another process is required, conditioned by the first and in its turn conditioning it. The subject-matter must be "translated" from the terms of reference of one culture into those of another. It must be detached from one substratum and grafted upon another—if such a thing is possible. It must—if the term is permissible—be "transculturated."[7]

What Van Nieuwenhuijze is saying, to take again the simple example used above, is that the concept of equal opportunity means different things in different cultures; in some, in fact, it may be altogether unknown. On the one hand, it may be so taken for granted, so submerged in the unconscious of those in one culture, that even they do not clearly understand it. On the other hand, before it can be understood by those to whom it is an alien concept, it must be, as it were, lifted from the context of a particular culture and transposed or seen as it might be in the learner's culture context. In the process of transculturation both the teacher and the learner come to a better understanding of what the concept means in its native culture and what it might mean, or how it might apply, in another. A concept which has become transculturated has become another concept in the process. If the concept conflicts too sharply with the basic values of the adopting culture, the learner will reject it as incompatible with his culture system. But in the exchange of ideas between the teacher and the learner, a new understanding will have arisen and genuine intercultural education will have taken place. The learner will know how the concept of equal opportunity came to be part of American culture, what it means, and how it functions. If he accepts the concept as valid, then he will do whatever is possible and necessary to incorporate it into his own thinking, to the extent of changing his own value system if he feels the new concept is that important and requires new thinking on his part.

The university cannot directly teach mutuality in intercultural education any more than it can directly teach a person to have an open mind or a sense of academic responsibility. A person either does or does not bring a feeling of mutuality to every intercultural encounter. But the university, even more than other institutions in society, has an obligation to encourage mutuality. At the university level, students are mature enough to understand the deeper meanings and processes of intercultural education; they are sufficiently reflective to know the techniques of incisive and perceptive questioning and of personal self-disclosure in an intercultural setting. If they see that their professors, after whom they often model themselves, possess a mutuality in their intercultural contacts and encounters, they will quickly acquire the same spirit.

Johnson and Colligan in their study of the Fulbright Program point out that this program has been an important exception to the generalization that most intercultural education programs are one-directional. They state:

One of the characteristic features of the Fulbright Program . . . was its provision for two-way traffic in exchanges—in a word, its reciprocity. In this it differed markedly from most of the other programs of the U.S. government and, more significantly, from those of most other countries as well. . . .

Even more important were reciprocity and mutuality in objectives and benefits. The two-way direction of the traffic was significant, but what mattered even more was that it was on the right street, that is, where the forces of education and scholarship could help generate the "expectancies of peace."[8]

A second premise on which intercultural education must be based, especially at the university level, is that it is necessarily pluralistic.

The traditional idea of the university has been that it is an institution in which the student finds for himself, with the assistance and guidance of his professors, a mature, consistent, and integrated view of life, a *Weltanschauung.* In theory, at the university the student comes to see more clearly the relationships and ordering among the intellectual disciplines, and to gain a fuller appreciation of the achievements of the human spirit as these are reflected in the great ideas, in all the forms of great art, and in the lives of those who are regarded as having lived worthily and well. The university is also the home of theory, as the human mind reaches ever further for ideas that will lead to the fuller development of man; no good or valid thought is alien to the university.

As the universities and the people in them come more to accept their responsibilities in intercultural education in and for the modern world, it is clear that any viable contemporary world view has to rest on the principle of cultural pluralism. One obvious fact of human experience is that there are many different world views offering themselves—often with competing and conflicting truth claims—to man's mind for its consideration. The university, or the community of universities, open to truth from all sources, seeks at one and the same time to preserve and strengthen all that is of value in each cultural world view and to create the bases on which people with fundamentally different world views can live together cooperatively and in a higher common outlook. While there are organizing and intergrating principles within each cultural world view that supply answers to basic theological and philosophical questions, what is now needed is a new kind of synthesis, an all-encompassing world view, that is, one which sees both the essential unity of all mankind and also the vitality and strength of man's culture differences.

The university, since it is the one institution formally designated by society to preserve, transmit, and extend man's higher learning, is the place in which efforts toward creating a workable transcultural synthesis or world view should continuously be moving forward. So much is this the case that no university that is not deeply engaged in and fully committed to this effort can be regarded as an integral or responsible university in this present stage of human development. The university is not the only institution in society which is concerned with intercultural or transcultural education, but it is the primary and major one. That part of the university's research effort which is devoted to this end must be given greater emphasis and corresponding financial support. The students, undergraduate and graduate, should have the opportunity to study other cultures in depth so that a synthesis based on universal human understanding could begin to emerge in their minds.

That the universities, in America and throughout the rest of the world, were well aware of their responsibilities in intercultural education was pointed out by Weidner as far back as 1962. He writes:

> The academic estate has for centuries engaged more than most other elements of society in international communication of scholarship and ideas. It would be strange indeed if the colleges and universities had not adjusted to play and did not themselves seek a leading role in adjusting the American sense of mission to the needs of a world become so small that its peoples must live together, if they live at all, peacefully and with mutual cooperation.[9]

But what was lacking in 1962, as is still lacking today, was a coherent theory of intercultural or international education. The universities have not yet evolved a clear enough picture of what intercultural education is, what it hopes to achieve, and what are the best means of achieving its goals. The attempt to achieve a human oneness, a universal culture, which is organic in itself and which makes due provision for an inevitable cultural pluralism is an immense task. It is not, however, impossible; it is in fact both possible and feasible once its full importance to the contemporary scene is realized.

Intercultural education does not aim at sameness, uniformity, or conformity, but rather at unity. Unity, in its turn, does not mean that everyone comes to see things in the same way; rather it means that

each culture comes to participate in an overall human culture, each in
its own way and each bringing to it the best ideas and values it has to
offer.

Tagore touched on this fundamental premise of any new theory of
intercultural education, namely that people of different cultures can
live together in a higher essential unity while preserving cultural
differences, when he wrote:

> The best way to union is to honour the separateness of what is really
> separate. . . . All development means the unfolding of diversity in
> unity. . . . It is because there is a stirring today all over the world,
> caused by the mutual impact of peoples upon one another, that the
> natural disparities of human society have been roused all around to
> an effort for self-preservation in accordance with an inviolable law
> of development.[10]

He added that in his experience, which by reason of his travels and
his reading was worldwide, the realization of the importance of the
concept of the unity of man through intercultural education was not
just a pious wish, but was gaining significant force, especially among
students. Tagore states:

> But even in the West a real concern to rise superior to material interests
> is now apparent. . . . Those are men who, freed of the petty bonds
> of nationalism, feel within them the inner oneness of all mankind, and
> are ready for every sacrifice in working for the fulfillment of the great
> ideal. . . . I have watched the faces of students in Europe, radiant
> with the hope of world unity, and bearing with patience and courage
> the blows they must suffer for their dream of the gold age ahead.[11]

On the one hand, the universities themselves are pluralist societies:
the ideas and the energies within them are diverse. On the other hand,
the modern world that the universities serve and mirror is also pluralistic. In serving the modern world and in seeking to answer some of
its most basic problems and needs, the university must look far beyond
the demands of the particular culture in which it happens to be located.
Perhaps the most urgent need of the modern world is for a new type
of intercultural education that will lead to profound consciousness of
the dignity and identity of all members of the human family. As
Constantine K. Zurayk has pointed out, "In aspiring towards this
'order' within itself and to its realization in the human community
the University will be fulfilling its own particular function and *re-
sponding to a vital, perhaps the most vital, 'need' of its society.*"[12]

What is essential is to accept the fact of differences as natural and inescapable and to realize that the world itself is diverse and complex and open to many honestly differing interpretations. No one set or system of answers is ever likely to satisfy everyone; different world views may be good and true in different ways. Pearl S. Buck, in speaking of differences between the Oriental and the Occidental, writes that "I shall say that what seems to me the greatest difference between Orient and Occident is that they are logically unalike, and what seems to be their greatest similarity is that they are emotionally alike. That is, we *think* differently and we *feel* the same. All differences in external ways are the result of this difference in thinking and of this similarity in feeling."[13]

The individual persons or the community of scholars at a university, in whatever country or culture, who think that they and they alone have all the best answers, are probably the greatest obstacles to genuine intercultural education, since one of its basic assumptions has to be that each culture has something to learn from all others. Even in those cultures in which some answers are accepted on faith as final, or on the authority of a supernatural revelation, the assent to such truths is regarded as a gift, the gift of faith. No person has a right to impose his interpretations on anyone else through any kind of force, other than the convincing power of the ideas themselves. Closed intellectual systems and ideologies, however, make intercultural discourse difficult if not impossible.

Nor is openness to ideas from sources other than one's own culture and its thought patterns the same as cultural relativism or subjectivism, that is, the theory that all world views are equally valid as long as they serve the purposes of those who are convinced of them. The fact is that different people hold to different world views, for reasons which they regard as valid, and that there are at present no indisputable criteria for evaluating them or distinguishing among them. It implies only that human intelligence has not yet evolved sufficiently precise ways of making such evaluations. Whether it will ever be able to do so is a question only the future can answer, but it would appear that even now certain criteria are emerging. For one clear and direct example, a culture which guarantees the rights of man as promulgated in the United Nations declaration of the "Universal Rights of Man" can be judged to be more human, and hence superior to cultures which do not.

A given individual may have what are for him perfectly valid grounds for adhering to a certain world view. He is under no obligation either to change his world view or to regard all others as equally valid. In fact, he has no choice other than to accept what appear to him to be the best and most honest answers he can attain in his individual pursuit of the truth. He has every right, further, to attempt to persuade others that his interpretations are the more correct, illuminating or conclusive and, indeed, in any acceptable theory of human unity, he owes it to his fellow men to share with them all ideas which he feels might be valuable or helpful to them. The treasury of human knowledge should be freely open to the scrutiny of all. The only final test of any idea or system of ideas is whether or not it conforms to canons of inquiry and the dictates of reason; no man is entitled to hold to an idea simply because he "wants" to or because it serves some individual privilege or purpose of his own. This is the meaning of Pearl Buck's statement that "we cannot help the history of the past, but we can shape the history of the future. We can move into a new era of common sense, the era of the world view. . . . We have not yet moved into that era. Many of our citizens have, but our government has not. Let us remember that our government is our servant, and not our master."[14]

The object of intercultural education is understanding, not necessarily agreement or consensus. Charles Frankel states the point well: "I think the object of this kind of understanding is to create conditions under which we are talking the same language, under which people can negotiate, live peacefully in disagreement, and retain their interdependence while remaining diverse."[15]

THE UNIVERSITIES AND THE PREPARATION OF TEACHERS FOR INTERCULTURAL EDUCATION

According to one of its most honored traditions, the university prepares the teachers of the future for all school levels from primary through universities to adult or continuing education. Much teaching takes place outside any academic setting, for example in the home, on the job, or through the media, but those who are to be professional teachers or educators must be specially prepared by the university for their important work. Intercultural education cannot be left to chance and this means that people must be explicitly prepared to teach it. Its content and its form, its substance and its processes, have to be planned, developed, systematically carried out, and evaluated.

The generalization has often been leveled at the teaching profession that its members, the teachers themselves, are not sufficiently well educated. To the extent that the generalization is correct, the universities are at fault, and it serves no purpose to blame the accrediting agencies, the state educational bureaucracies, or the society at large— which often neither sufficiently respects nor properly rewards its teachers. Neither is it altogether accurate to say that the schools of education or the pedagogical institutes have stressed process and technique to the detriment of substance and content in the preparation of teachers.

In more recent years the preparation of teachers has come to be regarded as a cooperative responsibility within the university, rather than as the exclusive domain of the school of education and the pedagogical institute or, as was generally the case in earlier years, the teachers colleges. Still more recently community representatives and representatives of the school systems have been included on the planning boards which design the programs of teacher preparation. On the assumption that most teachers tend to teach in the way they have seen other teachers teach and in the way they have been taught to teach, much attention is now being given to educating those who will be the teachers of future teachers. For example, in the United States, the Education Professions Development Act of 1967 includes a program with the rather improbable title of "Training of Teacher Trainers." At both the preservice and in-service levels much more attention is being given to the preparation of teachers and to improving the quality of teaching.

The one area of teacher preparation that has been, and still is, woefully neglected is intercultural education. Whatever other judgments, good and bad, that may be made about the members of the teaching profession, the one that is most easily documented is that most teachers are one-culture persons, that is, they do not as a group have an intercultural or transcultural outlook themselves, and they do not show genuine concern with developing intercultural understanding among their students. Harold Taylor spent three years studying the teacher preparation and education programs in the United States. He reports that "not more than three to five percent, according to the best estimates available, have had in the course of their preparation to become teachers in the social sciences or any other area of the curriculum, any formal study of cultures other than their own, or have studied in a field which could properly be described as world affairs."[16] In other words most teachers in the United States—the situation may be somewhat better in some other countries of the world—have themselves been educated and prepared for teaching in a one-culture system. Their own education may have included the learning of a foreign language but practically all of the theology, philosophy, history, literature, and social science they will have studied is limited to that of their own culture. A fair number of teachers will have traveled abroad, and a few will have studied abroad, but hardly any will have experienced or examined another culture in any depth.

In preparing teachers for intercultural education, what is most needed is a fundamental change in the thinking of how teachers are to be prepared, and a clearer understanding of the world in which they will be teaching. As Taylor points out:

> The principal fact of the modern world is not its massive unrest, although that is its most visible characteristic, but its growing and necessary unity—the interpenetration of all lives by every other, the coming together of peoples, cultures, and societies to accomplish common and contradictory purposes. The teacher is at the center of his own culture and of this process of interpenetration. By what he teaches and by what he learns, he has it within his power to join with other teachers and their students in every part of the world to create the elements of unity in a world culture. That is what he must now do.[17]

Taylor makes an important distinction between liberal and general education in the preparation of teachers. He maintains that general education has resulted in the student's having a broad exposure to the major fields of human knowledge, but that it has failed to give him the depth of knowledge in any one field which leads to the true freeing of the human mind and releasing its capacity for intellectual growth and the desire for further study and exploration. He insists that liberal education is education in depth, and in speaking of liberal education for teachers he writes:

> What is actually needed is a radical revision in the conception of culture and in the conception of what truly educates. . . . Since it is the attitude taken toward the world which is decisive in what one learns to think and to know about it, it is with the creation of attitudes that

the educator must be primarily concerned. By attitudes I do not mean agreement or disagreement with specific political or social doctrines or world views, but attitudes in support of rational inquiry as against acceptance of social norms, tolerance toward opposing views as against ethnocentrism, the achievement of a large view of world society as against a parochial view of one's own.[18]

Over and above the general knowledge that all teachers should have about the content and the process of intercultural education, the university must make provision in its curricula and in allied educational activities for the education of those for whom intercultural education and the creating of intercultural understanding will be a primary responsibility, field of teaching and research, and a continuing involvement. While in one sense it is true to say that ideally every discipline at any university, if properly taught and if understood in all its dimensions, is a part of intercultural education, it is also true that that which is everyone's responsibility is, in practice, no one's. There is little evidence to support the position that the universities at the present time are adequately handling the problems and opportunities of intercultural education. Rather it seems clear that what is required not only in the United States but throughout the world as well, is the identifying and educating of a large group of teachers who will come to know what intercultural education is, how it can best be carried on, and who, in their teaching and research, will in fact actually and deeply engage themselves in it.

Most universities have a number of scholars and students working on comparative studies and gathering information about the peoples of other cultures. But this information, these data, are not intercultural education so much as they are the raw material on which intercultural education is based. It may be intercultural knowledge but it is not intercultural education. Intercultural education at its best is not simply informational, though knowledge is essential to it; it involves a whole new kind of awareness as well as the creation of attitudes, emotions, feelings, skills, and the sensitivity and empathy through which genuine understanding is arrived at and new patterns of thought and behavior are established. In this profound sense intercultural education is very similar to religious education; it goes beyond knowledge to the actual experience of new values and new outlooks, to new ways of viewing, feeling, and doing things. The intercultural person does not simply *know* or observe another culture; he lives it, lives in it and with it, and to some extent, makes it part of his very being, even though this does not mean necessarily that he transfers cultures or abandons his own views and identifications.

As the name implies, intercultural education is the bringing of the peoples of two or more cultures together so that a new understanding emerges in the mutual interaction. Those who engage in intercultural education in any significant way do not come together, mutually educate one another for a period of time, and then go their separate ways untouched and unchanged. Each becomes newly acculturated in the sense that a kind of transformation takes place. He experiences profound intellectual and psychological changes within himself in that either he is more convinced than ever of his own cultural principles or he is open to modification or qualification of them in the light of what he has learned. Most often, as a result of intercultural education, the person becomes bicultural or multicultural, and increasingly in the modern world, intercultural education leads to an awakening to the need for, and the possibility of, a world culture, or a culture of man.

Intercultural education, taken seriously, is of such recent origin that it is an enigma to the modern university. Like so many other fields of modern knowledge, development for example, or ecology, it is and must be interdisciplinary. While it has a specific content, that is, learning about culture, the interaction of culture principles and the impact of one on the other, and the meaning of culture learning and understanding, it is also the process by which people of different cultures come to know and appreciate one another. For that reason intercultural education should not be in a single department or division within a university, as physics or even philosophy might be. For the same reason, intercultural education is not exactly a division within the school of education although, since it deals with the learning and communicating process, it is sometimes placed there for convenience. It does not properly belong in departments of international relations, foreign affairs or diplomacy since it is not dealing with national policy as such. So far, the universities throughout the world have tended to ignore intercultural education and simply leave it up to the initiative of concerned individuals on campus to handle in whatever ways they can devise.

How can a university go about educating those who want to specialize in intercultural education as both theoreticians and practitioners? Can one think, for example, of developing a doctoral program in intercultural education? If so, what would be its prerequisites, its content or program, and who would teach it? On the face of it, it would seem highly unlikely that anything as important to the modern world as intercultural education would not find a highly respected place within the university. By its very nature it would have to draw on resources of the university as a whole, however the program was administered and wherever it was located. Many of these resources are already available in most universities. A doctoral program in intercultural education would be similar in some ways to the present ones in area studies, but it would have as its focus the teaching and learning process rather than the one-way comparative or analytic process that so many of the area studies programs now have.

Intercultural education is based principally on a knowledge of culture and of the way it determines the lives of peoples in different cultures. A doctoral program in intercultural education would have to begin with a rigorous study of the general nature of culture. Such knowledge, important as it is, is impossible without an in-depth study of at least one culture other than one's own, including learning and using the language, and spending some extended period of time in directly experiencing the other culture in operation. The study of any one non-native culture, if properly undertaken, leads to a knowledge of the general principles, the structure and dynamics of culture, which makes intercultural education possible and effective.

Over and above a general knowledge of culture and of a specific knowledge of a culture other than one's own however, intercultural education is based on a knowledge of the way in which ideas and attitudes are formed, communicated, and exchanged, and for what purposes. It involves knowing what motivates people and which kinds of settings are most conducive to free and frank interchange, and of how to eliminate the obstacles or roadblocks to genuine learning. Intercultural education is, then, different from education carried on within one's own culture by those with the same cultural background, and even from that carried on by people from different cultures who are engaged in the learning of a specific subject-matter, for example, people from different cultures coming together to learn physics or medicine. Intercultural education, properly so called, takes place when people of different cultures set out precisely to learn one another's culture. Its parameters and its directions are thus different from any other kind of education.

The central responsibility of the university in the preparation of teachers for intercultural education should be, at least in the contemporary world if it has not always been the case, developing in the prospective teachers a sense of world culture, or a universal, human culture. Area or regional studies, important as they are, do not inevitably lead to an understanding of the basic unity of man. On the contrary, area studies frequently tend to concentrate on those ideas and culture characteristics which differentiate one grouping of people from another, or from all others. Differences there will always be, and these ought to be cherished and preserved, but it is the unity, the common elements, the ideas and feelings that all men share, which are ultimately the most important for the peace and happiness of the human race.

Huston Smith has given a brilliant analysis, from a historical perspective, of how the universities might proceed as they work toward developing world culture or a civilization of man. He notes that man is inescapably engaged in three basic conflicts, that is, with nature, with his fellow men, and with himself. He goes on to say that there are at present three great surviving cultural civilizations: the Chinese, the Indian, and the Western. Each of these three civilizations has concentrated on solving one of man's basic conflicts. Smith writes that " . . . generally speaking, the West has attended more assiduously and with higher expectations to the problems of nature, China with the social, and India with the psychological." Later in the same article he concludes: "Each of the three great civilizations has achieved notable results with one of man's basic problems, but each also has been brought to the brink of ruin by not attending sufficiently to the other two problems. The obvious conclusion is that an adequate world civilization must strike all three notes as a chord."[19]

And from a somewhat more philosophic point of view, Hajime Nakamura has written:

> We can expect to reach truth only when we compare the various concepts of philosophy and try to relate them to the utmost depths of human experience. . . . This kind of comparative study is inevitable because we live in a world moving toward unity, but we still lack the attempt to see the various streams of man's philosophical activity as one organic whole. Today we can no more escape from the reality that we are members of the world community than we can the air by which we are surrounded.[20]

Finally, it must be emphasized that the new world civilization, the building of which is now the deepest imperative of the modern university, is a human or world civilization that is both one and diverse. The attempt to find an overarching unity in the vast diversity of persons, places, and things has long been a major concern of philosophic thinking in the East as well as in the West. For example, speaking of Indian thought, Betty Heimann writes: "One of the main axioms of Hindu thinking is that of *Unity in Divergency*. All beings of the Universe are among themselves interrelated as manifestations of an underlying all-pervading Life-Force."[21]

If a world civilization is to emerge—and it must—it is in the universities of the world that it is most likely to be formulated and make itself felt. The university could make no more appropriate and yet magnificent contribution to the modern world than to insure that the teachers of the future have a sense of the need for, the meaning of, and the substance and process of a culture of all men on a unitary planet. In this effort the universities will find they have the complete support of the World Confederation of Organizations of the Teaching Profession, as evidenced in that organization's publications. They will also have the support of the UNESCO Institute for Education. Both of these have been greatly concerned about the preparation of teachers for intercultural education. There is general agreement that the understanding of foreign cultures must be part of teacher-preparation programs if the teachers are to transmit positive attitudes to their students. In speaking particularly of the developing nations a UNESCO Institute for Education report states the goals for all teacher-preparation programs in the modern era:

> Their full participation in the political and economic activities in the world community has made it necessary to bring about a new fabric of spiritual and moral relations, to co-operate on a fully accepted equality, and to develop a civilization compounded of original contributions from all cultures, welded into one by their enlightened understanding of each other and the universal recognition of their equal worth.[22]

A WORLD UNIVERSITY

Perhaps no institution in society has been under more worldwide attack in recent years than the university. Much of this criticism has

come from within the faculties themselves as they carry out their
traditional roles as critics of all of society's institutions, including their
own institution. From university students has also come much criticism, ranging all the way from questioning the basic purposes of the
university, to complaining about its size and its bureaucratic procedures. Still more of the criticism comes from the public sector from
a variety of sources which feel that the universities are not serving well
the intellectual and moral needs of society. Some indeed question
whether the university, as it has come to function in the modern world,
can or should survive.

Today's universities, depending on the country in which they are
located, find themselves in strangely contradictory positions. In some
countries they appear to be too closely linked to the needs and pressures of the particular society that supports them. They are often
controlled, directly or indirectly, by political considerations rather
than by intellectual or academic ones. They are literally creatures of
the political regime, teaching only what they are permitted to teach
and carrying on research only in politically sanctioned areas. In other
countries the universities appear to be so far removed from the political scene, the centers of power, and the decision-making process that
they are largely irrelevant and uninteresting.

In neither case can they be true to their inherent nature, which
calls for the unimpeded and independent search for knowledge in all
fields, and for the free dissemination of that knowledge. The university
that is too closely tied with the political system of which it is a part
cannot do justice to its proper role as critic of society and defender of
objectivity and the ways of reason. The university that is completely
cut off from the political conflicts and contexts of its time cannot fulfill
its function as a source of new ideas, and as a power for the improvement of society and the quality of human life. The good university
must be at one and the same time a part of the political process and
distinct from it.

In one sense every university, rightly conceived, is a world university. The domain of the university is all the knowledge possible to
man, not just knowledge in prescribed fields and not just official information. The campus of every university is literally as wide as the
world, because no valid idea is alien to it and no qualified human
being should be excluded from participating in it. Every true university
is founded on the assumption that above all the nations is humanity,

and that while it is located in a particular nation or culture, its best and fullest function is to serve humanity as a whole. The university will necessarily always have it foundations in a particular place and time, but if it is to be a genuine university its vision will not be limited to them.

It would be naïve, however, to think that a university, located in a particular culture or country and subject to all the political and financial controls this implies, could be a world university in fact as well as in theory. Even the most open and far-sighted of such universities are inevitably restricted by the national, social, and ideological interests they are expected to serve. For this reason, the idea of founding one, and eventually more, truly world universities has captured much recent favorable attention.

The discussion of a world university has usually centered, however, more on such questions as how it would be staffed, financed, and administered, and where it would be located, than on what its underlying purposes and philosophy would be. Many people who have not inquired deeply into the nature and meaning of a world university nonetheless see the desirability of a university that would have a completely international faculty and student body with an open library and open research opportunities. Whether the world university should be under the auspices of the United Nations or of some independent board or corporation is not a crucial matter, but would have to be settled. A world university could be located in some specific place, or the faculty and students could be free to travel from place to place; in fact one of the objectives of the university would be to make sure that its faculty and students experienced the world widely and came to a realization of its essential oneness. Any one of a number of ways of financing a world university on a multilateral or worldwide basis could readily be worked out.

The important question is what a world university would seek to achieve and how it would go about achieving it.

In the first place, the world university would be committed to the free and open exchange of ideas among all the members of the university community. Without in any way detracting from the insights, experiences, and achievements of the individual cultures, the world university would seek the many ways in which awareness of human unity could be heightened. In scientific and technological, as well as in humanistic, education it would be at the service of the world as a whole. It would be a start toward bridging the gap between East and West on the one hand and between the sciences and the humanities on the other.

Second, a world university would be a living symbol of the fact that man is a learning animal, capable of strong commitment to ideas and ideals of his own culture, but also willing to enter into dialog with his fellow men everywhere in the hope of finding ways further to integrate and synthesize his knowledge. The world university would be open to scholars and students of all nations, as both teachers and learners, but it would not be a political forum, nor would it be directly involved in political decision-making. It would be a world university, not an international one, in that faculty and students, while deeply conscious of their own cultural heritages, would not be representatives or delegates from particular nations. Rather, in its intellectual approach and in its human and social environment, the university would lay the groundwork for the emergence of a world consciousness and a true world culture.

Third, since most of the major issues and problems of the late twentieth century are in fact world issues and problems, there are few things that would be excluded from the purview of the world university. Its curriculum would be the world seen from a world perspective. Its formal emphasis would be on world issues precisely as global and unitary, and its aim would be to help students to come to see things as a whole through seeing the deeper interrelationships among the parts. All the known disciplines have a world dimension to them and those which will develop in the future are likely to be even more consciously world oriented. The study of law, for example, can no longer be limited to local or national law, or even to the law between nations, but now must be viewed as world law, applying to man wherever he is on the planet or in space.

The idea of a world university is not some improbable or impractical dream. The resources for bringing it into existence are at hand once the decision to do so has been made, and once sufficient worldwide support for the idea has been elicited.

An Action Program

In 1947, Julian Huxley, then Director General of the United Nations Educational, Scientific, and Cultural Organization (UNESCO), writing about the purposes and philosophy that organization stated: "Still more generally, it (UNESCO) will have to stimulate the quest, so urgent in this time of over-rapid transition, for a world philosophy, a unified and unifying background of thought for the modern world."[1] In any discussion of cultural and human values and intercultural education, stress must be placed on what Huxley calls "a unified and unifying *background* of thought." He is not suggesting that there will ever necessarily be a unified and unifying *body* or *system* of human thought so clear and certain that everyone would assent to it. When Huxley emphasizes the unifying background of thought he is talking about the essential elements in a human or universal culture. This background of thought, this human culture, is in itself a high value and it includes many things, especially learning how to live with and cooperate with people who have other sets of systems of values, and how to understand, respect, and be considerate of them. The common background of thought includes the very idea that people of different cultures will always have different values; it excludes the thought that the people of any one culture could forcibly impose their values on the people of another culture. To identify one's self with this unifying and unified background of thought about human values does not in any way minimize the values held by a particular person or culture.

It used to be generally held that values could not be formally taught, but were acquired only by example and through experiencing them and feeling them deep within the consciousness of the total person. But in recent years much more attention has been given in educational theory to developing within the individual the ability to make mature value judgments. One cannot be taught directly the act of valuing or appreciating, of putting high or low value on some thing or action. In a specific instance, whether the person values something or not will depend on a number of circumstances over which no teacher has any control. On the other hand, it is now becoming clearer that the ability to make mature value judgments can be taught and that such teaching is a legitimate and important part of the educational process. The value judgment remains, to be sure, in the intellectual order and there is always a big difference between judging that one *should* value something and actually doing so. Often, however, valuing will in fact follow from judgments about value.

Intercultural education is concerned with helping people make mature value judgments about the life of man, all men now together on this planet. If intercultural education is to be successful and if modern man is to learn the value of identifying himself both with his own culture and with a universal culture through participating in a unifying background of thought, what practical steps must be taken?

Although the judgment of value seeks primarily to decide whether some thing or action is good or bad, whether it is valuable and to what extent, rather than to decide about its truth, the individual person arrives at value determinations in much the same way as he arrives at truth determinations. Nothing can be seen as good or valuable unless it is, in fact, seen also as true. The searcher gathers data from all possible sources; he weighs the evidence pro and con, he considers feasibilities and advantages and disadvantages; he projects the possible usefulness of an object or the possible consequences of an action to himself and to other people. He then decides or judges whether the thing or the action is worthy of being valued, and to what degree. His value judgment is said to be mature in those cases in which what he decides is valuable, is in fact valuable, either intrinsically or extrinsically.

In the practical order, intercultural education involves new ideas with their own principles and structures but it does not involve any new or unique pedagogical techniques. The value of identifying with a human culture would be taught in the same ways that are used to teach students to make other kinds of value judgments. The work of intercultural education is to make the data available to the student in the best and most convenient form—books, articles, lectures, demonstrations and experiments, and specific projects where possible, exhibits and displays, video and audio tapes and recordings, psychodrama and role playing, and model-building. As is true of all good education, intercultural education seeks to get the student personally involved in what he is studying by active participation, not just abstract consideration. Direct experience of cultures other than his own, is one of the best ways of helping the student to arrive at a mature value judgment about his own values and those of other cultures. Specially designed seminars and discussions—in which the very meaning of intercultural understanding and of human culture in general, the advantages and disadvantages of different theories and courses of action, the psychological blocks, the stereotypes, the historical prejudices and antipathies are central themes, honestly and openly discussed—have proven to be excellent ways of helping students to arrive at mature value judgments about intercultural understanding and world culture.

Basic to any program of intercultural education, or to the building of a culture of man, is the assumption that each or any culture will have something of value, some deposit of truth, to present to the thinking of all mankind. All men can learn something from what each culture has to say about the basic problems of human existence. No culture could endure for very long if it were clear that the principles on which it rested were inhuman, grossly incorrect or inconsistent, unrelated to reality, or unresponsive to the needs, interests, and perplexities of the people. This is true in spite of the fact that some countries and cultures, led by powerful military or ideological cliques, have represented in the past—and do represent in the present—ideas which are totally unacceptable to the rest of mankind.

In the building of a culture of man, a human community, not all ideas will be considered of equal worth or validity, but all responsible ideas will be heard and contributions from various cultures will be weighed and considered on the basis of the depth of insight or the degree of wisdom they contain, without regard to the national or cultural background of the person presenting the idea. The simple fact that an idea, a cultural principle, has existed for a long time and that it has answered the needs of a large number of people over the years does not necessarily establish it as a good idea; it has to prove itself continually as times and conditions change. On the other hand, neither does the fact that an idea is new and revolutionary say anything about its truth or value; it may or may not contribute something to what is needed in the modern world. A world culture, then, would be drawn from new ideas and from old, from large cultures and from small; the single criterion being whether it is good and should be worked into man's thinking everywhere. An editorial in the *Christian Science Monitor* puts it this way:

> Nor do we believe that the judgment of history is automatically correct. It should be apparent to anyone who takes the trouble to look about him that vast tasks remain to be taken up, tasks which history was unable to cope with. We welcome the search for greater freedom, a deeper sense of brotherhood, a more expansive love for all mankind even if this results in shaking men out of their traditional comfort and placidity. . . . The time must come when men will recognize that it is impossible to ask for safety, security, happiness and progress and not be willing to demand those mental, moral and spiritual loyalties which alone can produce them.[2]

The very concept of a human culture, a human community, implies some kind of a synthesis, or, as Huxley called it "a unified and unifying background of thought," a recognition that although men of different cultures think and feel differently about many things, they are all thinking and feeling persons. A synthesis suggests an accommodation at a higher level of human thought, a new theory, a new intellectual structure, a new model, and a vaster plane of thinking. Up to this point there has never been a world culture based on the willingness of people openly, freely, and honestly to discuss their similarities and differences. Generally speaking, people of different cultures have either accepted their own culture views as the only correct ones or they have simply seen no need to search for any higher synthesis in which their culture views could and should play a part. Each culture has been as jealous and defensive regarding its cultural principles as each nation has been about its political sovereignty. They have felt, again generally speaking, that their self-interest, the achievement of their personal and cultural purposes, rested more on looking out for themselves than on cooperating and participating in any larger community of man. Intercultural education, however, seeks to show that personal and cultural self-interest is, in the modern world, served best in a culture which views all men as basically one though culturally diverse.

It would not be to the point to attempt to show here the specifics of what each culture might contribute to a human synthesis in the way of ideas, skills, attitudes, feelings, or special moral and spiritual insights. These specifics would emerge from the continuing writings, discussions, conferences, and conversations that would take place among scientists, theologians, philosophers, historians, artists, educators, and social scientists. Each culture would contribute its best thinking. The people of other cultures would be free to accept or reject this thinking and in so doing they would come to know what that thinking is and why they accept or reject it. In the very interchange, new ideas, larger and more significant principles, or modifications of old ideas would come to light. The process is an open one. There are creative thinkers in every culture; a true community of man needs ideas from all sources and the human culture at which it aims is a better and richer culture for everyone's contributing to it and participating in it. Just one specific example: the developing world culture might well find some new and higher way of reconciling the age-old problem of the relationship of the individual and the state. The two pure positions are, on the one hand, that the individual exists for the state and on the other, that the state exists for the individual. Both points of view say something worthwhile about the nature of the state and of the individual, but each, carried to its extreme conclusion, leads to distortion. It is possible that this conflict might be resolved in a new theory which safeguards the rights and responsibilities of both the state and the individual.

The developing of a higher synthesis, a culture of man, takes place ultimately, of course, in the minds and the hearts of individuals. Even now, except in those cultures in which thought is tightly controlled and directed, each individual decides for himself which ideas are valid and viable, including ideas and attitudes which come to him from other cultures. Indeed, no community of man is possible if thought is arbitrarily or ideologically censored and dictated. A human culture does not exist in any objective way, neatly defined and catalogued, apart from the people who participate in it and contribute to it. It will reflect itself in numberless ways: in the law, in literature, in international organizations, in social action, and even in the political sphere. But in itself a human culture, like all knowledge, exists within the individual person; it is what he thinks, feels, and loves, and how what he thinks and loves corresponds with what other people think and love. Intercultural education aims not at making all people think in a standardized or uniform way, but at making it possible for each person to contribute what he can to the fuller and wider enlightenment of all.

Writing of the social factors in intellectual development, Jean Piaget makes the important point that

> in fact, it is precisely by a constant interchange of thought with others that we are able to decentralize ourselves in this way, to co-ordinate internally relations deriving from different viewpoints. In particular, it is very difficult to see how concepts could conserve their permanent meanings and their definitions were it not for co-operation; the very reversibility of thought is thus bound up with a collective conservation without which individual thought would have only an infinitely more restricted mobility at its disposal.[3]

The education and the thinking of the monocultural person is centralized within one culture. Intercultural education seeks to increase the intellectual flexibility of the individual by making it possible for him to share in a universal culture that has its own language, its own content of intellectual and spirtual values, and a worldwide, rather than a one-culture, viewpoint on the nature of thought and ways of thinking.

CONTINUING EDUCATION

The impact of the continuing education movement on educational thinking in general is well stated in the report prepared by Henri Janne for the International Association of Universities. He writes:

> These various considerations explain the increase in adults' needs for "education," the inadequacy of the school and university system in a new context, as well as the rapid change in the very content of knowledge. This is so true that we see a new society emerging under our eyes and hence a new educational system, in spite of the resistance of the old system which is still charged with the weight of tradition. With the result that permanent education has become the key factor in the change of the educational system.[4]

If, as Professor Janne finds, permanent or continuing education has become a key factor in modern society and in the changing thinking about education, it may prove to be the case that continuing education programs will also have the greatest impact on intercultural thought and on the development of a community of man.

Intercultural education, as a specialized form of continuing education, could take advantage of all that has been learned up to now about the psychology and the processes of continuing education and direct them to the particular goals of intercultural learning and understanding. While it might be disputable whether intercultural education best takes place in the home, in the schools, colleges and universities, or while persons are still young and presumably open and receptive, there is ample evidence that intercultural education for adults is not only possible but also in many ways deeply effective and significant. In any event, intercultural education, like all forms of continuing education, involves a lifelong learning and living process which at its best grows out of the directions and the inspirations of the schools and universities.

Much of modern continuing education has a business or career orientation and, as business and trade become more international, they could provide great opportunity for further intercultural learning and understanding.

It has in recent years become a guiding principle of many companies located in one country, but doing business in and with other countries, that those who represent the company know as much as possible about the country or countries with which they are doing business. In one sense this is only good business, but in a far deeper sense it is a form of intercultural education on a continuing basis. The process is by no means one-way. Much intercultural knowledge and understanding develop as businessmen negotiate with one another. Those, for example, who are trying to manufacture or market a particular product in a given country have to know what its people think about manufacturing in general and about the specific product. Because a culture is a complex whole, the attitude of the people toward an individual product is closely interconnected with other attitudes and even with underlying cultural assumptions. The businessman needs to know these attitudes and premises before he can function effectively in the culture. He has to discover what social obligations, if any, attach to doing business together. He has to know, for example, what formalities attend the concluding of a business agreement, whether a handshake is sufficient or a formal contract is necessary. In short, since business entails cooperation and mutual advantage, the man who does business in another culture has to know how all of his actions will be interpreted by those with whom he deals. Finding this out, becoming aware of the similarities and the differences, and acting accordingly is a form of continuing intercultural education. That it is oriented to a career in business makes it no less educative, and many more companies are now having their executives and managers taught about the countries and cultures with which they do business.

Two illustrations will help to make clear the relationship between intercultural, continuing education as it relates to a career in business. Businessmen quickly learn that neither the philosophy of business nor the way it is carried on is always the same in another culture. The first illustration is from Japan. Speaking of the different ways of looking at the profit motive, Van Zandt states:

> American visitors are often surprised at the lack of enthusiasm shown for the profit motive. They can elicit more interest and more respect from their Japanese contacts by talking about helping them increase their market share, or achieving growth or benefiting Japan. The making of profits is not the main goal of Japanese business. Early in the Meiji period the old despised merchant class, which was profit-motivated, clashed ideologically with the sumurai, who were more concerned with public welfare. The samurai won out, and for nearly a hundred years the Japanese have soft-pedaled the idea that business exists to make a profit. Actually, of course, given the progressive spirit of the people, their preoccupation with growth and their hard work, profits have come automatically.[5]

The second illustration is taken from Latin America. Stanley M. Davis maintains that there is a different interpretation of individuality in the United States and in the Latin American countries. He writes:

> Both the North American and the Latin American have a strong sense of individuality but the word "individuality" means something different in each case.
>
> On the one hand, the U.S. executive's notion of individuality stresses a basic equality of people. His belief is that each person has (or should have) equal rights, an equal job opportunity, and an equal chance to find his own place in the sun. Paradoxically, it is his belief in his very sameness, vis-a-vis others, that makes him distinct and defines his individuality.
>
> On the other hand, to the Latin sense of individuality, the notion that "each person is just as good as the next" is untrue, irrelevant, and contradictory.[6]

The examples could be multiplied many many times over. The point, however, is clear. The businessman who continues his education in order to advance his international business career is and should be deeply committed to intercultural education, if for no other reason than to make sure his business is successful.

One particular kind of business venture deserves special consideration in any discussion of how the modern business world requires continuing intercultural education and could lead, presumably, to greater intercultural understanding. This is the business known as tourism, a business that is already large and growing rapidly as travel becomes more economical and convenient, as greater affluence creates more leisure during the working life and earlier retirements, and as more people gain a sense of wanting to see the world.

In the past, tourism has most often been regarded as an escape, a change, a kind of recreation, or a pilgrimage. Today it is increasingly thought of as a means of continuing education and much more could be done to make it such. It is also, where other cultures are involved, a form of intercultural education. More and more people, whether individually or in groups, are visiting other lands not merely for recreation but because they want to learn at first hand more about how other people think and live, work and play. A tour, even a relatively short one, could begin with reading as much as possible about the country or countries to be visited; such preparation should also include trying to gain a basic functional knowledge of the language. A well-organized tour might include the possibility of getting to know some people in the countries to be visited. Well-informed guides could help tourists understand the history of the country and could explain, for example, its styles of architecture, its works of art, and the meaning of certain of its customs.

The tourist himself is thus clearly engaging in intercultural education in a continuing way. But even more importantly, those for whom tourism is a business need to know more about the cultures within which they are arranging tours. They need to know the impact of tourism, for example, on the local economy, whether tourists are welcome and why, and any special feelings, attitudes, and thoughts the residents might have about the tourist trade. It is coming to be taken for granted that those whose business is travel management will make it possible for their travelers to have a genuine intercultural learning experience while on tour. One way in which this is particularly manifested is in the so-called special interest tour, in which groups of people join together to visit the museums, or the theaters, or the schools and universities, or the libraries, or the national monuments, or even the sporting events in various countries. Those who are preparing for careers in the tourist business have to plan to develop a broad and intercultural outlook as part of their continuing education in their own business.

A second type of career-oriented and continuing intercultural education is that connected with the diplomatic corps. Much more can and should be done to make sure that education for the diplomatic service entails genuine intercultural understanding.

As long as nation-states exist it will be necessary for each of these to have a corps of persons who officially represent the government of one nation in others. The League of Nations and the United Nations created the need, as well, for a kind of diplomat who can represent his own country and the common interests or welfare of all men in the forum of all nations. Although many of the same ideas apply to persons in the Peace Corps and to educational or technical advisors and consultants in foreign lands, these persons are not officially representing their governments. Needless to say, any national of one country, who lives in or even visits another country, unofficially represents his country and its culture, and is creating either a good or a bad impression on the people of the country in which he is residing.

That the members of the diplomatic corps should be thoroughly informed about both their own culture and that of the country to which they are assigned should almost be taken for granted. That this has not always been the case has led to great misunderstanding, on the one hand, and to missed opportunities for cooperative action, on the other. To represent his country intelligently and effectively the diplomat must undertake a study of the patterns of thought and behavior of the people with whom he is dealing. To know what the people of the host country think and feel, and why; what their history has been; and to be able to anticipate what their reactions are not likely to be: these are of the very essence of diplomatic efficacy. Unless the diplomat is in this sense an intercultural person, he is not going to be able to explain well his own country's thinking, its principles and positions, and he is not going to be able to interpret the policies and actions of the foreign culture back to the people of his native land.

He who is to be a career diplomat must engage in intercultural education on a continuing basis. Not only does his own career depend on it, but also, since he is involved in policy making and execution, the diplomat's accurate understanding of the peoples of other cultures might be the grounds on which friendly rather than hostile attitudes among nations could develop. Kingdon W. Swayne points out one important aspect of this process of continuing intercultural education for career diplomats, whose very career is to be devoted to intercultural understanding, when he writes:

> The relationship of language to culture, the effect of language structure on meaning, differing value systems, differing concepts of the nature of the universe and of man, patterns of interpersonal relationships . . . all are relevant to this inquiry. . . . For rhetoric is the art of persuasion, and the ability to persuade is the *sine qua non* of the effective diplomat. . . . Our cultural provincialism inclines us to view Aristotelian rhetoric not only as *the* rhetoric of the West, but as the rhetoric of the world.[7]

Continuing intercultural education takes many forms. Though much of it is career or vocation oriented, much of it is also liberal or humanistic in form and content. The aim and intention of this kind of continuing intercultural education is to make it possible for adults to continue to grow intellectually and spiritually so that their lives will be richer and more rewarding, more satisfying to them personally and more significant to the world at large. It seeks to create a greater awareness and sensitivity to human problems whatever one's particular career, vocation, or profession. It seeks precisely a greater knowledge of other peoples and cultures as a way of communicating with and understanding them, and of joining with them in a shared effort to make the world a better place for all.

Unlike continuing intercultural education with a career orientation, liberal or humanistic continuing intercultural education requires a special desire and effort on the part of those who would engage in it. For a great many adults in all lands, intercultural education is outside the ordinary demands and preoccupations of their life patterns. Complacent within their own culture—and in some cases limited and even blinded by it—they are happy with family and friends who share their background and views, and they feel little need to know about or understand other peoples. They have not yet felt the full impact of the inevitable drawing together, for good or ill, of the peoples of the world. Intercultural education does not enter their consciousness for they rarely, if ever, encounter people of other cultures.

Yet, though their number is relatively small taken on a world scale, there are many adults participating in continuing intercultural education programs in the hope of finding a new form of humanism that will illuminate the modern world, and in the hope of building a world civilization that will be adequate to the world's present and future spirit. These are not only the professional theologians, philosophers, detached intellectuals, artists and poets, but also workaday adults who, in the midst of fulfilling their responsibilities in life, also see a new type of world emerging, for which they want to be prepared and which they want to help shape. These intercultural activities take many forms, some supported by various governments, and some privately financed. The United Nations and its component UNESCO have naturally been interested in continuing intercultural education and have taken the initiative in organizing and in supplying materials to study and action groups. Many universities throughout the world have arranged intercultural conferences and seminars for both their students and the general public, as part of their continuing education programs.

In those continuing intercultural education programs which are primarily information centered, the adults are seeking deeper and more comprehensive knowledge and understanding of other cultures. They are interested in learning for the sake of learning. They know, however, that no matter how remote from their lives the peoples of other cultures may at first appear, their general culture has meaning for all humans, since they all experience the same universe, though interpreting it differently. They want to see what other persons think, not only to compare it with their own thinking, but also to broaden their view of the total human condition and experience, and to see what new ideas may lie ahead.

Although one can learn much about another culture simply by reading about it, genuine intercultural learning takes place best in direct interchange between persons of different cultures. Because it is often difficult for adults to experience another culture directly, at least for any period of time, they experience it indirectly through its representatives. Thus, for example, adult discussion groups that are interested in intercultural education will often invite in a foreigner in order to learn more about his native culture. They will also make it a point to view foreign films and television shows, listen to foreign broadcasts, and discuss the ideas and interpretations presented.

A number of continuing intercultural education programs, moreover, are action oriented, on the theory that one best comes to know another culture by working with persons from that culture on projects of common interest. Such programs are organized to encourage continuing education, to develop intercultural understanding, and at the same time, to achieve some desired religious, political, social, or economic change. A number of churches have such programs aimed at helping adults understand their own and other religions better, and at bringing combined strength to bear on religious and social problems. In the same way, various civil-rights and political-action groups, labor organizations, and fraternal societies make adult intercultural education part of their organized educational programing. One example, taken from hundreds of action-oriented adult intercultural education programs, is that of the Panel of American Women. By no means the best known or most extensive such organization, it is an excellent illustration of what can be done in a systematic way and at a basic, practical level. Founded in Kansas City, Missouri, by Mrs. Esther Brown in 1957, the Panel of American Women seeks to combat prejudice and to secure civil rights for minorities. The panelists are all women, mostly housewives and mothers, and each panel is made up of a Catholic, a Jew, a Negro, a white Protestant or another minority representative depending on the community, and a moderator. At the time of Mrs. Brown's death in 1970 there were sixty-three such panels in the United States and Canada. The panelists themselves are deeply committed to continuing intercultural education and also serve as teachers of other prospective panelists in speaking to audiences all over the United States and Canada and in discussing with them questions regarding various kinds of prejudice.

Continuing education, particularly that which is liberal and humanistic, tends to be voluntary and spontaneous. The person is learning because he wants to, not because he is being forced to; this is in fact an essential precondition to true intercultural education. He feels that he has something to gain through learning, which, in turn, will help him contribute more. His interest prompts him to be more active in the learning process, more concerned with seeing what is to be learned, and with making sure he gets answers to his questions and problems. His learning is more life related than bookish, more germane to his personal needs, and more concentrated on finding realistic and workable solutions.

Continuing intercultural education, unlike some other more formal or academic disciplines, requires that one proceed at his own pace and does not easily lend itself to rigid structuring. It does not follow any necessary sequence and it cannot, at least at present, be subjected readily to objective examination. For these reasons, intercultural education fits well in programs of continuing education which are more informal, experimental, and open ended. The research now being done in processes of continuing intercultural education will also help clarify how intercultural education ought to be approached and handled in the schools. Especially in intercultural education, the rhythms or cycles of education, that is, romance, precision, and generalization, which Whitehead[8] wrote about must be respected and must be allowed to unfold naturally.

THE UNITED NATIONS AND INTERCULTURAL EDUCATION

In October of 1970 the United Nations celebrated the twenty-fifth anniversary session of its General Assembly, the only body in that organization in which all members are represented. This anniversary was the occasion for an extensive reevaluation of the accomplishments and the potential of the United Nations and its specialized agencies since the time of its inception. As would be expected, with an organization as new as this, and with its history filled with problems, crisis, and changing world conditions, including the fact that its membership has more than doubled, world opinion was decidedly mixed. The *Christian Science Monitor* could write that "it remains the globe's most prominent forum. It is the center to which the world's leaders most frequently and persistently repair. Above all, it is the one organization which can be termed the earth's collective conscience."[9] Though the UN can look back over some successes and some exceptional leadership, particularly that of Dag Hammarskjold, serious doubt exists in the minds of many people throughout the world as to whether the organization as now constituted could ever achieve the crucial purposes for which it was created. The reason for this doubt is well expressed in this way:

> Of fundamental importance is the place accorded to the United Nations in the general context of a state's foreign policy. And, insofar as governments generally have become increasingly inclined to give precedence to their alliance obligations and regional loyalties over their commitments to United Nations, one might well expect General

Assembly resolutions to carry rather less weight today than they did say ten or fifteen years ago.[10]

Those who feel that the United Nations will have to be restructured before it can become truly effective in its efforts at world peace and human welfare see its basic flaw precisely in that it is an organization of governments rather than of people or of private citizens. Representatives of governments tend to put national policies and interests above those of the community of man, and even above those of the "organized international community" of which Mr. Hammarskjold spoke so often. The United Nations General Assembly, based as it is on the principles of the sovereign equality of states and of national self-determination, can hope to do no more than enlighten and persuade. The weight of the Assembly's moral judgment cannot be discounted—in a number of specific cases it has proven to be a powerful force—but the United Nations still has to work through governments, one of whose inherent drives is to preserve themselves and to promote the interests of their own people rather than those of the larger community of man. Even before the United Nations came into being, the League of Nations had moved in the direction of abandoning efforts to bring about formal agreements among governments and of concentrating its attention on the needs and interests of individual citizens. But those who founded the United Nations felt that the only possibility for establishing any kind of world political organization was to bring together the already existing governments. To build a world government based on the sovereignty of the individual citizen and on the comity or community of man did not appear to be at all realistic at that time. Even if the idea had been considered at all, it would have been apparent that no such community of man existed in fact. On the contrary, while the building of a community of man has greatly increased in tempo and in quality during the last twenty-five years, the member states in the United Nations have also increased rather than diminished their assertions of sovereignty.

To speculate on whether the United Nations in its present form will eventually disappear and be replaced by some new organization based on an altogether different principle of political organization is not, however, the main point at issue here. Intercultural education, to be sure, is deeply concerned with the ideas, values, attitudes, and sensitivities that would bring about a form of international government truly representative of, and responsive to, the needs and desires of all men, a form of government in which the common interests of men rather than the particular interests of governments would be paramount. Political thinking and political action are important parts both of intercultural education and of a world culture or civilization.

The central consideration for the moment is that the United Nations, both as concept and as organization, has been a powerful means of intercultural education throughout its history. In its present form it may or may not be the best, or the best possible, structure for achieving its purposes, but it has helped immensely to make possible the emergence of a new type of person, the genuinely international person who, because of his position, function, and responsibilities, is forced to look at things more from an international than a national point of view. One can question how much intercultural learning takes place, for example, in the formal meetings of the General Assembly—the heavy and perhaps somewhat untrue presumption being that speakers for the most part follow lines dictated by national policy, and that their listeners do so perfunctorily without any real effort at understanding and without any intention of changing their thinking, no matter what is said—but even then at least the possibility of some amount of learning and understanding is there. Simultaneous translations make it possible to follow the speaker, and even casual listening leads to some better understanding of how the speaker's mind works and what his central concerns are.

But it is more in informal conversations and discussions, in lounges, offices, and caucus rooms, and in working on specific resolutions and projects, that most intercultural education in the UN takes place. And it is deep and realistic learning. It is in these processes that a person of one culture comes to know what the representatives of another culture are thinking, how they have arrived at this way of thinking, and what the relationship is between their thinking and their actions. Further, this intercultural learning and thinking extends far beyond the interactions of the official delegates. As Sydney D. Bailey puts it: "Today the United Nations and its agencies employ tens of thousands of professional men and women in the secretariats and in field operations. These persons, at their best, are citizens of the world, seeking to substitute large for narrow interests. The 'international man' now exists."[11]

Yet the fact is that the work of the UN, the theory behind it and the intercultural education which takes place because of it, is not well known throughout the world. One specific program of action for intercultural education is to undertake to instill a better understanding and fuller knowledge of United Nations and all that it represents. Implicit in this understanding is the realization that the organization might eventually need to be restructured, but in the meantime the fullest attention should be given in intercultural education to what the UN has done and can still do to create wider intercultural understanding and mutual trust.

While the United Nations was never designed to be an agency of intercultural education, though this is a necessary consequence of its existence, its specialized agency, UNESCO, was established precisely for that purpose. Realizing, among other things, that since wars begin in the minds of men, it is in the minds of men that the defenses of peace must be constructed, the United Nations created UNESCO to further educational, scientific, and cultural collaboration among the peoples and nations of the world. UNESCO is only one of several hundred governmental and nongovernmental agencies and organizations directly involved in intercultural and transcultural education. It works closely with a number of these organizations—in fact it depends on cooperation with them for achieving specific goals. Its overall objective, as agreed to by the states which are party to its constitution, is to achieve world peace and to promote the common welfare of all, while striving to promote a realization of the intellectual and moral solidarity of mankind. Without going into detail, it is possible to say that UNESCO, in its own programs and in those it has inspired and cooperated with, has, in spite of vast difficulties, emerged as a vital primary force in intercultural education throughout the world.

DEVELOPMENT: INTERNATIONAL AND HUMAN

There are many close interrelationships between intercultural education and international development. Development programs are a means of intercultural education and a strong motivating force for it, and, in turn, they depend largely on it for their success. More study must be given to what action programs are necessary in order that the peoples of the world gain the fullest benefit of intercultural understanding from the international development programs that are now under way and from the new directions that these programs may take in future. The United Nations declared the 1960s the first decade of development, but it is certain that development will be a major concern of the UN and of all peoples throughout the rest of this century and on into the next one as well. In fact, the gap between the developed nations and the developing nations still appears to be growing wider rather than narrowing. The individual governments of practically all countries and many private organizations and institutions as well are engaged in one or the other of the many facets of development, but the UN development program has the distinct advantage of appearing to the recipient governments and peoples as supranational and not as an arm of the foreign office or the foreign policy of any particular nation.

Economic development has occupied center stage in most international development thinking and programing. Finding the ways of making capital and technical know-how available to the people of developing countries to enable them to solve their food and health problems, so that they can modernize their production of consumer goods, so that they can improve their transportation and communication facilities, so that they can carry forward their modernization programs, so they can extend their educational systems, and in general, so that they can take their places in proportion to their numbers and their potential in the world economy, has in itself taxed the thinking of the best economic theorists and has called for the fullest cooperation and understanding on the part of those in a position to give assistance and on that of those who would like to receive it. Economic development in many of the developing countries is still in its infancy stage in spite of the billions of dollars that have gone into it through both government and private sources and through such agencies as those of the International Bank for Reconstruction and Development, the International Finance Corporation, and the International Development Association, the World Bank, and the International Monetary Fund.

The phase of international economic development most directly connected with intercultural learning and understanding is technical assistance. A sound theory of economic development in any underdeveloped country calls for a three-pronged approach, all closely interrelated: (1) the building of a sound infrastructure with all that this implies in the way of attitudes, managerial skills, work habits, equipment, and facilities; (2) securing development capital; and (3) acquiring technical competence. It is the latter that calls for the greatest amount of intercultural learning, experience, and understanding. It necessitates the coming together of persons from different cultures; one may be skilled and the other unskilled, but the interaction is basically a human one that is sometimes made even more difficult by the differences in technical skill. Technical assistance can be an impediment to intercultural understanding if it appears to imply superiority or domination by one side, or if the motives for the assistance are suspect. At first, those who already have the technical competence, whether for example in building an irrigation system or in servicing it, go to the underdeveloped country to teach these competences to others, or, those who want to acquire such competences do so by visiting the cultures of those who have them. Either way, a vast amount of intercultural learning can and should take place. Eventually a multiplier effect takes over, and those who have acquired the competences can teach them to others within their own country. Every technical skill, if it is to be fully effective in the development process, should be evaluated against the background of the culture of which it is to be a part. In general, technical assistance must be kept in balance with other phases of development; frustration and disenchantment frequently follow from acquiring technical skills for which there is no outlet in the economy.

Important as technical assistance is, the concept and operation of most such programs have in the past been too narrowly gauged. Programs have tended to concentrate on the teaching of given skills on a short-term basis to meet a specific need. There have been, of course, numbers of longer-range programs in which experts from one country go to another country to help in the establishing of technical and vocational schools and colleges of engineering, but these are usually thought of as educational assistance rather than as technical assistance. Plano and Riggs give some indication of the scope of technical assistance programs when they point out that the Expanded Program of Technical Assistance (EPTA) of United Nations had by the fifteenth year of its operation ". . . extended technical assistance to some 150 states and territories in expending a budget of $54 million contributed by 109 governments. Over its fifteen years, it offered training and new skills to an estimated 150,000 persons and included almost every developing society in its program. Services contributed by EPTA amounted to the equivalent of 32,000 man-years of experts, 31,000 fellowships, and $36 million worth of equipment, with a total cost for the period of $450 million."[12] It must be remembered that during this same period many governments, private businesses, universities, and other institutions were also engaged in technical assistance. EPTA represents simply the United Nations involvement.

In evaluating the technical assistance programs it is only fair to point out that their objectives have been limited and that, although much more needs to be done, they have succeeded in calling attention to the need for greater intercultural education and understanding even if they have not always achieved their own goals. Seldom, however, have programs of technical assistance been able to take into account the broader economic problems of the developing country, to say nothing of considering the even broader underlying cultural patterns of the country. Only rarely have these programs been viewed as excellent opportunities for participants to come, by putting the programs in their proper context, to a deeper intercultural understanding and appreciation; on the contrary, experts all too often go to another culture, perform their assigned tasks as well as they can, and leave again without any direct attempt to understand the people and their culture. Technical assistance programs generally are aimed at solving particular problems, not at helping people of different cultures learn more about each another. One specific action program for intercultural education for the future is to seek the best ways to broaden the view of technical assistance, both so that it will itself have more long-range effectiveness and so that it may contribute more to intercultural learning and understanding.

But it is a mistake, frequently made, to identify international or human development exclusively with economic development. Economic development is so essential that it is easy to assume it is the whole of international and human development—even in the face of the immense human problems that the developed countries, which have somewhat succeeded in surmounting their economic difficulties, are facing. Human development is much broader and more comprehensive than economic development, and it is to the total development of the human person, in a world of diverse cultures, that those engaged in intercultural education should devote more attention.

Human development, fulfilling the person, actualizing all his potentials, attaining humanity and humaneness—in that one achieves maximum happiness in his own life and contributes what he can to the happiness of others—is not limited to social, political, and economic progress. Human development is also a matter of intellectual and spiritual enrichment: it involves the search for knowledge and the creation and enjoyment of beauty; it includes love, family, friendship, appreciation, and an openness toward, and an affirmation of, existence. Human development, in this sense, is achievable and achieved differently by different individuals in different cultures. Each society and its general level of culture, the processes and purposes of its education, either impedes or promotes a fuller and higher human development.

At the international level, UNESCO aims to promote human development through greater cooperation in education, natural and social sciences, in cultural affairs, and in the humanities. And in addition to its own efforts, UNESCO is in direct relationship with some 225 non-governmental organizations (NGOs) whose efforts are directed in one form or another toward the widest possible human development. To give just a few examples: the International Council for Philosophy and Humanistic Studies, the International Federation of Library Associations, the International Association of Universities, the International Theatre Institute. Many NGOs also have a large number of affiliated organizations with which UNESCO is in indirect relationship. Because UNESCO, at least in part, is tied into governmental structures, the NGOs have certain advantages in their work of promoting human development. Among these, as stated in the report of one seminar is that

> They are a proven instrument for opening and maintaining contact between professional people in spite of both cultural and ideological barriers; and [they] provide a means to continue communication at times when political contacts are at a minimum. They provide a non-political arena and mechanism for unofficial discussion and possible trial of new ideas, in cases where official commitment would be premature. They demonstrate and extend the free world concepts of an open democratic society, in which private citizens can freely organize themselves to carry forward their private and professional interests.[13]

In spite, however, of the immense international and intercultural activity already taking place through UNESCO and the NGOs, much remains to be done; the most that can be said is that good beginnings have been made. Even with all the conferences being held, the projects and studies being undertaken, and the journals being published, only a small percentage of the world's people are now being directly influenced by any program of intercultural education. The task of changing the directions of education from a nearly total concern with one specific culture to an intercultural orientation is, to be sure, a formidable one. Many of the UNESCO programs, and the conferences, studies, and projects of the NGOs suffer seriously from inadequate financing and from the lack of highly skilled, full-time leadership. Programs are often based on false assumptions about the willingness and readiness of participants from different cultures to seek genuine intercultural understanding and, often enough, there is insufficient preliminary planning, preparatory work, and subsequent evaluation. UNESCO and the NGOs, taken together, constitute one already existing program of action in intercultural education. Their activities should be strengthened and expanded and new programs should be developed. The whole area of intercultural exchange and dialog on a person-to-person basis, apart from formal organization of any kind, also needs to be more fully explored and further ways of making it possible should be found.

COOPERATION AMONG RELIGIONS

The new era of intercultural education has witnessed in the recent past a much more serious effort on the part of world religions to understand one another and to work more closely together. This trend is almost sure to be accentuated in the future. Religion often plays a central role in defining a culture; religious commitments are often among the most deep and meaningful ones. One simply cannot understand India without understanding Hinduism, China without understanding Confucianism and Buddhism, the Middle East without understanding Islam, or Europe without understanding Christianity. José Ortega y Gasset wrote that "thus we may now say that the diagnosing of any human existence, whether of an individual, a people, or an age, must begin by an ordered inventory of its system of convictions, and to this end it must establish before all else which belief is fundamental, decisive, sustaining and breathing life into all the others."[14] The understanding of religious beliefs and convictions is one key to intercultural understanding and is an essential part of intercultural education.

The new emphasis on interreligious understanding and education is, at least in part, a reaction to growing world secularism. Those who share an interest in religious concepts and practices are finding it both more necessary and much easier than had earlier been thought possible to come together to meet a common challenge: the denial or the neglect of religious values and meanings in human life. Harvey

Cox, in his analysis of this trend, makes an important distinction between secularism and secularization. He states that

> secularization implies a historical process, almost certainly irreversible, in which society and culture are delivered from tutelage to religious control and closed metaphysical world views. We have argued that it is basically a liberating development. Secularism, on the other hand, is the name for an ideology, a new closed world view which functions very much like a new religion. . . . It menaces the openness and freedom secularization has produced; it must therefore be watched carefully to prevent its becoming the ideology of a new establishment.[15]

Cox, following Dietrich Bonhoeffer, sees in the secularization process the possibility of a rebirth of a more authentic, vital, and illuminating religious experience—in his context a truly biblical and Christian one. He illustrates this point by noting:

> Thus it is now possible for the United Nations to develop a Declaration of Human Rights based on a consensus of all the nation-states involved. It does not, like the American founding documents, rest on affirmations concerning the inalienable right with which men are 'endowed by their Creator.' Nor is it based on some theory of natural law. It is the expression of a consensus which draws together several cultural and religious traditions including those which believe neither in a Creator nor in any form of natural law.[16]

Secularization may very well turn out to have given a new form, substance, and significance to the world's religions. Nonetheless, many of the leaders of those religions see both secularization and secularism as the turning away from religious beliefs and practices and a much too pronounced focusing of man's attention on the things of this world, this time, and this life. The modern challenge to religion ranges all the way from the avowed atheism of the Communist party, for example, to the simple neglect of it as an institutional force in man's life. In the summary report prepared by UNESCO for the 1970 volume of *International World of Learning* there is only one mention of religion and that is under the heading "Interdisciplinary Co-operation and Philosophy," in which reference is made to studies of the concept of human rights in different religions, traditions, and cultures. These studies, to be sure, culminated in the book *Birthright of Man*.

It would be incorrect to conclude that the leaders of the world's religions are seeking ways of achieving greater understanding and co-operation simply as a way of gaining strength in the struggle against the forces of irreligion or nonreligion, or, to put it a little too bluntly, that they are coming together in order to meet on a common foe. The trend has a much deeper reason and significance. The religions of the world are themselves coming more fully to understand and appreciate what has always been a clear doctrine of the major religions, namely, that all men are indeed one. No one has seen this more vividly or put it more beautifully than Teilhard de Chardin, but he is by no means alone. He writes:

> The enrichment and ferment of religious thought in our time has undoubtedly been caused by the revelation of the size and unity of the world all around us and within us. All around us the physical sciences are endlessly extending the abysses of time and space, and ceaselessly discerning new relationships between the elements of the universe. Within us a whole world of affinities and interrelated sympathies, as old as the human soul, is being awakened by the stimulus of these great discoveries, and what has hitherto been dreamed rather than experienced is at last taking shape and consistency. Scholarly and discriminating among serious thinkers, simple or didactic among the half-educated, the aspirations towards a vaster and more organic *one,* and the premonitions of unknown forces and their applications in new fields, are the same, and are emerging simultaneously on all sides. It is almost a commonplace today to find men who, quite naturally and unaffectedly, live in the explicit consciousness of being an atom or a citizen of the universe.[17]

Prompted, then, both by the feeling that the religions of the world must understand each other better if religion is to continue to be a significant feature of modern life and that, as Teilhard explains, there is on the face of the earth an awakening to man's essential oneness, many efforts are being made at interreligious education and cooperation. In the hope that each person will come to a fuller acceptance and practice of whatever religion is his, the interfaith programs are now leading to more vital forms of both intellectual and operational cooperation. At the very least it is clear that religious people now have in common their concern for religion and its place in man's life.

The modern ecumenical movement is an attempt to emphasize what the religions of the world have in common rather than what their differences are. The word *ecumenical,* which means general or universal, is being used more and more to designate understanding and working together among all religions.

Dostoevsky, with the eye of a novelist rather than of a philosopher, suggests one aspect of man's religious history against which modern ecumenism is a sharp revolt.

> But man seeks to worship what is established beyond dispute, so indisputably that all men would agree at once to worship it. For these pitiful creatures are concerned not only to find what one or the other can worship, but to find something that all would believe and worship; what is essential is that all may be *together* in it. This striving for *community* of worship is the chief misery of every man individually and of all humanity from the beginning of time. For the sake of common worship they've slain each other with the sword. They have set up gods and challenged one another, "Put away your gods and come and worship ours, or we will kill you and your gods!"[18]

All religions have the common bond or denominator that they are seeking an ultimate reality, or a ground of being, in human life and world experience. Ecumenism is the means by which the religions of the world try to learn from one another to the great benefit of all. The ecumenical spirit represents a gigantic step forward, since it has not been too long ago that some religions forbad their members to co-operate in religious matters with members of other religions, to say nothing of worshiping with them. Above all, ecumenism is the straightforward effort to break through the barriers of defensiveness, exclusiveness, and the arcane so that what a given religion really believes and practices can be examined by all who wish to do so. Ecumenism, still in its infancy, seeks to reinvigorate religion and make it more contemporary the world over. A completely viable theory of ecumenism remains to be worked out.

The liturgy or forms of public worship are highly educative and those who are ecumenically minded have sought to open up the possibility for persons of different religions to learn from each other by coming together in worship. Prior to the spread of the ecumenical movement, many religions had their own more or less private and distinctive liturgy, their own way of worshiping. These individual liturgies still exist, of course, and have great value and meaning for those who share most intimately in them. In the past, however, most such liturgies were closed to those who were not members. Nonmembers might well attend liturgical services, and in some cases they were urged to do so, and made welcome, but usually they came as observers and out of curiosity, not to learn or participate. In some cases liturgical services are now composed in such a way that mutual education is a direct objective, on the theory that in the very act of common worship people can come to know, respect, and understand one another.

Socioeconomic action also offers wide opportunity for ecumenical cooperation. Here, the representatives of the major religions or churches come together to work on basic human problems. The problems of race or caste, health, poverty, education, population, technology, war, natural disaster, and the city all have religious and theological dimensions. People working together and from a basic religious inspiration have done much in these areas to show the force of religion at work. In such work the aim is not so much to instill religious ideas directly as simply to bear religious witness among those who need help.

The concept was once widely held in some religious circles that each person, even each theologian, had all he could do to learn his own religion thoroughly and that the study of other religions might even be a dangerous or a corrupting influence. But now, in keeping with ecumenism, many of the seminaries and theological schools have broadened their curricula to include the serious study of other religions and of the religious experience generally. This type of intercultural education is sure to strengthen and enhance the spirit of human community.

The ecumenical movement is not concerned about institutional forms, except insofar as they might symbolize a sense of coming together in an open ecumenical intention. Ecumenism, like the religious dimension in life itself, may not be amenable to institutionalization and its bureaucracies. To try to organize it might mean to defeat it altogether. In any event, there is within the ecumenical movement little if any discussion of the emergence of a superchurch which would have its own dogmas, ethical systems, and liturgies. The feeling generally is that the religions of the world have to find their own way of coming together in an organic unity that will continue to preserve the individuality of its many authentic expressions.

Ecumenism, in the broadest meaning, is not as much a problem among the major religions of the East as it is among those of the West. Hinduism, Buddhism, Taoism, and Confucianism, for example, are not monotheistic religions. Although they differ among themselves, they have in common the fact that they are based much more on religious insight, awareness, and feeling than on specific intellectualized creeds. They are open to all who would find *the way* and they regard the universe as a whole, man and nature, as one. The name of no particular individual is associated with the founding of Hinduism, and the Buddha, Lao Tzu, and Confucius are thought of as wise and holy men rather than as divine or the prophets of the divine.

An ecumenism that seeks to encompass the religions of both the East and the West will find the major Eastern religions broad, tolerant, and accommodating, rather than dogmatic. In the unity that they already see in all things there is great room for diversity, including religious diversity. For these religions salvation is not limited to those who are chosen or who are called, but, however defined, is available to all who seek it. In this sense the Eastern religions are, by their very nature, universal and ecumenical in contrast to the theistic Western religions, which, while increasing their ecumenical understandings and efforts, are constrained by a more or less closed credal system.

Participation in the ecumenical movement is clearly one of the many important practical and action-oriented ways in which people can further their own intercultural education and contribute meaningfully toward the development of a common humanity.

THE COMMUNICATIONS MEDIA

The twentieth century generally has come to a greatly heightened realization of the importance of communications in the life of the individual, of society, and of culture. For example, John McHale writes that "man is human by virtue of his social existence; he lives in, by, and for his communication with others," and, "we may, more accurately, characterize the key evolutionary stage of man not as tool making or using, but as communication through symbolic language."[19] The communications media are a vital and powerful force in the development of any practicable concept of human solidarity and civilization, and they are an integral part of it. Men communicate in a number of ways other than through symbolic language, important as that is; much of the clearest communication is nonverbal.

The communications media are the means by which we communicate with one another, and the better they are, the greater the ease of communication. The modern world is not without its communications breakdowns, but the media have reached a high stage of technological development that can be expected to improve further in future. It is not the medium, but the message itself that is of central concern, regardless of how much the medium may influence and shape the message. What is said and what is heard and how it is being interpreted is the communications message, however it is transmitted.

By far the most important and powerful contemporary means of communication are the mass media such as newspapers, television, radio, and films. Not only do these media enable the communicator to send his message quickly to millions of people at the same time, but also to get an almost instantaneous feedback as to how well or poorly, how favorably or unfavorably, the message is being received, so that desired corrections can be made. Modern communications technology is flexible enough that the message can be directly pointed toward the specific receiver for whom it is intended. The message can be made as permanent as desired and can be used over and over again without change. It is entirely possible, for example, that the same videotape could be seen by every person in the world, not only once, but as many time as anyone might like.

At the present time, however, most messages sent and received through the various communications media are intended for persons of the same culture. Communication, like education itself, is still mostly *intracultural* rather than *intercultural*. Even though simultaneous translation in all media is more and more feasible, for the most part those who control them do not serve broad, intercultural interests, but respond to provincial or one-culture interests. The situation is changing slowly and, for example, certain educational television programs are devoted to the news or its interpretation as seen by those outside the particular culture involved. It is possible as well to see a film produced in another culture with the necessary translation supplied, yet the percentage of Americans, for example, who have seen a Japanese or Russian film is very small. Moreover, newsmen stationed abroad usually regard themselves as representatives of their own culture or nation rather than as objective observers trying to weigh the news according to standards of its value and importance for the world as a whole. Rarely, if ever, for example, does an American hear an interpretation of the conflict between Russia and China by anyone other than an American. There is at present no international or intercultural newspaper that truly attempts to see mankind as a whole.

The complaint of those who control the media is that people generally will read only that which interests them, and that the majority of people are not now interested in world affairs or even in anything having to do with another culture, unless it involves some kind of threat or advantage. On the one hand, the gatherers and disseminators of news and information, tend, by reason of their own education, to be one-culture persons, though the best of them make it a point to learn the language and the ways of the culture within which they are working. On the other hand, the public at large is busy about its own affairs and is interested only in those things which they feel will affect their lives immediately and directly, not realizing how much in fact the events in what used to be regarded as far-off places do, in the modern world, make a difference to them. The situation with the media is thus circular: the controllers of the media limit their messages to a one-culture view, and their audience, not being presented with messages from outside cultures, have little chance to acquire an interest in them.

The result has been a great lag between the potential the media have for increasing intercultural understanding, and the actual development of that understanding. It is, in fact, far from clear how the media might best be used or what kinds of messages are best suited to which of the media. There is always the possibility that overcommunication might be as bad as undercommunication, in that the human receiver can handle only a limited number of messages at the same time without confusion and distortion. At the present time, the information the people of one culture have about another ordinarily derives from communicators who interpret events in the light of their own cultural background, rather than as those same events are viewed by the members of the other culture. Stanley Karnov, who spent more than a decade in Asia, illustrates this point:

> For, it seems to me in retrospect, the principle wisdom a Westerner can acquire about this part of the world is the recognition of his own ignorance. In short, I have learned over the years, the East really is inscrutable. . . . In contrast, prime cause of America's setbacks in the Far East from the Communist takeover of China to the present quagmire in Indochina has been the delusion of our policymakers that they understood Asia. Two elements, I would suggest, contributed to this delusion. . . . The first was the conviction that there must be measurable facts in Asia because, regarding ourselves to be rational, we had to operate on the basis of facts. . . . The second flaw in our approach has been to rely on Asian Allies who spoke our language and imitated our mannerisms even though we were never quite sure whether they shared our values.[20]

The media should be used as a means of genuine communication and education rather than of propagandizing or of simply reinforcing and confirming ideas already held by the people of individual cultures. They can help to let the peoples of one culture know what other people really think, not what some one person thinks they think. The *forms* of the media themselves are neutral; they can open the way to further understanding and appreciation or they can be used to communicate distortions and half-truths to larger and larger numbers of people, thus perpetuating ancient prejudices and creating further hostilities among people. To make sure the messages transmitted by the media are accurate and reliable is a fundamental responsibility of those who manage and direct them.

Television, as probably the most effective and comprehensive of the various communications media, gives ample evidence that the master teachers of today are those who control media programing, just as the master teachers of the past were those who wrote important books. Altogether apart from whether television is publicly or privately owned, programing and editing are always a matter of selection and perspective. Although television makes it possible for millions of people around the world to see a live telecast of a major world event, whether they will see it at all and what they will see of it are determined by those who control the medium. Television particularly has a profound educative impact, and the perceptions and attitudes that the people of one culture have about the people of another culture can be deeply influenced by what they see and hear on it. As one example, Merrill Panitt, editor of *TV Guide,* reports after a recent intensive study that Europeans tend to have a greatly distorted image of the United States because of what they see about the U.S. on television. He says that the U.S. television news programs, in their tradition of critical news reporting, are concerned with what is wrong with such things as government structure, political leaders, prisons, schools and universities, the roads and traffic systems, race relations, and pollution laws. Europeans, seeing the news presented in this way, easily can and do conclude that what they see represents the whole, rather than a partial picture of life and culture in the United States.

The modern communications media open up windows on the world in a way never before possible. These media could and should be used to create among all people a greater intercultural understanding and an awareness of the basic unity of man everywhere. The media can only reflect, however, the intelligence and the motivations of those who program them. Used with responsibility and integrity, the media could help to correct prejudices and false impressions and to reveal deeper underlying human realities. Part of any action program for the intercultural education of the future will be the search for better ways of employing the media to these ends, including the communicators and their recipients, in an open and mutual exchange of feelings and points of view. An international or world television network, sponsored by the United Nations or a similar agency, could carry programs of interest and value to peoples all over the world.

The communications media are only one of many technological developments suggesting the possibility of a contemporary realization of the community of man. Whether modern man will find sufficient wisdom, and the depth of moral and spiritual commitment to the idea of a community of man, to achieve in fact what is now a technical possibility is the great challenge to intercultural education and to the very survival of any form of human civilization.

Notes

CHAPTER 1

1 Henry Steele Commager, *Intercultural Education,* An Information Service of Education and World Affairs, vol. 1, no. 4 (New York, March 1970), p. 2.
2 Letter of Rabindranath Tagore to Gilbert Murray, September 16, 1934; quoted in *International Education: A Documentary History,* ed. David G. Scanlon (New York: Teachers College, Columbia University, 1960), p. 113.
3 F. S. C. Northrop, *The Meeting of East and West* (New York: Macmillan Co., 1946), p. 376.
4 Ibid., p. 101.
5 John Stuart Mill, *Autobiography* (New York: Bobbs-Merrill Co., The Library of Liberal Arts, 1957), p. 153.
6 Arthur W. Hummel, "Chinese Culture," in *Understanding Other Cultures,* ed. William A. Parker (Washington, D. C.: American Council of Learned Societies, 1954), p. 63.
7 Milton Rokeach and Seymour Parker, *Annals of the American Academy of Political and Social Sciences,* March 1970; reported in the *Christian Science Monitor,* June 11, 1970, p. 8.
8 Sarkar Bhupendra Nath, *Tagore, the Educator* (Calcutta: Progressive Publishers, n.d.), p. 59.
9 Thomé H. Fang, "The World and the Individual in Chinese Metaphysics," in *The Status of the Individual in East and West,* ed. Charles A. Moore (Honolulu: University of Hawaii Press, 1968), p. 43.

CHAPTER 2

1 John C. H. Wu, "Chinese Legal and Political Philosophy," in *Philosophy and Culture East and West,* ed. Charles A. Moore (Honolulu: University of Hawaii Press, 1962), p. 627.

2 For an excellent discussion of this point and an extensive bibliography see Richard A. Falk, *This Endangered Planet* (New York: Random House, 1971).

3 N. K. Devaraja, *The Philosophy of Culture* (Allahabad: Kitabl Mahal Private Ltd., 1963), p. 139.

4 Perhaps along the lines proposed in *A Constitution for the World* (Santa Barbara, California: Center for the Study of Democratic Institutions, 1965). But other models might also emerge in the course of discussions on this point.

5 Betty Heimann, *Facets of Indian Thought* (New York: Schocken Books, 1964), p. 149.

6 *U. S. Foreign Assistance in the 1970s: A New Approach* (Washington, D. C.: U. S. Government Printing Office, March 4, 1970), p. 7.

7 Barbara Ward, "A Summing Up," in *The East and West Must Meet,* ed. and with an introduction by Benjamin Houston Brown (East Lansing, Michigan: Michigan State University Press, 1959), pp. 126, 129.

8 Gunnar Myrdal, *The Challenge of World Poverty* (New York: Random House, Pantheon Books, 1970).

9 Quincy Wright, "War and Peace," in *The Challenge of the '60s* (Palo Alto, California: Palo Alto Unified School District, December 1961), p. 69.

10 Georges Fradier, *East and West towards Mutual Understanding* (Paris: UNESCO, 1959), p. 37.

CHAPTER 3

1 Khin Maung Win, "The Burmese Language: An Epistemological Analysis," in *Cross-Cultural Understanding: Epistemology in Anthropology,* ed. F. S. C. Northrop and Helen H. Livingston (New York: Harper & Row, 1964), pp. 226–228.

2 Ibid., p. 233.

3 *The Holy Qur-an,* text, translation, and commentary by Abdullah Yusuf Ali Sh. Muhammad Ashraf (Lahore, Pakistan: Kashmiri Bazar, n.d.), vol. 1, p. 83.

4 Theodore Brameld, *Education for the Emerging Age: Newer Ends and Stronger Means* (New York: Harper & Row, 1965), p. 132.

5 S. Radhakrishnan as quoted by Bhabani Bhattacharya in *Gandhi the Writer* (New Delhi, India: National Book Trust, 1969), pp. 280–281.

6 Hajime Nakamura, *Ways of Thinking of Eastern Peoples: India, China, Tibet, Japan,* rev. English translation ed. Philip P. Wiener (Honolulu: East-West Center Press, 1969), p. 3.

7 John Ulric Nef, ed., *Bridges of Human Understanding* (New York: University Publishers, 1964), pp. 7–8.

8 Mortimer J. Adler, *The Time of Our Lives: The Ethics of Common Sense* (New York: Holt, Rinehart, and Winston, 1970), pp. 122–123.

9 S. Radhakrishnan, "The Indian Approach to the Religious Problem," in

Philosophy and Culture East and West, ed. Charles A. Moore (Honolulu: University of Hawaii Press, 1962), p. 255.

10 Clyde Kluckhohn, "The Philosophy of the Navaho Indians," in *Ideological Differences and World Order,* ed. F. S. C. Northrop (New Haven: Yale University Press, 1949), p. 356.

11 Edwin O. Reischauer and John K. Fairbank, *East Asia, The Great Tradition,* vol. 1 (Boston: Houghton Mifflin Co., 1958), p. 6.

12 Robert Rossow, Jr., "Natural Man, Philosophy, and Behavior," in *Philosophy and Culture East and West,* ed. Charles A. Moore (Honolulu: University of Hawaii Press, 1962), p. 121.

CHAPTER 4

1 Jerome S. Bruner, *The Process of Education* (New York: Random House, Vintage Books, 1963), p. 25.

2 Ibid., p. 20.

3 A. N. Whitehead, *The Aims of Education and Other Essays* (London: Williams & Norgate, 1936), p. 23.

4 Joseph K. Yanagiwa, "Approaches to the Study of Japanese Literature," in *Twelve Doors to Japan,* ed. John Whitney Hall and Richard K. Beardsley (New York: McGraw-Hill, 1965), p. 247. .

5 Theodore Brameld, *Cultural Foundations of Education: An Interdisciplinary Exploration* (New York: Harper & Brothers, 1957), p. 205.

6 Wilbur L. Schramm, "Imaginative Writing," in *Literary Scholarship,* ed. Norman Foerster et al. (Chapel Hill: The University of North Carolina Press, 1941), pp. 184–185.

7 Northrop Frye, *The Educated Imagination* (Bloomington: Indiana University Press, 1964), pp. 63–64.

8 Boris Pasternak, *Doctor Zhivago* (New York: New American Library, Signet Books, 1958), p. 417. Quoted by permission of Pantheon Books, a division of Random House, Inc.

9 Ibid., p. 406.

10 Ibid., p. 402.

11 Ibid., p. 60.

12 Nikos Kazantzakis, *Report to Greco* (New York: Bantam Books, 1966), p. 97. Quotations from this work reprinted by permission of Simon and Schuster, Inc.

13 Ibid., p. 73.

14 Ibid., p. 156.

15 Ibid., p. 158.

16 Ibid., p. 98.

17 Ibid., p. 138.

18 Ibid., pp. 140–141.

19 *Antigone* in *The Oedipus Plays of Sophocles,* trans. Paul Roche (New York: New American Library, Mentor Books, 1958), p. 167. Copyright © 1968 by Paul Roche. Quoted by permission of New American Library, Inc.

20 Ibid., p. 182.
21 Ibid., p. 187.
22 Ibid., p. 187.
23 Ibid., p. 179.
24 Ibid., p. 181.
25 Tsao Hsueh-chin, *Dream of the Red Chamber,* trans. Wang Chi-chen (Garden City: Doubleday and Co., Anchor Books, 1958), p. xx. Quotations from this work reprinted by permission of Twayne Publishers, Inc.
26 Ibid., p. 92.
27 Ibid., p. 167.
28 Ibid., p. 322.
29 Ibid., p. 323.
30 Ibid., pp. 13–14.
31 Kamala Markandaya, *Nectar in a Sieve* (New York: New American Library, Signet Books, 1954). Copyright © 1954 by The John Day Company. Quotations from this work reprinted by permission of The John Day Company, Inc., publisher.
32 Ibid., p. 91.
33 Ibid., p. 136.
34 Ibid., p. 83.
35 Ibid.

CHAPTER 5

1 Edwin O. Reischauer, "Asia, the Pacific, and the United States," from a hearing before the Committee on Foreign Relations, United States Senate (Washington, D. C.: U. S. Government Printing Office, 1967), p. 3.
2 John McHale, *The Future of the Future* (New York: George Braziller, 1969), p. 300.
3 *Measures Designed to Promote among Youth the Ideals of Peace, Mutual Respect, and Understanding between Peoples* (Paris: UNESCO/Ed/189, May 1962), p. 7.
4 C. A. O. Van Nieuwenhuijze, *Cross-Cultural Studies* (The Hague: Mouton & Co., 1963), p. 127.
5 Ketty A. Stassinopoulou, "Communication and Education," in *Education in World Perspective,* ed. Emmet John Hughes (New York: Harper & Row, 1962), p. 85.
6 William E. Vickery and Stewart G. Cole, *Intercultural Education in American Schools* (New York: Harper & Row, 1943).
7 Don Adams and Robert M. Bjork, *Education in Developing Areas* (New York: David McKay Co., 1969), p. 37.
8 Gunnar Myrdal, *The Challenge of World Poverty* (New York: Random House, Pantheon Books, 1970), p. 133.
9 Ritchie Calder, "The Speed of Change," as quoted in McHale, *The Future of the Future,* p. 294.
10 *Measures Designed to Promote among Youth the Ideals of Peace, Mutual*

Respect, and Understanding between Peoples (Paris: UNESCO/Ed/189, May 1962), p. 4.

11 Alexis de Tocqueville, *Democracy in America,* trans. Henry Reeve (New York: Schocken Books, 1967), pp. lxviii and lxxv.

12 *Education for International Understanding* (Tournai, Belgium: UNESCO, 1959), p. 14.

13 Carl R. Rogers and Barry Stevens, *Person to Person: The Problem to Being Human* (Lafayette, California: Real People Press, 1967), p. 20.

CHAPTER 6

1 William W. Marvel, "The University in World Affairs: An Introduction," in *The University Looks Ahead: Approaches to World Affairs at Six American Universities* (New York: Walker and Co., 1965), p. xiii.

2 *International Education Act* (Washington, D. C.: U. S. Government Printing Office, 1966), pp. 20–21. Italics mine.

3 Mario Pei, *One Language for the World* (New York: Devin-Adair Co., 1961), p. 18.

4 R. Freeman Butts, *American Education in International Development* (New York: Harper & Row, 1963), p. 27.

5 Walter H. C. Laves, *Toward a National Effort in International Educational and Cultural Affairs,* Department of State Publication 7238, International Information and Cultural Series 78 (Washington, D. C.: Government Printing Office, July 1961), p. 11.

6 J. W. Fulbright, "Education for a New Kind of International Relations," in *Diversity and Interdependence through International Education,* ed. Allan A. Michie (New York: Education and World Affairs, 1967), pp. 18–19.

7 C. A. O. Van Nieuwenhuijze, *Cross-Cultural Studies* (The Hague: Mouton & Co., 1963), pp. 52–53.

8 Walter Johnson and Francis J. Colligan, *The Fulbright Program: A History* (Chicago: The University of Chicago Press, 1965), p. 313.

9 Edward W. Weidner, *The World Role of Universities* (New York: McGraw-Hill, 1962), p. 2.

10 Rabindranath Tagore, *Towards Universal Man* (New York: Asia Publishing House, 1961), pp. 142–143.

11 Ibid., pp. 272–273.

12 Constantine K. Zurayk, "Preface" to *The University and the Needs of Contemporary Society,* a report prepared by Henri Janne (Paris: International Association of Universities, 1970), p. xiv.

13 Pearl S. Buck, *China as I See It,* comp. and ed. Theodore F. Harris (New York: John Day, 1970), p. 61. Italics hers.

14 Ibid., pp. 279–280.

15 Charles Frankel, "The Role of Government," in *Diversity and Interdependence through International Education,* ed. Allan A. Michie (New York: Education and World Affairs, 1967), p. 45.

16 Harold Taylor, *The World as Teacher* (Garden City: Doubleday and Co., 1970), p. 21.

17 Ibid., pp. 4–5.

18 Ibid., pp. 16–17.

19 Huston Smith, "Toward a World Civilization," *Center Diary* 17 (March–April 1967): 45–49. Center for the Study of Democratic Institutions (Palo Alto: Fund for the Republic, 1967).

20 Hajime Nakamura, "The Vision of a Universal History of Thought," in *International Christian University Publication III-A, Asian Cultural Studies 5.* (Tokyo: Mitsuki, October 1966), p. 55.

21 Betty Heimann, *Facets of Indian Thought* (New York: Schocken Books, 1964), p. 155. Italics in original.

22 Carole Methven, *School and Community in Education for International Understanding* (Hamburg: UNESCO Institute of Education, 1964), p. 63.

CHAPTER 7

1 Julian Huxley, UNESCO: *Its Purpose and Philosophy* (Washington, D. C.: Public Affairs Press, 1948), p. 41.

2 "The Root Problem," editorial, *Christian Science Monitor,* October 21, 1970.

3 Jean Piaget, *The Psychology of Intelligence,* trans. Malcolm Piercy and D. E. Berlyne (New York: Harcourt, Brace & Co., 1950), pp. 164–165.

4 Henri Janne, *The University and the Needs of Contemporary Society* (Paris: International Association of Universities, 1970), p. 63.

5 Howard F. Van Zandt, "Japanese Culture and the Business Boom," *Foreign Affairs,* January 1970, pp. 348–349.

6 Stanley M. Davis, "U. S. versus Latin America," *Harvard Business Review,* November–December 1969, p. 89.

7 Kingdon W. Swayne, "The Bridge between Peoples," *Foreign Service Journal,* November 1969, p. 31.

8 See A. N. Whitehead, *The Aims of Education and Other Essays* (London: Williams & Morgate, 1936), pp. 27–30.

9 "The UN's Potential . . . ," editorial, *Christian Science Monitor,* October 16, 1970.

10 "Decade of Development?" editorial, *Christian Science Monitor,* September 24, 1970.

11 Sydney D. Bailey, "The United Nations Secretariat," in *The Evolution of International Organizations,* ed. Evan Luard (London: Thames and Hudson, 1966), p. 102.

12 Jack C. Plano and Robert E. Riggs, *Forging World Order: the Politics of International Organization* (New York: Macmillan Co., 1967), p. 445.

13 "The Role of Non-Governmental Organizations in International Intellectual Cooperation," in *Report of a Seminar Sponsored by the American Council of Learned Societies and the United States National Commission for UNESCO, April 28–30, 1964* (New York: Gould House), p. 15.

14 José Ortega y Gasset, *History as a System and Other Essays Toward a*

Philosophy of History (New York: W. W. Norton & Co., 1941 and 1962), p. 168.

15 Harvey Cox, *The Secular City* (New York: Macmillan Co., 1965), p. 18.

16 Ibid., p. 31.

17 Pierre Teilhard de Chardin, *The Divine Milieu* (New York: Harper & Row, 1960 and 1968), p. 45.

18 Fyodor Dostoevsky, *Notes from Underground and the Grand Inquisitor*, trans. Ralph E. Matlaw (New York: E. P. Dutton and Co., 1950), p. 128.

19 John McHale, *The Future of the Future* (New York: George Braziller, 1969), p. 85.

20 Stanley Karnov, "Wisdom Is in Recognizing Ignorance," *Honolulu Advertiser*, July 25, 1970, p. A–16.

Index

DATE		